BUSINESS STRATEGIES AND MANAGEMENT FOR SUSTAINABILITY

宝库山精选：可持续性经营战略与管理

Digital editions

Business Strategies and Management for Sustainability is available through most major ebook and database services (please check with them for pricing). Special print/digital bundle pricing is also available in cooperation with Credo Reference; contact Berkshire Publishing (info@berkshirepublishing.com) for details.

For information, contact:
Berkshire Publishing Group LLC
122 Castle Street
Great Barrington, Massachusetts 01230-1506 USA
www.berkshirepublishing.com
Printed in the United States of America

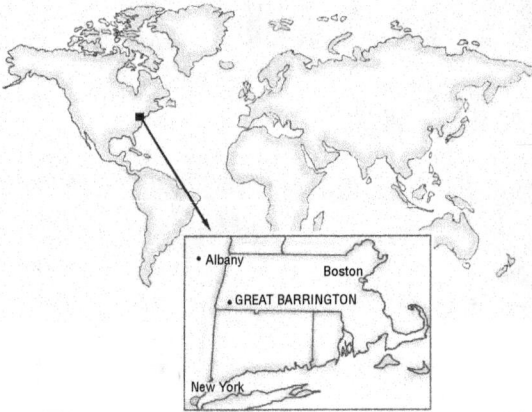

Library of Congress Cataloging-in-Publication Data

Business strategies and management for sustainability / Chris Laszlo, general editor.
    p. cm. — (Berkshire essentials)
    Includes index.
    ISBN 978-1-61472-964-8 (pbk. : alk. paper) — ISBN 978-1-61472-965-5 (ebook)
    1. Social responsibility of business.   2. Business enterprises—Environmental aspects.   I. Laszlo, Christopher.
    HD60.B887 2013
    658.4'012—dc23   2012049800

BERKSHIRE 宝库山

Essentials

BUSINESS STRATEGIES AND MANAGEMENT FOR SUSTAINABILITY

宝库山精选：可持续性经营战略与管理

General Editor Chris Laszlo

BERKSHIRE
A global point of reference

About *Business Strategies and Management for Sustainability*

Business Strategies and Management for Sustainability, a Berkshire Essential, explores how a green economy can be created and sustained. A team of well-known authors looks at business in terms of both environmental and financial sustainability. Articles are designed and written for the nonexpert reader, covering topics such as green gross domestic product, "greenwashing," risk management, and the economics of renewable energy and "going local." An article on corporate social responsibility (CSR)—and what some hail as its more realistic successor, CSR 2.0—assesses the ways in which we can make a measurable difference in how business is conducted.

THE **BERKSHIRE** *Essentials* SERIES

Berkshire Sustainability Essentials, distilled from the *Berkshire Encyclopedia of Sustainability*, take a global approach to environmental law, energy, business strategies and management, industrial ecology, and religion, among other topics.

- Religion and Sustainability
- Business Strategies and Management for Sustainability
- Energy Resources and Sustainability
- Energy Industries and Sustainability
- Ecosystem Services for Sustainability
- Environmental Law and Sustainability
- Finance and Investment for Sustainability
- Industrial Ecology

Distilled for
the classroom
from Berkshire's
award-winning
encyclopedias

BERKSHIRE ESSENTIALS from the *Berkshire Encyclopedia of China* and the *Berkshire Encyclopedia of World History, 2nd Edition* also available.

Contents

About Berkshire Essentials

For more than a decade, Berkshire Publishing has collaborated with a worldwide network of scholars and editors to produce award-winning academic resources on popular subjects for a discerning audience. The "Berkshire Essentials" series are collections of concentrated content, inspired by requests from teachers, curriculum planners, and professors who praise the encyclopedic approach of Berkshire's reference works, but who still crave single volumes for course use.

Each Essentials series draws from Berkshire publications on a big topic—world history, Chinese studies, and (in the case of this book) environmental sustainability, for instance—to provide thematic volumes that can be purchased alone, in any combination, or as a set. Teachers will find the insightful articles indispensable for stimulating classroom discussion or independent study. Students, professionals, and general readers all will find the articles invaluable when exploring a line of research or an abiding interest.

These affordable books are available in paperback as well as ebook formats for convenient reading on mobile devices.

Editors, Editorial Advisory Board, and Production Staff

Editors

The following people served as Editors for the source of these articles, *The Business of Sustainability*, Volume 2 of the *Berkshire Encyclopedia of Sustainability*.

General Editor: Chris Laszlo
Case Western Reserve University

Karen Christensen
Berkshire Publishing Group

Daniel S. Fogel
Wake Forest University

Gernot Wagner
Environmental Defense Fund

Peter Whitehouse
Case Western Reserve University

Editorial Advisory Board

Ray Anderson, *Interface, Inc.;* Lester Brown, *Earth Policy Institute;* Robert Costanza, *University of Vermont;* Luis Gomez-Echeverri, *United Nations Development Programme;* John Elkington, *SustainAbility;* Daniel Kammen, *University of California, Berkeley;* Ashok Khosla, *International Union for Conservation of Nature;* and Christine Loh, *Civic Exchange, Hong Kong*

Production Staff

Project Coordinator
Bill Siever

Copy Editors
Linda Aspen-Baxter
Mary Bagg
Kathy Brock
Barbara Resch
Chris Yurko

Editorial Assistants
Echo Bergquist
Hillary Cox
David Gagne

Designer
Anna Myers

Base of the Pyramid

The Base of the Pyramid refers to the huge proportion of humanity who are mired in poverty, as well as to the business strategies that are evolving to connect this segment of the population into the formal global economy as consumers, suppliers/producers, and entrepreneurs.

A concept developed in the late 1990s, the Base (bottom) of the Pyramid, or BOP, refers simultaneously to the socioeconomic demographic representing the 3–4 billion poorest people inhabiting the globe and to the private-sector business models meant to address the poverty of these people. The idea of the BOP as a business opportunity came about as a convergence of two streams of thought within strategic management. The first is premised on a new model of global economic expansion within international business that uses innovation and technology management. This perspective challenges assumptions regarding the source of innovation and creativity—shifting it from home offices and headquarters based in developed nations to subsidiaries and competitors based in developing countries. The second stream of thought is a model of the global economy that emerged from work on organizations and sustainability. This view describes the global economy as consisting of three distinct demographic categories (the layers of the pyramid) that transcend geographic boundaries, organized by the sustainability challenges that each faces (Hart and Milstein 1999).

Three Layers of the Pyramid

The first demographic category, the tip of the pyramid, is composed of the "mature" economy made up of the world's wealthiest individuals who represent about 15 percent of the global population. These individuals are able to afford all the goods and services they need as well as any or most of what they might want. Although these individuals tend to be found mostly in developed countries, a good percentage exist in less-developed countries as well. The challenge and opportunity for business is to develop goods and services that reduce the large environmental footprint that occurs through consumption in this market. Business can achieve this by applying renewable forms of energy, "green" building and design, and other advancements that offer significant reductions in energy usage, toxicity, and emissions.

The second demographic group represents the aspiring middle class that makes up approximately 20 percent of the global population. While found in many countries throughout the world, the majority of this demographic reside in China, India, Brazil, and other countries undergoing rapid economic transformation. These individuals are able to afford most goods and services they need and some of those they want. The challenge for businesses here is to develop innovative products and services that prevent further contributions to environmental degradation as the aspiring economy develops. Most efforts by companies to penetrate emerging economies are attempts to adapt the mature economy's expensive products and services to make them more affordable. They often do this by introducing earlier-generation technologies or stripped-down product offerings into the marketplace. Such products—for example, cars without catalytic converters—may be cheaper, but they are also dirtier. The incremental revenue generated from sales of such products is often lower than expected, and the impact on the environment can be high.

The third group represents the "survival economy" made up of the nearly two-thirds of humanity, living all over the globe, who earn between $1 and $3 a day. (It should be noted that poverty lines set by specific income levels suggest definitive levels at which poverty does and does not occur; such figures tend to conceal the variety of circumstances affecting the human condition.) Demographically, this is the BOP. These individuals are barely able or unable to meet their most basic needs, such as clean water, health care, education, housing, and nutrition. For the most part, the economic system has overlooked, ignored, or even exploited this market segment. Existing business models, products, and services have little relevance in this market because the logistical, cultural, technical, and political characteristics are so different from the mature economy for which the products were developed. What goods do exist are usually more expensive and of lower quality than comparable items available to the wealthy. The *poverty penalty* is a term used to describe the premium the poor have to pay for basic services—such as water, electricity, and sanitation—that are often of inferior quality to those available at lower costs to the rich (Prahalad and Hammond 2002).

BOP as a Business Opportunity

While the term BOP itself refers to the socioeconomic demographic of the world's poorest, the paradigm of the BOP that is being taught in many management education programs refers to private-sector activity where poverty is addressed when low-income markets become engines for entrepreneurship and business growth. This view is very contentious for those suspicious of the motivations of companies, such as Unilever and Procter & Gamble, who have been pursuing BOP initiatives. The concern is that such initiatives are simply another way to sell unnecessary goods to poor people in a way that extracts what little wealth exists in those markets. Other concerns are that successful BOP strategies will lead to increased consumption patterns that place even more pressure on critical ecosystem services and further environmental decline.

Another viewpoint, however, promotes BOP ventures as a way to unlock the latent vitality and ingenuity of robust, informal markets, thus releasing the poor from economic imprisonment. This view rejects the idea of the poor simply as a source of revenue for new business growth and instead sees the poor as capable partners and resources for technology development and innovation. The BOP is not advocated as simply the opportunity for increasing sales through the marketing of existing products and services in forms that are smaller and cheaper than their upmarket cousins (e.g., sachets and single servings of products such as shampoo or detergents). Instead, the BOP is conceptualized as a holistic, long-term investment process in business model innovation.

It is based on partnerships and need-based product and service development as articulated by the poor themselves and built on the local resource base, infrastructure, and cultural institutions. The most progressive concepts of BOP business are premised on the idea that the poor can provide markets for commercializing next-generation technologies that offer social, environmental, and economic value. For example, high-tech cookstoves can allow people to use the sun's energy to prepare meals rather than requiring the poor to further deplete vital wood supplies or breathe in noxious fumes from dung, kerosene, or coal.

Mark B. MILSTEIN, Erik SIMANIS,
Duncan DUKE, Stuart HART
*Johnson Graduate School of Management,
Cornell University*

This article is adapted from the article "Base of the Pyramid (BOP) Model" that appears in Wayne Visser, Dirk Matten, Manfred Pohl, & Nick Tolhurst (Eds.), *The A to Z of Corporate Social Responsibility: The Complete Reference of Concepts, Codes and Organisations*, Chichester, UK: John Wiley and Sons.

See also in the *Berkshire Encyclopedia of Sustainability* CSR and CSR 2.0; Development, Sustainable; Fair Trade; Investment, Socially Responsible (SRI); Poverty; Social Enterprise; Triple Bottom Line; United Nations Global Compact

FURTHER READING

Hart, Stuart L. (2005). *Capitalism at the crossroads: The unlimited business opportunities in solving the world's most difficult problems*. Philadelphia: Wharton School Publishing.

Hart, Stuart L., & Christensen, Clayton M. (2002). The great leap: Driving innovation from the bottom of the pyramid. *Sloan Management Review*, *44*(1), 51–56.

Hart, Stuart L., & Milstein, Mark B. (1999). Global sustainability and the creative destruction of industries. *Sloan Management Review*, *41*(1), 23–33.

Prahalad, C. K. (2004). *The fortune at the bottom of the pyramid: Eradicating poverty through profits*. Philadelphia: Wharton School Publishing.

Prahalad, C. K., & Hammond, Allen. (2002). Serving the world's poor profitably. *Harvard Business Review*, *80*(9), 48–57.

Prahalad, C. K., & Hart, Stuart L. (2002). The fortunate at the bottom of the pyramid. *Strategy+Business*, *26*, 2–14.

Simanis, Erik, & Hart, Stuart L. (2009). Innovation from the inside out. *Sloan Management Review*, *50*(4), 77–86.

Simanis, Erik; Hart, Stuart L.; & Duke, Duncan. (2008). The Base of the Pyramid protocol: Beyond "basic needs" business strategies. *Innovations*, *3*(1), 57–84.

Community Capital

Community capital comprises the economic, cultural, and social resources that communities must access to foster their sustainable development. Emerging from nineteenth-century social thought, community capital financial networks such as cooperatives, credit unions, and local alternative currencies benefit both individuals and businesses, while social networks support feelings of well-being and belonging. Corporate social responsibility (CSR) in community capital extends the corporate sector's focus beyond profit margin toward sustainable and pro-community activities.

Community capital is the sum of the various elements of capital upon which a community relies and from which it benefits. It draws on all the areas underpinning community life: human, social, environmental, economic, and cultural. In addition, community capital includes indigenous resources, regional amenities, and a local skills base; these, combined with corporate and civic forms of philanthropy and volunteerism, are necessary to make a community sustainable in its most extensive aspects. Community capital comprises the significant forms of capital outlined by the theorist Pierre Bourdieu (1986) in "The Forms of Capital": economic, cultural, and social. At the center of this understanding of community capital, Bourdieu outlined a series of "relationships of mutual acquaintance and recognition." Within this context, community capital can be understood as the kinds of economic, cultural, or social capital that link social groups who provide due concern for the well-being of their counterparts, and who do so without immediate recourse to the usual concerns about profit or other compensation.

Community Capital and Networked Finance

One significant outcome of the global economic downturn that began in late 2007 was the emergence of community capital networks to replenish flows of finance to local businesses. A number of initiatives have extended community capital in local or regional contexts over time. These enterprises have included cooperatives, credit unions, and local alternative currencies. Community capital may also include those assets that can be held in common by a community for their mutual benefit. Such assets may include the provision of labor, technologies, equipment, factory space, or land banks that could be used in commonage. While the reasons for this pooling of resources may vary, ultimately programs that create flows of community capital are devised to have universal benefits for society.

The Cooperative Movement

The cooperative movement emerged during the Industrial Revolution to facilitate the economic plight of workers exposed to the vagaries of nascent capitalism. One of the earliest exponents of the cooperative movement was Robert Owen (1771–1858), who developed the concept of utopian cooperative villages in Britain and the United States. The ethic of pooled labor and resources was common in agrarian societies, and the cooperative movement developed these concepts by establishing a framework for mutual cooperation in a planned community. Throughout the eighteenth and nineteenth centuries, cooperatives, intentional communities, workers' collectives, and religious communes were developed through the promotion of an ethic of community capital. Owen founded the rationalist cooperative in New Harmony, Indiana, in 1825. The

Brook Farm experiment of the 1840s in Massachusetts was frequented by utopians, transcendentalists, and intellectuals such as Nathaniel Hawthorne, Ralph Waldo Emerson, and Henry David Thoreau, under the influence of Charles Fourier (Leonard 2007).

Credit Unions

Credit unions represent another form of community capital. One key idea underpinning the credit union is that ownership remains in the hands of the group membership. In addition, credit unions extend financial services such as loans to their members at reasonable rates without the emphasis on profits that characterize the mainstream banking sector. The role of credit unions in maintaining access to credit and direct finance has been an important aspect of localized responses to the economic challenges that have emerged since the collapse of the corporate banking sector.

In the United States credit unions are classified as nonprofits, while in Canada credit unions are free to return a profit from their enterprise. In the United Kingdom, "mutual friendly societies" were established to extend credit to poorer sectors of society, while "building societies" were created to extend credit for housing to the same sector. Credit-union directors are volunteers and are democratically elected by members without an emphasis on their assets. Credit unions also provide a microfinance service based on the provision of financial services to low-income clients who may not have access to mainstream banks. Corporate credit unions provide a clearinghouse service for the wider corporate sector.

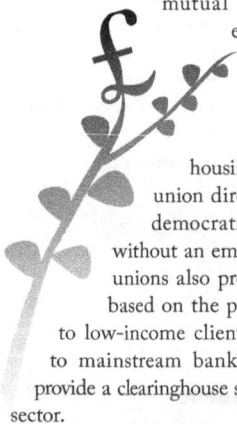

Both cooperatives and credit unions continue to play a significant role in contemporary society. In many countries, cooperatives and credit unions have contributed to alternative economic activity since the onset of the global "credit crunch" and subsequent downturn. Cooperatives continue to play a significant role in rural development, while credit unions are expanding their influence, with new credit unions opening across the world at a rapid rate.

Alternative Currencies

Alternative currency movements are often conceptualized as an object of protest or a tool for constructing alternative communities, economies, and societies. Contemporary alternative-currency networks have attempted to use new forms of money as a tool for building more fair and balanced economies and societies. Traditionally, community capital initiatives have included concepts such as social credit or the paying of a dividend to equalize incomes in free societies. Since the homestead movement of the Great Depression, supporters of alternative currencies have advocated a supply of credit based on principles of bartering or exchanging goods and services (North 2007). In contemporary society, the Local Exchange Trading System (LETS) in North America, or local currencies such as "favours" in the United Kingdom, promote local self-sufficiency. Greens have advocated replacing welfare with a program that would guarantee recipients a basic income and allow them additional earnings, whether in local or traditional currencies, and thereby provide an incentive to work.

The Role of Business

One further area of community capital is witnessed in the moves to engage business with sustainable and pro-community activities. Writers such as Fritjof Capra and Gunter Pauli (1995) have outlined the significant role business plays in creating more sustainable pathways for communities and their environments. The active role played by businesses in developing community capital is best understood though an examination of the concept of corporate social responsibility (CSR). Essentially, corporate social responsibility extends the corporate sector's focus beyond mere concerns with profit margins and allows for recognition of the world beyond the business–customer relationship.

As multinationals increase their presence across the globe, this move toward increased integrity in the relationship between corporations and communities has become more significant. Corporations have also moved toward contributing to communities through increased charitable philanthropy. This process of making donations to help communities develop has been described as "cause marketing." Jocelyne Daw (2006) described the emergence of the cause-marketing phenomenon in international business. Representing a market worth $1.4 billion, Daw outlined the manner in which cause marketing has become a sophisticated contemporary trend that creates deeper links between the corporate sector, communities, and the groups or foundations that enhance the lives of others.

Community Culture

Community culture emerges from a process of socialization whereby inhabitants are indoctrinated with distinct values by social institutions including parents, schools, peers, work colleagues, religious groups, media, and state apparatus. The creation of these bonds of socialization lies at the heart of community capital. For Bourdieu, the local characteristics that underpin socialized community cultures are part of that region's "habitus," or the identity born of shared forms of local experiences and environments. Community capital is then derived from a system of mutual exchange built from what Bourdieu describes as "all the goods, material and symbolic, without distinction, that present themselves as rare and worthy of being sought after in a particular social formation" (Harker, Mahar, and Wilkes 1990, 1).

According to Robert Putnam, author of *Bowling Alone: The Collapse and Revival of American Community* (2000), the social version of capital "refers to the collective value of all *social networks* and the inclinations that arise from these networks to do things for each other." In his study of American community, Putnam set out two main components of social capital: bonding capital and bridging capital. Bonding capital refers to the value attributed to the social networks that exist within homogeneous communities, while bridging capital refers to the social networks that exist between socially heterogeneous groups. Relevant examples are utilized by Putnam to demonstrate the consequences of the existence or nonexistence of community capital. For instance, adolescent gangs may create forms of bonding social capital with negative consequences, while sports groups such as the bowling clubs referred to in Putnam's title may create bridging forms of social capital with positive outcomes. Bridging social capital may be beneficial for society in a number of ways; democratic deficit and social breakdown can be addressed as participatory activity is enhanced in the civic sector. Alternatively, the absence of community capital may lead to the further eroding of civil rights and the loss of public amenities, creating negative consequences for wider society and the environment.

The formation of community capital is dependent on the existence of a "sense of community," which is a shared psychological experience of community rather than its tangible or structural frameworks. Such experiences are multifaceted and interwoven with the experiences of others, and it is within this "imagined community" (Anderson 1983) that community capital emerges in its nascent form. This sense of community engenders shared feelings of belonging that are supported by a mutual respect and sense of commitment. Ultimately this sense of social cohesion can be understood by examining the social relations found within a neighborhood, where socialized forms of influence are crucial to the formation of norms and values. The shared values, both imagined and acted upon, form the social cohesion (or "glue") that binds communities.

Internet communities have developed the imagined community further, with the technological capital that has emerged from such innovations central to the contemporary concept of community diffusion.

From a social psychological perspective, David McMillan and David Chavis (1986) set out a theory within the field of community psychology; it argues that a prevailing "sense of community" comprises the following four key elements:

- membership that includes boundaries, emotional safety, a sense of belonging and identification, personal investment, and a common symbol system
- influence that is reciprocal because participants have some influence over the wider group and the group has influence on participants in order to maintain wider cohesion
- integration and fulfillment of needs that occurs when participants attain benefits or rewards for their contribution to the group
- a sense of shared emotional connection that includes shared histories and experiences borne from participation and engagement with the group

Classical Theory and Community Capital

Further understanding of community capital can be gained from the works of classical social theorists. The philosopher, social scientist, and revolutionary Karl Marx (1818–1883) extolled a concept of collectively pooled "species being," or the group-based aggregate of skills passed on within a community from the skilled exponents of communal-based crafts. The social theorist Max Weber (1864–1920) outlined an understanding of "status and association" whereby social networks and mobility could be derived from the groups with which a person associated, with status being bestowed by the community for contributions rather than earnings or profit. Credited by many to be the father of sociology, Émile Durkheim (1858–1917) identified the central role of "organic and social solidarity networks" in the development of society, as different types of social solidarity came to correlate with different types of society. Durkheim divided these into mechanical and organic solidarity in his seminal study *The Division of Labour in Society* (1893). Mechanical solidarity comes from the homogeneity of individuals connected by shared location or common goals and is an attribute of traditional societies. Organic solidarity emanates from the interdependence that arises from specialized activities in modern societies. This interdependence is therefore based on the sum of a community's component elements. In modern societies, social solidarity develops through the interaction stemming from the complexities and interdependence of the industrial age.

The sociologist Ferdinand Tönnies (1855–1936) contrasted social groups formed through personal and social ties—in families, villages, and towns, for instance—that link like-minded individuals sharing values and belief systems (*gemeinschaft*) with the impersonal, formalized, and engaging links, such as economy and industry, that exist across society (*gesellschaft*). The pluralism set out by the French political thinker Alexis de Tocqueville (1805–1859) in *Democracy and America* (2000) depends on the creation of public space for such forms of community capital to exist. Community capital is formed through the tapping of reservoirs of key elements and resources in and around the community by those who comprise the community, and through the value placed on this process. This value is supported by the public-spirited impulse that survives without recourse to preexisting alignments or alliances, avoiding what de Tocqueville described as "the tyranny of the majority." From the work of the historian and philosopher Michel Foucault (1926–1984), community capital can be understood through the nodes of "local governmentality" that emerged from regional forms of power.

Key Indicators

The conditions that point to whether sufficient degrees of community capital exist in a social group include levels of pluralistic activism within participatory democracy and an active civil society with associated nongovernmental organizations (NGOs) and community-foundation groups with access to Internet resources. Economic capital augments community capital in the form of credit unions and cooperative movements, corporate social responsibility movements engaged with cause marketing, and alternative financial networks. Cultural-capital contributions to community capital incorporate "the engaged campus" with enhanced opportunities for volunteerism, knowledge sharing and pooling of existing educational resources, smaller school sizes with literacy programs, and equal access to education for all sectors in society. Particularistic elements within a region such as pedestrian access to commercial, residential, and public structures, as well as the availability of park benches, sports facilities, woodlands, and cycle lanes, play a significant role in the development and retention of levels of community capital. Therefore, spatial planning for public spaces and amenities becomes a crucial part of community-capital projects. Due to the costs involved, public/private partnerships have emerged around community projects, enhancing corporate engagement with the public sector and local municipalities.

Ecological capital is provided through the establishment of sustainable practices such as recycling, community

farming, cooperative markets, pooled labor, and alternative or green-living practices. The corrosive results of poor urban planning and neglect were outlined in David Harvey's book *Spaces of Hope* (2000). He presented the significance of good planning practice and the development of the public space as an antidote to the urban breakdown that has become characteristic of major cities such as Baltimore. The development of social ecology and ecological capital is also a significant element of the concept of sustainable development. End-of-pipe solutions are replaced with green processes that incorporate sustainable practices into the chain of production, from the product-planning stage through to recycling of used parts, with integrated forms of management and production being utilized for the benefit of the environment and wider community.

Various forms of mutual engagement create community capital that can be measured through a series of indices to quantify quality of life, happiness, health, longevity, optimism about the future, employment and wealth, civic engagement, and neighborliness. Religious participation and family interaction may also be measured as part of a community-capital index. These indices can be referenced during societal upheavals, such as economic downturns, demographic shifts, increased ethnic diversity, and spatial developments, or in wider events such as climate change, to create better understandings of community-capital reservoirs. The creations of horizontal public networks are at the core of the quest to enhance or retain levels of community capital. Public-spirited concepts such as civic leadership, egalitarian volunteerism, philanthropy, and social responsibility are crucial to this initiative. Once sufficient levels of these civic virtues are attained, the subsequent civic engagement provides an effective bridging function between nonlinear and nonaffiliated networks and the wider population. This connectivity between social networks and community capital has provided a local and interpersonal response to the anomie, or the social instability and personal uncertainty, formed from trends in globalization and accelerated change that is a characteristic of the post-modern condition.

In Chinese culture, the concept of *guānxi* is used to describe the interpersonal networks that exist between two people whereby one person is able to rely on another for assistance, favors, or other forms of community benevolence, regardless of preexisting levels of social status. *Guānxi* can also be used to describe a network of prevailing contacts that can be mobilized within the community. In addition, influence for the common good can

be maintained in this way. This form of community capital can become an unspoken norm, part of the manners or etiquettes of what the sociologist Norbert Elias (1897–1990) called *The Civilizing Process (2000)*. Ultimately a key component of sustainability is derived from the sharing of practice and knowledge that emerges from community discourse, as when innovative solutions and best practices evolve from such flows of knowledge.

Recent discussions of community capital have dealt with demographic diversity. Ethnic diversity is on the increase across developed nations. The imparting and learning of new languages and cultures is an important aspect in the development of community capital. Multicultural-based community capital creates opportunities for new forms of economic and development entrepreneurialism. This is the basis for the study *Better Together: Restoring the American Community* (Putnam and Feldstein 2003), which explores social cohesion and civic engagement within the context of shifting demographics and increased migration. Community capital is built as different cultures merge to form new identities based on the exchange of cultural norms and values, and as they develop bonds through institutions and practices such as educational pursuits and volunteerism.

Using Civic Intelligence to Address Issues

Another element in the formation of community capital is civic intelligence, or the pooled expertise devoted to addressing public or civic issues by organizations, public bodies, or individuals. Within the framework of the community, civic intelligence is the understanding that there is a value in the contribution made by all members of the community regarding the decisions affecting the community. According to the sociologist Jared Diamond in his study *Collapse: Why Some Societies Choose to Fail or Succeed* (2005), significant levels of civic intelligence are required for humankind to solve the planet's major problems such as climate change or the energy crisis.

Community capital can be seen in a range of social engagements and interactions, from community-development initiatives to intentional communities, to credit unions, cooperatives, and the social responsibility of the corporate sector. The shared experiences and values formed from community capital create a pool of human and natural resources that can be drawn upon to meet the many challenges facing neighborhoods, societies, and nations on this ever-changing planet.

Liam LEONARD
Institute of Technology, Sligo

See also in the *Berkshire Encyclopedia of Sustainability* Corporate Citizenship; CSR and CSR 2.0; Development, Sustainable; Ecological Economics; Municipalities; Public Transportation; Smart Growth; Social Enterprise

FURTHER READING

Anderson, Benedict. (1983). *Imagined communities: Reflections on the origin and spread of nationalism*. London: Verso.

Bourdieu, Pierre. (1986). The forms of capital. In John G. Richardson (Ed.), *Handbook of Theory and Research for the Sociology of Education* (pp. 241–258). New York: Greenwood Press.

Capra, Fritjof, & Pauli, Gunter. (Eds.). (1995). *Steering business towards sustainability*. New York: The United Nations University Press.

Daw, Jocelyne. (2006). *Cause marketing for non-profits: Partner for purpose, passion and profits*. Hoboken, NJ: John Wiley & Sons.

Diamond, Jared. (2005). *Collapse: Why some societies choose to fail or succeed*. New York: Viking.

Durkheim, Émile. (1893). *The division of labour in society*. New York: Free Press.

Harvey, David. (2000). *Spaces of hope*. Berkeley: University of California Press.

Harker, Richard; Mahar, Cheleen; & Wilkes, Chris. (1990). *An introduction to the work of Pierre Bourdieu*. London: Macmillan.

Leonard, Liam. (2007, Winter). Sustaining ecotopias: Identity, activism and place. *Ecopolitics Online Journal 1*(1), 105–122. Galway, Ireland: Greenhouse Press.

McMillan, David W., & Chavis, David M. (1986). Sense of community: A definition and theory. *Journal of Community Psychology, 14*(1), 6–23.

North, Peter. (2007, Winter). Alternative currencies as localised utopian practice. *Ecopolitics Online Journal 1*(1), 50–64. Galway, Ireland: Greenhouse Press.

Putnam, Robert. (2000). *Bowling alone: The collapse and revival of American community*. New York: Simon & Schuster.

Putnam, Robert, & Feldstein, Lewis M. (2003). *Better together: Restoring the American community*. New York: Simon & Schuster.

Tocqueville, Alexis de. (2000). *De la démocratie en Amerique* [Democracy in America]. (Harvey C. Mansfield & Delba Winthrop, Trans. & Eds.). Chicago: University of Chicago Press (Original work published 1835).

Consumer Behavior

Researchers have found that social, economic, and biological factors contribute to consumer behavior. Consumption of consumer goods has increased since the beginning of the twentieth century, largely because of social factors (desire for social and sexual status, displays of wealth, personal identity, and symbolic meaning). The increase affects sustainable consumption, and policy makers need to examine social contexts when addressing pro-environmental behavioral change.

U nderstanding mainstream consumer behavior is a prerequisite for understanding how to motivate or encourage pro-environmental consumer behavior. Although the terminology and the context of sustainable consumption were developed during the twentieth century, the debates about consumption, consumer behavior, and consumerism are much older and much deeper.

Consumption, in the words of the social scientist Daniel Miller (1995), has become the "vanguard of history." To question consumption is, at one level, to question history itself. To engage in attempts to change consumption patterns and consumer behaviors is to tinker with fundamental aspects of our social world. To proceed without acknowledging this degree of complexity and sophistication, many thinkers believe, is to invite an inevitable failure.

The wider debates on consumption can be traced back (at least) to classical philosophy. They encompass the critical social theory of the nineteenth and early twentieth centuries, the consumer psychology and "motivation research" of the early postwar years, the "ecological humanism" of the 1960s and 1970s, the anthropology and social philosophy of the 1970s and 1980s, and the sociology of modernity, popularized in the 1990s. Each different avenue of exploration asks slightly different questions about consumption and consumer behavior.

Consumption and Well-Being

Consumption can be viewed as a functional attempt to improve individual and collective well-being by providing the goods and services necessary to meet people's wants and desires. This linear view of consumption is generally the one encoded in conventional economics (Mas-Colell, Whinston, and Green 1995; Begg, Fischer, and Dornbusch 2003). (See figure 1. on page 9.) Stressing the "insatiability" of consumer desire and the "sovereignty" of consumer choice, economics takes a broad, utilitarian approach to evaluating consumer goods and services.

A consumer buys a particular commodity because it offers certain useful functionalities. A new car gets a person from A to B more efficiently, cheaply, and pleasantly than an old car does. A wide-screen plasma TV is easier to see and hear. People are willing to spend more money on these purchases because they value these additional services. But a consumer can never be considered entirely satiated, because new and better products and more and different ways of satisfying appetites and tastes will always be offered.

Though based on the assumption that consumers have a certain set of preferences or tastes, the economic view of consumption does not address the underlying motivations for them. The economic view goes only so far as to "reveal" the ways in which consumers spend their money in the market. Economics makes key assumptions about the rationality of consumers' ability to choose products that offer them utility and thereby contribute to their well-being.

Figure 1. A "Supply Chain" View of Well-Being

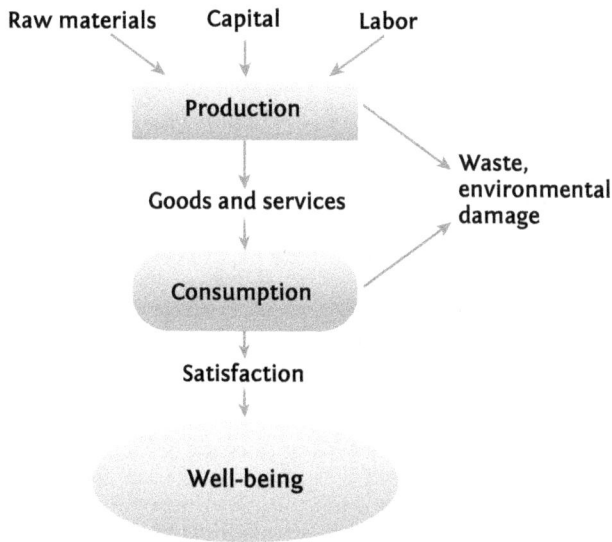

The "supply chain" view of consumption illustrates the inherent unsustainability of depending on material things for a feeling of well-being.

Consumption and Needs

Over the years, numerous critics have attacked the conventional economic position on consumption and needs. One of the most telling critiques draws heavily on the concept of human needs. Needs theorists suggest that, in contrast to the "insatiability" of desire, "true" human needs are finite, few, and universal (Max-Neef 1992; Maslow 1954, 1968).

Classifications and typologies of human needs tend to distinguish between material needs (such as subsistence and protection) and social or psychological needs (such as self-esteem, autonomy, and belongingness). They also distinguish between needs themselves and satisfiers, things that produce satisfaction. They suggest, crucially, that not all satisfiers are equally successful at meeting the underlying needs. Food, for example, is a satisfier of the need for subsistence. But not all foods have equal nutritional value, and some are positively bad for us in anything more than very small quantities.

The possibility that some of what we consume does not satisfy our needs provides the basis for a long-standing critique of consumer society (Springborg 1981). Social critics maintain that, far from meeting our needs, commercial interests in modern society have created sets of "false" or "unnatural" needs that have come to alienate consumers from their own well-being, and in the process threaten the environment (Fromm 1976; Illich 1978; Marcuse 1964;

Scitovsky 1976). According to this critique, the consumer way of life is deeply flawed. It neither serves our own best interests nor protects the environment. Proponents of this argument call on the so-called life-satisfaction paradox in defense: real consumer expenditure has more than doubled in the last thirty years, but reported life satisfaction has barely changed (Donovan, Halpern, and Sargeant 2002).

The debate about human needs has generated protracted and sometimes fierce disagreements. Cultural theorists and sociologists tend to be skeptical of this discourse on needs, arguing that it is naive, rhetorical, and moralistic. Nonetheless the language of needs has popular appeal, and it links with the discourse of sustainable development. Indeed this needs-based critique of consumer society appears to offer considerable hope for achieving sustainable consumption. If social and psychological needs really are ill served by modern commodities, then it should be possible to live better by consuming less, and in the process reduce our impacts on the environment.

On the other hand, if consumerism fails to satisfy, why do we continue to consume? The social critique of consumer society tends to point to the power of commercial marketers—the "hidden persuaders" in the sociologist Vance Packard's (1956) terminology—to "dupe" consumers into buying things that do not serve their needs. But there are a number of other equally powerful and sometimes more sophisticated responses to the question.

Consumption and Desire

One response to the question of why we continue to consume is that human needs have been overemphasized. Consumers are not driven much by coherent attempts to satisfy well-defined sets of needs and wants, according to this view. Instead many of our tastes and preferences are informed by desire. And desire, it is argued, has a different character from need. Desire is associated with powerful emotional or sexual drives and motivations, rather than with "rational" efforts to match the functional character of goods with specific personal or social requirements.

The idea that consumption is connected to sexual desire is supported by ethnographic research (Belk, Güliz, and Askegaard 2003) and bolsters the wisdom of advertising executives that "sex sells." From cigarettes to chocolate, and from underwear to cars, sexual connotation has been widely employed in advertising, both directly and indirectly, to render goods and services attractive to prospective consumers. But this association of objects with sexual desire is not an arbitrary or artificial device concocted by marketers. If it were, it would be highly unlikely to succeed. What advertising attempts to exploit is a widespread association of material commodities with sexual and social status. Therefore, for well over a century, sociological and psychological discourses on consumption have focused on displays of wealth and income and the status they bring.

This is where accounts of consumer desire sometimes call on evolutionary biology to explain and understand display- and status-oriented consumption (Wright 1994; Ridley 1994). The theory of evolution suggests that animal behaviors are the result of evolutionary adaptation under pressure from the forces of natural selection and sexual selection. (Natural selection is inter- and intraspecies competition for scarce resources, and sexual selection is intraspecies competition for sexual partners). This explanation suggests that consumer behavior is conditioned, at least partly, by social and sexual competition. It also suggests a biological basis for consumption that makes behavioral changes in consumption difficult.

Ordinary and Inconspicuous Consumption

Sociology studies suggest that the conspicuous and status-seeking aspects of consumer behavior have been overemphasized. According to this view, a great deal of consumption takes place inconspicuously as a part of the ordinary, everyday decision making of millions of individual consumers.

Ordinary consumption, argue these studies, is not oriented toward individual display. Rather it is about convenience, habit, practice, and individual responses to social norms and institutional contexts (Gronow and Warde 2001; Shove 2003; Shove and Warde 1997). Instead of acting as willing partners in the process of consumerism, consumers are "locked in" to a process of unsustainable consumption over which they have little individual control (Sanne 2002).

The concept of *inconspicuous consumption* is important to understanding consumer behavior. In particular, it connects with our day-to-day experience of consuming. Shopping for high-fashion goods may explicitly engage our display motivations on selected occasions. Apart from compulsive or addictive shoppers, however, we do not as a rule spend our day-to-day life engaged consciously in this kind of consumption. Much everyday consumption is almost invisible, even to ourselves. The regular payments that leave our bank accounts to cover our mortgages, insurance payments, utility bills, and local taxes do not appear to be associated with display or status. Even when we change electricity or gas suppliers, for example, few of us are motivated to choose a new supplier by any attempt to improve our social standing.

In this analysis, consumers are a long way from being willing actors in the consumption process, capable of exercising either rational or irrational choice in satisfying their own needs and desires. More often they find themselves locked in to unsustainable patterns of consumption, either by social norms that lie beyond individual control or by institutional constraints in which individual choice is negotiated.

Consumption and Identity

There is a broad agreement that, in modern society, consumption is in some sense inextricably linked to personal and collective identity. According to Yiannis Gabriel, a former professor of organizational theory, and Tim Lang, a food-policy professor, identity is the "Rome to which all discussions of modern Western consumption lead, whether undertaken by Marxist critics or advertising executives, deconstructionists or liberal reformers, advocates of multiculturalism or radical feminists" (1995, 81).

Certain sociologists and social philosophers believe that consumer goods are important to processes of identity creation, a belief that forms the basis for a specific view of consumer society. According to this view, the individual consumer is engaged in a continuous process of constructing and reconstructing personal identity in a continuously renegotiated universe of social and cultural symbols.

Authors take different positions on the extent to which this relationship between identity and consumerism is a good or a bad thing. The sociology professor Colin Campbell (1997) argues that an open choice of consumer goods is vital to enabling consumers to be autonomous individuals in modern society. The historian and psychotherapist Phillip Cushman (1990) argues that the "empty self" of the modern consumer, which constantly needs "filling up," is a cultural artifact, or human-made object, generated explicitly by and for the commercialism of modern society. The philosopher Jean Baudrillard (1998) condemns the "social logic" of consumption, in which people consume for status, as a "luxurious and spectacular penury."

Despite these differences, the link between the consumption of material goods and the construction and maintenance of personal identity is one of the most prominent and perhaps most important elements in modern understanding of consumer behavior. Whereas in earlier times we were what we did (or sometimes who we knew), in modern society we are what we consume.

Symbolic Role of Consumer Goods

Embedded within the idea that consumption and identity are linked lies an important insight into our relationship to consumer goods: consumer goods play vital, symbolic roles in our lives. We value goods for what they can do, but also for what they represent to us and to others. Without this belief, it is doubtful that plain "stuff" could serve such a key role in our lives. This insight resonates with popular psychology about our relationship with material possessions (artifacts). A favorite teddy bear, a wedding dress, a favorite set of golf clubs, the souped-up sports car: all these examples suggest that more is at stake in the possession of material artifacts than simple functional value.

Over the second half of the twentieth century, this popular wisdom was given more credence. The symbolic importance of consumer goods has been underlined by a wide range of intellectual sources; the evidence from anthropology is perhaps the most convincing. Societies throughout the ages have used material commodities (things of value to exchange or sell, such as cattle, for example, in early societies) as symbolic resources to denote a wide variety of different meanings in a wider variety of situations and contexts.

The lesson from the huge body of literature on the symbolic roles of goods is clear: material commodities are important to us, for what they do and for what they signify to others and to ourselves about us and about our lives, loves, desires, relationships, successes, and failings. Material commodities are not just artifacts. Nor do they offer purely functional benefits. They derive their importance, in part at least, from their symbolic role in mediating and communicating personal, social, and cultural meaning.

The symbolic role of material artifacts is not unique to modernity. In the light of the anthropological evidence, we must see the symbolic role as an essential feature of human

societies with long roots in antiquity. Any understanding of consumer behavior not built on this insight likely underestimates the social and psychological importance of consumer goods and services.

Consumption as Social Conversation

The symbolic function of consumer goods allows them to play a key role in "social conversations"—the continuing social and cultural dialogues and narratives that keep societies together and help them function. "Forget that commodities are good for eating, clothing and shelter," argue the anthropologist Mary Douglas and the economist Baron Isherwood (1996). "Forget their usefulness and try instead the idea that commodities are good for thinking; treat them as a non-verbal medium for the human creative faculty."

Douglas and Isherwood draw attention to the importance of material goods in providing "marking services." These are social rituals—dinner parties, work functions, or festive celebrations, for example—that embed people in their social group, cement social relations, and help maintain information flows within the social group. These information flows, claim Douglas and Isherwood, go far beyond the "display consumption" mentioned in the above discussion about status- and display-oriented consumption. Information flows are crucial to helping the individual maintain and improve social resilience in the face of cultural shifts and social shocks, and in helping the group maintain its social identity and negotiate intergroup relationships.

Consumption and the Pursuit of Meaning

The ability of consumer goods to operate as a form of social conversation means that they become embedded in a wide variety of different personal, social, and cultural narratives. The anthropologist Grant David McCracken (1990) argues that one of the most pressing problems a culture must deal with is the "gap between the 'real' and the 'ideal' in social life," the distance between our aspirations (for ourselves, for our society, and for human nature) and daily reality. He suggests that consumer goods help overcome this problem. Material artifacts, he says, are "bridges" to displaced

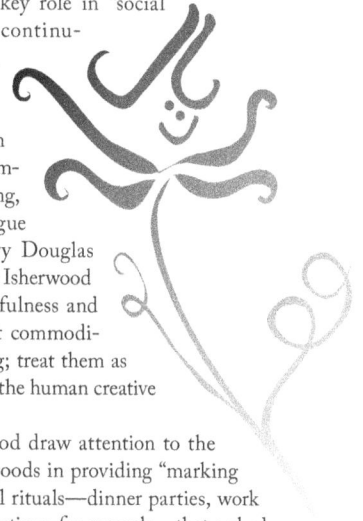

meaning (a coping strategy people use to sustain hope). Designer sunglasses, the new car, the wedding outfit, the seaside vacation are more than satisfiers of functional needs. They are bigger than the objects themselves or even than their use value. They are material representations of our expectations for the future, of the status to which we aspire, of the comforts that we deserve, of the rewards that we fervently hope will be showered upon us. They are bridges to our displaced ideals.

The concept of the pursuit of meaning is vital to understanding consumption. No purely functional account of material goods will deliver a robust model for understanding consumer behavior, because functionality is not the point (or not exclusively the point). We consume not just to nourish ourselves or protect ourselves from the elements or maintain a living; we consume in order to identify ourselves with a social group, to position ourselves within that group, to distinguish ourselves with respect to other social groups, and to communicate allegiance to certain ideals. We consume in order to communicate. Through consumption, we communicate not only with each other but with our past, with our ideals, with our fears, and with our aspirations. We consume, partly, in pursuit of meaning.

Implications for Behavioral Change

The psychological, sociological, and anthropological literature on consumption is rich. Its richness has long been recognized in marketing, consumer studies, and motivation research. Business and commercial interests have drawn widely on this depth to design products and devise strategies for persuading people to buy them. Importantly, the same literature is a resource for policy makers attempting to deal with the problem of unsustainable consumption. But the vast literature is dogged with disagreements and intellectual tensions, and its understandings straddle some well-entrenched and rather intractable debates with very long histories. Nonetheless, it is possible to draw out two or three important themes in relation to understanding unsustainable consumption.

The first theme is that we are living in a consumer society. There has been a massive expansion in the availability of consumer goods in developed economies since the mid-twentieth century. These economies have a structural reliance on consumption growth, and previously public goods and services have been extensively commercialized.

Fundamental aspects of our modern cultural identity are different than they were in the nineteenth century. Modern consumer society has its own logic, its own dynamics, its own epistemologies and ethics, its own myths and cosmologies. All of these are different from those of other times and places. Policy makers addressing the large-scale shifts in consumption patterns will be well served to examine the history of consumption.

In certain respects, however, modern consumer society is much like any other society before it. The second theme to be drawn from the consumption literature is that material artifacts have important symbolic roles and, accordingly, can negotiate crucial psychological and social functions in our lives. The main objective of consumption by the individual is, in Mary Douglas's words (1976), "to help create the social world and to find in it a credible place."

The symbolic role of material artifacts appears to be shared by every society for which there is anthropological evidence. But modern society's extensive appropriation of this symbolic role for key social and psychological purposes does appear to be a distinguishing feature of modernity. The social-psychological and cultural complexity associated with this relationship is a main reason for the apparent difficulty in analyzing consumer behavior and consumption patterns.

The third theme is equally important, because the evidence indicates that consumer motivations are often embedded in a variety of ordinary, routine, and habitualized behaviors. The behaviors are heavily influenced by social norms and practices and constrained by institutional contexts. These factors emphasize that consumers are not able to exercise free choice in the selection of goods and services, and they often find themselves locked in to specific consumption patterns by a variety of social, institutional, and cognitive constraints.

These understandings highlight the difficulty and complexity associated with negotiating pro-environmental behavioral change. They also point to the importance of understanding and influencing the social context within which consumer choice is negotiated. Policies that seek to promote pro-environmental behavioral change will need to engage the social context that shapes and constrains social action and the mechanisms of individual choice equally.

Tim JACKSON
University of Surrey

This article is based on chapter two of *Motivating Sustainable Consumption: A Review of Evidence on Consumer Behaviour and Behavioural Change*, a report to the Sustainable Development Research Network (2005) by Tim Jackson. That chapter, in turn, draws from an earlier paper published by the Sustainable Development Commission (Jackson and Michaelis 2003).

See also in the *Berkshire Encyclopedia of Sustainability* Development, Sustainable; Green Gross Domestic Product (GDP); Marketing; True Cost Economics

FURTHER READING

Baudrillard, Jean. (1998). *The consumer society: Myths and structures*. London: Sage Publications.

Begg, David; Fischer, Stanley; & Dornbusch, Rudiger. (2003). *Economics* (7th ed.). Maidenhead, UK: McGraw-Hill.

Belk, Russ; Güliz, Ger; & Askegaard, Søren. (2003). The fire of desire: A multi-sited inquiry into consumer passion. *Journal of Consumer Research, 30*(3), 325–351.

Campbell, Colin. (1997). Shopping, pleasure and the sex war. In Pasi Falk & Colin Campbell (Eds.), *The shopping experience* (pp. 166–176). London: Sage Publications.

Cushman, Philip. (1990). Why the self is empty: Toward a historically constituted psychology. *American Psychologist, 45*(5), 599–611.

Donovan, Nick; Halpern, David; & Sargeant, Richard. (2002, December). *Life satisfaction: The state of knowledge and implications for government*. Retrieved September 28, 2009, from http://www.cabinetoffice.gov.uk/media/cabinetoffice/strategy/assets/paper.pdf

Douglas, Mary. (1976). Relative poverty, relative communication. In A. H. Halsey (Ed.), *Traditions of social policy: Essays in honour of Violet Butler*. Oxford, UK: Basil Blackwell.

Douglas, Mary, & Isherwood, Baron. (1996). *The world of goods: Towards an anthropology of consumption* (Rev. ed.). London: Routledge.

Fromm, Erich. (1976). *To have or to be?* New York: Harper & Row.

Gabriel, Yiannis, & Lang, Tim. (1995). *The unmanageable consumer: Contemporary consumption and its fragmentations*. London: Sage Publications.

Giddens, Anthony. (1991). *Modernity and self-identity*. Stanford, CA: Stanford University Press.

Gronow, Jukka, & Warde, Alan. (2001). *Ordinary consumption*. London: Routledge.

Illich, Ivan. (1978). *Toward a history of needs* (1st ed.). New York: Pantheon Books.

Jackson, Tim, & Michaelis, Laurie. (2003). *Policies for sustainable consumption*. Retrieved September 28, 2009, from http://www.sd-commission.org.uk/publications/downloads/030917%20Policies%20for%20sustainable%20consumption%20_SDC%20report_.pdf

Marcuse, Herbert. (1964). *One-dimensional man: Studies in the ideology of advanced industrial society*. Boston: Beacon Press.

Mas-Colell, Andreu; Whinston, Michael D.; & Green, Jerry R. (1995). *Microeconomic theory*. New York: Oxford University Press.

Maslow, Abraham H. (1954). *Motivation and personality*. New York: Harper & Row.

Maslow, Abraham H. (1968). *Toward a psychology of being* (2nd ed.). Princeton, NJ: Van Nostrand Reinold.

Max-Neef, Manfred. (1992). Development and human needs. In Paul Elkins & Manfred Max-Neef (Eds.), *Real-life economics: Understanding wealth creation* (pp. 197–213). London: Routledge.

McCracken, Grant David. (1990). *Culture and consumption: New approaches to the symbolic character of consumer goods and activities*. Bloomington: Indiana University Press.

Miller, Daniel (Ed.). (1995). *Acknowledging consumption: A review of new studies*. London: Routledge.

Packard, Vance. (1956). *The hidden persuaders*. New York: D. McKay.

Ridley, Matt. (1994). *The red queen: Sex and the evolution of human nature* (1st American ed.). New York: Maxwell MacMillan International.

Sanne, Christer. (2002). Willing consumers—or locked in? Policies for sustainable consumption. *Ecological Economics, 42*(1–2), 273–287.

Scitovsky, Tibor. (1976). *The joyless economy: An inquiry into human satisfaction and consumer dissatisfaction*. New York: Oxford University Press.

Shove, Elizabeth. (2003). *Comfort, cleanliness and convenience: The social organization of normality*. Oxford, UK: Berg Publishers.

Shove, Elizabeth, & Warde, Alan. (1997, April). *Noticing inconspicuous consumption*. Paper presented at the European Science Foundation TERM programme workshop on Consumption, Everyday Life and Sustainability, Lancaster University, UK Retrieved September 28, 2009, from http://www.lancs.ac.uk/fass/projects/esf/inconspicuous.htm

Springborg, Patricia. (1981). *The problem of human needs and the critique of civilisation*. London: Allen & Unwin.

Wright, Richard. (1994). *The moral animal: Why we are the way we are: The new science of evolutionary psychology*. New York: Pantheon Books.

Cradle to Cradle

"Cradle to cradle" (sometimes abbreviated C2C) is a concept for sustainable waste management and natural resource conservation that aims to utilize 100 percent of all waste produced. This economic concept may be applied to such areas as urban environments, buildings, and manufacturing processes.

In 1987 Walter Stahel and Max Börlin published "Economic Strategies of Durability—Longer Product-Life of Goods as Waste Prevention Strategy." The report demonstrated how companies operating in a loop economy, which focuses on the reuse and recycling of materials over the life a product, could achieve higher profits than competitors whose continued economic growth depended on abundant sources of raw materials and resources. Some experts countered Stahel and Borlin's findings by proposing that a "cradle to grave" concept, in which a product would be responsibly monitored at every stage of its life cycle from design to disposal, was more compatible with the existing economic model used in industrialized countries. Stahel, an architect by training, insisted that the only sustainable solution was to use durable goods in a "loop" from cradle back to cradle.

Michael Braungart and William McDonough began to promote their own cradle to cradle concept based on research they contributed to *A Technical Framework for Life-Cycle Assessment* (1991), a publication that grew from a Society of Environmental Toxicology and Chemistry (SETAC) workshop with participants of various backgrounds. Braungart and McDonough agreed with Stahel that the rapid depletion of our natural resources makes the cradle to grave approach unsustainable. They also pointed out that the cradle to cradle model can be applied to any system in modern society—urban environments, buildings, and manufacturing processes—and they used many case studies to prove their point.

In their cradle to cradle model, all materials used in manufacturing processes are classified as either technical nutrients or biological nutrients. Technical nutrients are inorganic or synthetic materials manufactured by humans (such as plastic, glass, and metals) that can be used many times in a continuous cycle without any loss in quality. Biological nutrients are organic materials that, after use, can be disposed of in any natural environment to decompose.

How the Model Works

Harmful materials and chemicals continue to be used in the manufacturing (or appear in the ingredient lists) of many products. The cradle to cradle model seeks to remove dangerous technical nutrients, which may cause undesirable health effects or environmental damage, from product life cycles. This is can be achieved by producing another nontoxic product that has the same function or by replacing hazardous raw materials with a harmless substance.

Nike Considered products are an example of how a cradle to cradle business model can reduce a company's environmental footprint. From the design stage onward Nike measures its Considered lines—both apparel and footwear—according to a company index that evaluates and predicts the sustainability level of a product: a shoe will be "Considered," for example, on the basis of substantially reduced use of solvents and toxic glues during assembly (and in the application of design elements) as well as by the tanning methods used to on the principle that

a product must go back to the cradle at the end of its life, Nike's Reuse a Shoe program collects athletic footwear of any brand—whether discarded, defective, or counterfeit—from a variety of sources. The recycled shoes are then ground with scrap material from prior Nike manufacturing processes and purified; the mix, under the moniker of Nike Grind, becomes a part of a new manufacturing cycle.

C2C Companies

In 1995, McDonough and Braungart founded a consulting firm, McDonough Braungart Design Chemistry (MBDC), now based in Charlottesville, Virginia. MBDC promotes a worldwide cradle to cradle (C2C) certification program so that companies have a means to tangibly and credibly measure their achievements in environmentally friendly design. This proprietary program (i.e., it is privately sponsored and service marked), also helps customers identify and purchase products that meet C2C guidelines. MBDC corporate clients include Nike, Herman Miller (the Aeron chair manufacturer), and the United States Postal Service.

Another organization, the Product-Life Institute, is a nonprofit independent organization. Founded in 1982 in Geneva, Switzerland by Orio Giarini and Walter R. Stahel, the institute conducts contract research as consultants to industrial companies, government authorities, and universities. It develops strategies and policies for projects related to sustainability. These studies include optimization of the product-life of goods and services, improvement of the economic feasibility of goods by extending their useful life through product design, reconditioning and remarketing, selective recycling, and long-life component or product design. The institute's clients include Kodak, DuPont, and Caterpillar.

Criticisms

Some critics have stated that McDonough and Braungart keep the C2C consultancy and certification within its small proprietary circle. They point out that, with only 150 certifications, MBDC's program has so far only achieved limited effectiveness. Critics have also suggested changing the closed and proprietary approach of C2C certification to enhance competition and growth. Efforts in education, public participation, and international cooperation are important to the success of this concept.

Experts in the field of environmental protection have questioned the practicability of the concept. George Tchobanoglous, Hilary Theisen, and Samuel Vigil wrote in their 1993 book *Integrated Solid Waste Management: Engineering Principles and Management Issues* that plastics are the least recycled material in developed nations; unfortunately, there has been little change since then. Recycling and reuse are still labor-intensive processes. Because of the expensive labor costs and influential political lobbying that occurs in developed nations, recycling, reuse, and recovery of the waste have not improved much since the 1990s, especially in the United States. Another hurdle to C2C implementation is the existing technology in recycling. With plastics, for example, thermoplastics such as PETE, PVC, and HDPE are softened when heated and can be recycled and remolded. But other types of plastics, such as thermosetting plastics, are not recyclable due to their properties and the limited research on recycling them. Because of plastics' low cost, their light weight, and their ability to be formed in any shape, their use will increase, but 100 percent recycling of plastics will not be achieved in the near future. C2C is a goal and a process that cannot be reached in a short time and without considerable investment. In the long run, however, the concept of C2C may be achieved through more research in product development, proper material utilization, government regulation, public participation, and waste management.

Hsin-Neng HSIEH
New Jersey Institute of Technology

See also in the *Berkshire Encyclopedia of Sustainability* Design, Industrial; Development, Urban; Energy Efficiency; Life Cycle Assessments (LCAs); Manufacturing Practices; Natural Step Framework, The (TNSF); Remanufacturing; Sporting Goods Industry; Supply Chain Management; True Cost Economics; Zero Waste

FURTHER READING

Barnthouse, Larry; Fava, Jim; Humphreys, Ken; Hunt, Robert; Laibson, Larry; Noesen, Scott; et al. (Eds.). (1997). *Life-cycle impact assessment: The state of the art* (2nd ed.). Pensacola, FL: Society of Environmental Toxicology and Chemistry.

Börlin, Max, & Stahel, Walter. (1987). Wirtschaftliche Strategien der Dauerhaftigkeit, Betrachtungen über die Verlängerung der Lebensdauer von Produkten als Beitrag zur Vermeidung von Abfällen. Schweizerischer Bankverein-Heft Nr. 32 [Economic strategies of durability—Longer product-life of goods as waste prevention strategy. Swiss Bank Corporation Paper No. 32.]. Basel, Switzerland: Schweizerischer Bankverein.

Considered design and the environment. (2009). Retrieved October 15, 2009, from http://www.nikebiz.com/responsibility/considered_design/features/

Cox, Roger, & Lejeune, Bert. (2009, February 23). Cradle to cradle urgently needs a Dutch private partnership. Retrieved October 14, 2009, from http://www.duurzaamgebouwd.nl/index.php?pageID=3946&messageID=1751

Cradle to cradle. (2009). Retrieved October 16, 2009, from http://www.product-life.org/en/cradle-to-cradle

Fava, James; Consoli, Frank; Denison, Richard; Dickson, Kenneth; Mohin, Tim; & Vigon, Bruce (Eds.). (1993). *Conceptual framework for life-cycle impact assessment*. Pensacola, FL: Society of Environmental Toxicology and Chemistry.

Fava, James; Denison, Richard; Jones, Bruce; Curran, Mary Ann; Vigon, Bruce; Selke, Susan; et al. (Eds.). (1991). *A technical framework for life-cycle assessment*. Pensacola, FL: Society of Environmental Toxicology and Chemistry.

Lovins, L. Hunter. (2008). Rethinking production. In Worldwatch Institute (Eds.), *State of the world 2008: Innovations for a sustainable economy* (pp. 38–40). New York: W. W. Norton.

McDonough, William, & Braungart, Michael. (2002). *Cradle to cradle: Remaking the way we make things* (1st ed.). New York: North Point Press.

McDonough Braungart Design Chemistry (MBDC). (2009). Cradle-to-cradle design certification by MBDC. Retrieved October 1, 2009, from http://www.c2ccertified.com/

Tchobanoglous, George; Theisen, Hilary; & Vigil, Samuel. (1993). *Integrated solid waste management: Engineering principles and management issues*. New York: McGraw-Hill, Inc.

Vogtländer, Joost G.; Brezet, Han C.; & Hendriks, Charles F. (2008). Allocation in recycling systems: An integrated model for the analyses of environmental impact and market value. *International Journal of Life Cycle Assessment, 6*(6), 344–355.

CSR and CSR 2.0

Despite its good intentions, corporate social responsibility (CSR) has largely failed to make a significant positive impact on the world's most serious social, environmental, and ethical challenges over the past fifty years. The CSR 2.0 model presents an evolution of CSR concept and practice that is connected, scalable, and responsive—one that hopes to make a real, measurable difference in how business is conducted.

The concept of corporate social responsibility, or CSR as it is commonly known, has existed in one form or another for more than four thousand years. Several world religions have taught the immorality of usury, or the charging of excessive interest, as well as the morality of caring for those who are less fortunate. The modern concept of CSR can be traced to the last few decades of the 1800s, when industrialists and philanthropists began setting a charitable precedent that is echoed more than a hundred years later in figures such as Bill Gates of Microsoft and Warren Buffett of Berkshire Hathaway.

CSR's Recent History

CSR entered the popular lexicon in the 1950s with the US economist and college president Howard Rothmann Bowen's landmark 1953 book, *Social Responsibilities of the Businessman*. The concept took further shape in the 1960s with the birth of the environmental movement, following the US environmental scientist Rachel Carson's 1962 critique of the chemicals industry (in particular the widely used pesticide DDT) in *Silent Spring*. The consumer movement took shape with the activities of the US consumer advocate (and subsequent presidential candidate) Ralph Nader's social activism, most famously over General Motors's safety record.

The 1970s saw the first widely accepted definition of CSR emerge in the form of the US business and management ethicist Archie Carroll's four-part concept of economic, legal, ethical, and philanthropic responsibilities, later depicted as a CSR pyramid. It also was implemented in the first CSR code, the Sullivan Principles, named for the Reverend Leon H. Sullivan. He successfully challenged US businesses with South African ties to deal more forcefully with apartheid in South Africa. The 1980s brought the application of quality management to occupational health and safety and the introduction of CSR codes like Responsible Care, an initiative of the global chemical industry with the stated aim of improving health, safety, and environmental performance.

In the 1990s, CSR became institutionalized with standards like ISO 14001 (part of the International Organization for Standardization's system of voluntary industry standards for particular products and for environmental management issues) and SA8000 (overseen by Social Accountability International, a nonprofit affiliate of the Council on Economic Priorities). Guidelines like the Global Reporting Initiative (GRI) and corporate governance codes like the Cadbury and King reports (from the United Kingdom and South Africa, respectively) brought attention to the importance of stakeholders (as opposed to shareholders), among other issues.

The twenty-first century has spawned a multitude of CSR guidelines, codes, and standards addressing the industry sector and climate change variations. (*The A to Z of Corporate Social Responsibility* by George Visser et al. [2007], for instance, lists more than a hundred standards.)

An understanding of where CSR has come from is important in seeing where it is headed and what it might become in the twenty-first century. Because the term is used by such a variety of people and organizations there is a risk that it will cease to be meaningful, in the same way that the word "green" loses its luster when seemingly every product under the sun is marketed as being green.

CSR is a dynamic movement that has been evolving over decades, if not centuries, but despite this seemingly impressive progress, some would argue that CSR has failed and that we are witnessing its decline. Those who make this claim say that the concept needs to be reborn and rejuvenated. They make this claim because although CSR has had many positive impacts for communities and for the environment, it should be judged by the total impacts of business on society and the planet. Viewed this way, on every measure of social, ecological, and ethical performance that is available, the negative impacts of business (with a few notable exceptions) have been disastrous. CSR has not averted or even substantially moderated these impacts. The reasons CSR fails are threefold:

1. The incremental approach of CSR has not made any impact on the massive sustainability crises that the world faces, many of which are worsening at a pace that far outstrips any CSR-led attempts at improvement.
2. CSR is usually a peripheral corporate function, even when a company has a CSR manager or a CSR department. Shareholder-driven capitalism is pervasive, and its goal of short-term financial measures of progress contradicts the long-term stakeholder approach to capitalism that is needed for CSR to have any meaningful results. (In shareholder-driven capitalism, a company's primary purpose is to generate profits for its shareholders.)
3. Despite the rhetoric about the "business case for CSR," as practiced at the beginning of the twenty-first century, CSR remains uneconomical. Most of the difficult CSR changes that are needed to reverse the misery of poverty and mass species extinction require strategic change and massive investment. These necessary changes may be lucrative in the long term and economically rational over a generation or two, but the financial markets do not work this way—at least not yet.

A fourth point might be the old adage, "the path to hell is paved with good intentions." Although no one could possibly accuse the original framers of CSR of ill will, the fact remains that numerous corporations have used CSR to highlight their good points—providing jobs to communities or cheap goods to the consumer—in the hopes of playing down their less desirable points: environmental degradation or the promotion of an unsustainable, consumption-based economy. A classic example is Walmart, which has made significant environmental progress recently, but still leaves many questions on labor and social issues unanswered. Another is Exxon, which has strong

social programs, but has a poor reputation on environmental and climate change issues. A new model of CSR that will actually work—one that is measurable and grounded in environmental sustainability—is being delineated and developed by those who would like to avoid the mistakes made by the misguided application of CSR.

CSR 2.0

The CSR 2.0 model, first suggested by the business author and CSR expert Wayne Visser in 2008, proposes keeping the acronym CSR but rebalancing the "scales." In this new model, CSR stands for "corporate sustainability and responsibility." This change acknowledges that *sustainability* (with roots in the environmental movement) and *responsibility* (with roots in the social activist movement) are really the two main components that we should care about. A cursory look at companies' nonfinancial reports will rapidly confirm this: they are mostly either corporate sustainability reports (which typically adopt a "triple bottom line" approach of reporting social and environmental impacts along with economic performance) or corporate responsibility reports (which typically reflect a stakeholder approach).

CSR 2.0, however, also proposes a new interpretation on these terms. Like two intertwined strands of DNA, sustainability and responsibility can be thought of as different, yet complementary, elements of CSR. Hence sustainability can be conceived as the destination (challenges, vision, strategy and goals, i.e., what we are aiming for), while responsibility is more about the journey (solutions, responses, management, actions, i.e., how we get there).

If we admit the failure of previous CSR efforts at tackling our most pressing social, environmental, and ethical challenges, then the world may find itself on the cusp of a revolution, in much the same way as the Internet transitioned from the static Web 1.0 technology to the interactive Web 2.0. The emergence of social media networks, user-generated content, and open-source approaches are a fitting metaphor for the changes CSR will have to undergo if it is to redefine its contribution and make a serious impact on the social, environmental, and ethical challenges the world faces.

For example, Web 1.0 moved from a one-way, advertising-push approach to a more collaborative Google–Facebook–Twitter mode. In the same way, CSR 2.0 is starting to move beyond the outmoded approach of CSR as philanthropy or public relations (which has been widely criticized as "greenwashing") to a more interactive, stakeholder-driven model. Similarly, Web 1.0 was dominated by standardized hardware and software, but Web 2.0 encourages co-creation and diversity. So too in CSR, we are beginning to realize the limitations of the generic CSR codes and standards that have proliferated in the past ten years. The similarities between Web 1.0 and CSR 1.0 are illustrated in table 1 (below).

If this is where we have come from, where do we need to go to? The similarities between Web 2.0 and CSR 2.0 are illustrated in table 2 (below table 1).

Embracing the Future

Let us explore in more detail this revolution that will, if successful, change the way CSR is talked about and practiced and, ultimately, the way business is conducted. Five principles make up the "DNA" of CSR 2.0: connectedness to multiple stakeholders; scalability for expanding projects; responsiveness to the beneficiaries' needs; duality for balancing local concerns with larger principles; and circularity for closing the production loop so that there is no waste. Table 3 (on page 20) summarizes some of the shifts in these principles that are occurring between CSR 1.0 and CSR 2.0.

Hence, paternalistic relationships between companies and the community that are based on philanthropy give way to more equal partnerships. Defensive, minimalist responses to social and environmental issues (e.g., implementing carbon reductions only when climate legislation forces this action) are replaced with proactive strategies and investment in growing responsibility markets (e.g., investing in clean technology, as General Electric is doing with its ecomagination program). Image-conscious, public-relations approaches to CSR are no longer credible, and so companies are judged on actual social, environmental, and ethical performance (i.e., are things improving in absolute, cumulative terms?).

Although CSR specialists still have a role to play, each dimension of CSR 2.0 performance is embedded and integrated into the core operations of companies. Standardized approaches remain useful as guides to consensus, but CSR is implemented at the small-scale, local level. CSR solutions, including responsible products and services, go from niche "nice-to-haves" to mass-market "must-haves." And the whole concept of CSR loses its Western conceptual and operational dominance, becoming a more culturally diverse and internationally applied concept.

TABLE 1. Web 1.0 Compared with CSR 1.0

Web 1.0	CSR 1.0
Characterized as a vehicle for companies to connect to customers and use a new medium to present information and advertising	Characterized as a vehicle for companies to establish relationships with communities, channel philanthropic contributions, and manage their images
Saw the rise to prominence of innovators like Netscape, but these were quickly outmuscled by corporate giants like Microsoft, with its Internet Explorer browser	Included as a component of many start-up pioneers like Traidcraft, which is both a trading company and charity, but ultimately turned into a strategy for large multinational corporations like Royal Dutch Shell
Focused largely on the standardized hardware and software of the PC as its delivery platform, rather than on multilevel applications	Followed a "one size fits all" standardization through codes, standards, and guidelines to shape its offering

TABLE 2. Web 2.0 Compared with CSR 2.0

Web 2.0	CSR 2.0
Is being defined by watchwords like *collective intelligence, collaborative networks*, and *user participation*	Is being defined by terms like *global commons, innovative partnerships*, and *stakeholder involvement*
Includes tools such as social media, knowledge syndication, and beta testing	Includes mechanisms such as diverse stakeholder panels, real-time transparent reporting, and new-wave social entrepreneurship
Is as much a state of being as a technical advance—is a new philosophy or a way of seeing the world differently	Is recognizing a shift from centralized to decentralized power; a change in scale from a few large initiatives to many small ones; and a change from single, exclusive applications to multiple, shared ones

TABLE 3. Shifting CSR Principles

CSR 1.0	CSR 2.0
Paternalistic	Collaborative
Risk based	Reward based
Image driven	Performance driven
Specialized	Integrated
Standardized	Diversified
Marginal	Scalable
Western	Global

TABLE 4. Shifting CSR Practices

CSR 1.0	CSR 2.0
Premium markets	"Base of the Pyramid" (i.e., the poor) markets
Charity projects	Social enterprise
CSR indexes	CSR ratings
CSR departments	CSR incentives
Ethical consumerism	Choice editing
Product liability	Service agreements
CSR reporting cycles	CSR data streams
Stakeholder groups	Social networks
Process standards	Performance standards

How might these shifting principles manifest as CSR practices? Table 4 (above) summarizes some key changes to the way in which CSR would be implemented.

CSR would no longer manifest as luxury products and services (like many green and fair trade options) but as affordable solutions for those who most need quality-of-life improvements. Investment in self-sustaining social enterprises would be favored over donations, or "checkbook charity." CSR indexes, which rank the same large companies over and over (often revealing contradictions between indexes), would make way for CSR rating systems. These systems would turn social, environmental, ethical, and economic performance into corporate scores (A+, B–, etc., similar to credit ratings) that analysts and others could compare and integrate into their decision making.

Reliance on CSR departments would disappear or disperse as responsibility and sustainability are increasingly built into corporate performance appraisal and market-incentive systems. Whether consumers choose, or self-select, ethical products would become irrelevant, as CSR 2.0 companies would begin to "choice edit." In choice editing, companies stop offering implicitly "less ethical" product ranges, thus allowing guilt-free shopping. Liability at the end of products' life cycles would become obsolete, as the service-lease and take-back economy

becomes mainstream. Annual CSR reporting would be replaced by online, real-time CSR performance data flows. Feeding into these live communications would be Web 2.0–connected social networks, instead of periodic meetings of rather cumbersome stakeholder panels. And typical CSR 1.0 management systems standards like ISO 14001 would be less credible than new performance standards that set absolute limits and thresholds, such as those emerging in climate change.

The Purpose of Business

CSR 2.0 comes down to one thing: clarification and reorientation of the purpose of business. It is inaccurate to believe that the purpose of business is to be profitable or to serve shareholders. These are simply means to an end. Ultimately the purpose of business is to serve society by providing safe, high-quality products and services that enhance our well-being without eroding our ecological and community life-support systems.

Making a positive contribution to society is the essence of CSR 2.0—not just as a marginal afterthought, but as a way of doing business. It is not about bailing out the *Titanic* with a teaspoon—which is the effect of CSR 1.0—but about turning the whole ship around and heading back to port for a structural overhaul. CSR 2.0 is about designing and adopting an inherently sustainable and responsible business model. That business model is supported by a reformed financial and economic system that makes creating a better world the easiest and most natural and rewarding thing to do.

Wayne VISSER
CSR International

See also in the *Berkshire Encyclopedia of Sustainability* Activism–NGOs; Climate Change Disclosure; Fair Trade; Global Reporting Initiative; Greenwashing; Information and Communication Technologies (ICT); Investment, CleanTech; Investment, Socially Responsible (SRI); Stakeholder Theory; United Nations Global Compact

FURTHER READING

Achbar, Mark; Abbot, Jennifer; & Bakan, Joel. (2009). *The corporation* [Video clip]. Retrieved September 3, 2009, from http://www.thecorporation.com/

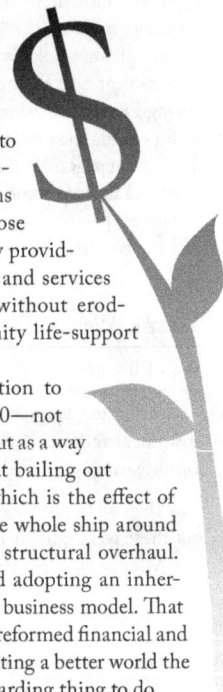

Bakan, Joel. (2004). *The corporation: The pathological pursuit of profit and power.* New York: Free Press.

Benyus, Janine M. (2002). *Biomimicry: Innovation inspired by nature.* New York: Harper Perennial.

Biomimicry Institute. (2009). Retrieved September 3, 2009, from http://www.biomimicryinstitute.org/

Bowen, Howard Rothmann. (1953). *Social responsibilities of the businessman; with a commentary by F. Ernest Johnson.* New York: Harper.

Carroll, Archie B. (1979). A three-dimensional conceptual model of corporate social performance. *Academy of Management Review, 4,* 497–505.

Carroll, Archie B. (2008). A history of corporate social responsibility: Concepts and practices. In Andrew Crane; Abagail McWilliams; Dirk Matten; Jeremy Moon; & Donald S. Siegel (Eds.), *The Oxford handbook of corporate social responsibility* (pp. 19–46). Oxford, UK: Oxford University Press.

Carson, Rachel. (1962). *Silent spring.* New York: Houghton Mifflin.

CSR International. (2009). *Welcome to CSR International—the incubator for CSR 2.0.* Retrieved September 3, 2009, from www.csrinternational.org

Elkington, John, & Hartigan, Pamela. (2008). *The power of unreasonable people: How social entrepreneurs create markets that change the world.* Boston: Harvard Business School Press.

Hawken, Paul; Lovins, Amory; & Lovins, L. Hunter. (1999). *Natural capitalism: Creating the next industrial revolution.* Boston: Little, Brown.

Henriques, Adrian. (2003, May 26). Ten things you always wanted to know about CSR (but were afraid to ask): Part 1: A brief history of corporate social responsibility (CSR). Retrieved November 4, 2009, from http://www.ethicalcorp.com/content.asp?ContentID=594

Leon H. Sullivan Foundation. (2005). *The global Sullivan principles.* Retrieved November 11, 2009, from http://www.thesullivanfoundation.org/gsp/principles/gsp/default.asp

McDonough, William, & Braungart, Michael. (2002). *Cradle to cradle: Remaking the way we make things.* New York: North Point Press.

McDonough Braungart Design Chemistry. (2009). *Transforming industry: Cradle to cradle design.* Retrieved September 3, 2009, from http://www.mbdc.com/c2c_home.htm

Natural Capitalism Solutions. (2009). Retrieved September 3, 2009, from http://www.natcapsolutions.org/

Skoll Foundation. (2009). Retrieved September 3, 2009, from http://www.skollfoundation.org/

United States Environmental Protection Agency. (2009). *Voluntary environmental management systems/ISO 14001.* Retrieved November 11, 2009, from http://www.epa.gov/OWM/iso14001/isofaq.htm

Visser, Wayne. (2010). CSR 2.0: The evolution and revolution of corporate social responsibility. In Manfred Pohl & Nick Tolhurst (Eds.), *Responsible business: How to manage a CSR strategy successfully.* Chapter 21. Chichester, UK: John Wiley & Sons.

Visser, Wayne. (2011). *The age of responsibility.* London: John Wiley & Sons.

Visser, Wayne; Matten, Dirk; Pohl, Manfred; & Tolhurst, Nick (Eds.). (2007). *The A to Z of corporate social responsibility: A complete reference guide to concepts, codes and organisations.* Chichester, UK: John Wiley & Sons.

Visser, Wayne, & McIntosh, Alastair. (1998). A short review of the historical critique of usury. *Accounting, Business & Financial History, 8*(2), 175–189.

Yunus, Muhammad, & Weber, Karl. (2007). *Creating a world without poverty: Social business and the future of capitalism.* New York: PublicAffairs.

Ecolabeling

Beginning in 1978, various countries started volun-
tary national product ecolabeling programs based on
environmental-impact assessment criteria. To increase
uniformity in European countries, the European Union
authorized a voluntary ecolabeling program for "envi-
ronmental excellence" in the 1990s. In order to provide
global standards for environmental labeling procedures,
the International Organization for Standardization
defined the ISO 14020 series of environmental labels and
declarations.

Ecolabeling is both a benchmarking tool for assessing enterprise sustainability performance and a fundamental guide to consumer choice in terms of the eco-efficiency of a process, product, or service. Besides being an acknowledged communication tool for promoting management strategies on an environmental and social scale, ecolabeling is also a marketing tool.

The complexity and rapid diffusion of socioenvironmental issues has created new challenges in production and consumption sectors in terms of adequate strategies for promoting ecological and social product compatibility and encouraging more purchase-conscious models. This approach has resulted in the proliferation of tools at international, national, and European levels that contribute to sustainability initiatives from an economic, environmental, and ethical perspective (i.e., the triple bottom line approach coined by John Elkington in 1994).

Background

The first relevant initiatives in the field of nonmandatory ecolabeling developed in Europe in the early 1980s, initially as self-declared claims by companies that attested to vague "ecological" characteristics of their products; certifications by private-sector bodies that proclaimed specific characteristics of a product (for example, chlorofluorocarbons free); or dubious declarations concerning the environmental compatibility of some types of goods (for example, green detergents, recycled paper). This kind of ecolabeling was utilized as a marketing tool, and it was often not based on valid scientific criteria. Consequently, contrary effects and market misinformation were the result.

To curb the diffusion of unofficial labels listing vague claims, many countries started voluntary national ecolabeling programs based on strict environmental-impact assessment criteria associated with production processes and accountability tools. The initiative guaranteed the diffusion of accurate information, but above all, it represented a significant instrument for firms to measure the eco-efficiency of process improvement and/or product performance.

Gradually, different environmental labeling systems were established at the national level including Blauer Engel (Blue Angel) in Germany (1978), considered by many to be the precursor of subsequent programs; EcoLogo in Canada (1988); Eco Mark in Japan (1989); White Swan in Scandinavia (1989); NF—Environnement in France (1991); Green Seal in the United States (1992); Green Label in Israel (1993); Green Label: Thailand (1994); Green Label in Hong Kong (2000); and Environmental Choice Australia (2001).

In the 1990s, the European Union (EU) authorized a voluntary ecological labeling program with Regulation EEC 880/92 (Ecolabel I), later modified by Regulation EC 1980/2000 (Ecolabel II), known as the EU "flower." The program resolved difficulties arising from the many different national nonmandatory ecolabeling systems available in Europe by creating an EU brand of "environmental excellence" for products that respected the strict requirements set out by the European Community based on the methodology of life cycle assessment (LCA).

LCA is characterized by its holistic approach "from cradle to grave" and applies life cycle thinking in quantitative terms to the environmental-overview analysis of activities related to processes or products (goods and services). In LCA, the use of resources, raw materials, energy sources, and electricity is identified as input, while emissions to air, water, and land as well as waste and by-products are recorded as outputs. The LCA procedure consists of four interrelated phases: goal and scope, life cycle inventory analysis, impact assessment, and interpretation of results.

State of the Art

Delineating the specifics of particular categories of current environmental labels is quite complex. Each system is characterized by specific programs and varies in terms of ecological criteria and standards on which product and process conformity is assessed. In addition, the ecolabeling process is still evolving in many product and service sectors. Consequently, identifying adequate systematic indicators for the evaluation of a product's true environmental impact is not always easy.

Nevertheless, within the context of the various types of ecolabeling available, systems that require certification of conformity awarded by an independent body are distinguished from those that merely portray a firm's self-certification, and nonmandatory programs are differentiated from mandatory programs such as those that require energy labeling. Taking into account the different certification and label-issuing procedures, an alternate classification can be made of the various systems on the basis of the public or private nature of the certifying body. Ecolabeling systems can be classified at international, community, and national levels.

On an international scale, many systems of nonmandatory ecolabeling are available. In order to standardize procedures in these systems, the International Organization for Standardization (ISO) has defined a set of standards regulated by the ISO 14020 series (environmental labels and declaration). As of 2009, ISO has defined three different labeling categories in this series: ISO 14024 for environmental excellence brands (type I); ISO 14021 for self-declared environmental claims (type II); and ISO 14025 for Environmental Product Declaration (EPD) (type III).

Type I Labeling

In the different type I environmental labeling systems, the EU flower—the Ecolabel logo—represents "excellence." The product groups benefiting from this label have to represent a wide sector of the market, demonstrate significant positive environmental impact at a global and/or regional level, favor research for competitive advantage among manufacturers, and satisfy real consumer expectations. Nowadays the EU Ecolabel covers a wide range of products and services that include cleaning products, appliances, paper products, textile and home and garden products, and lubricants, as well as services such as tourist accommodations and campsites.

Although the EU Ecolabel program has developed positively in recent years, it is clear that more can be done to streamline its procedures. The July 2008 proposal for the revision of the EU Ecolabel regulation introduced significant changes, including a simplified assessment procedure, a broader range of product groups, the reduction of annual fees, and the introduction of measures to encourage uniformity and synergies with other national ecolabeling programs.

Type II Labeling

The type II environmental labeling programs, based on the ISO 14021 standard, include self-declared environmental claims. The personal integrity of the producer (or the importer, distributor, and/or any subject that can benefit) is the only guarantee for this type of ecolabeling, in addition to the assumption that a series of requisites guarantee the validity of the declaration. In order to avoid excessive differences in personal declarations, which can generate confusion and consumer disorientation, the ISO 14021 standard sets out specific requisites and terms for the description, defines assessment procedures to be followed, and sets out specific guidelines that confirm the validity of the declarations on the part of the manufacturer. The requisites for self-declarations include accountability, precision, validation, detail, and clarity of reference, as well as the use of concise, straightforward language. Self-declared environmental claims range from "reduced energy (or water) consumption" to "recyclable" or "designed for recycling" to "compostable" to "recovered energy" and "reduced resource use."

Type III Labeling

The Environmental Product Declaration (EPD), known as type III environmental labeling and standardized by ISO 14025, establishes principles and specifies procedures for product development. The EPD is a document that accompanies a product and outlines the characteristics associated with environmental impact, quantified in LCA methodology, and validated by an independent body. The information is objective, quantified, verifiable, comparable, and credible, and it is primarily intended for use in business-to-business communication. Moreover, the

EPD is a tool that does not refer to predefined indicators to communicate the environmental performance of a product or service.

Implications

Ecolabeling programs can become an effective driving force in the transition process towards ecosustainability when current critical elements are eliminated. The main critical factor is undoubtedly consumer disorientation that results from the vast range of environmental labeling systems available on the market. This factor, unfortunately, affects numerous sectors including tourism, which in recent years has seen the eruption of ecolabeling certification programs and procedures characterized by very different content and impact in many areas of the world.

Moreover, this negative element is accentuated if it is taken into account that the consumer is not always capable of fully understanding the information on the label, which often requires specific competence. The reason for this is that criteria used in the different programs are not uniform and frequently far too complex or too superficial.

The combination of these elements together with the price factor, which is generally upgraded, limits the diffusion of ecocompatible products and services, especially as consumers are not always willing to pay a higher price for the purchase of goods of low environmental impact.

Another element to consider is the difficulty of assessing the "real" effects generated by using ecolabeling programs. As of 2009, there is no official published data that supplies information on volumes of sales and market shares, nor are there qualitative and quantitative indicators that refer to the reduction of environmental impact. No doubt standardization of the methodologies used by ecolabeling programs would help in implementing more efficient standards and practices. Then information on environmental protection could be streamlined with feedback from relevant data on results obtained.

A strong commitment is needed on the part of many of the participants involved to coordinate the different initiatives in order to establish a multilevel framework—based on distinct levels of sustainability—that favors rating activities within the international ecolabeling scenario.

Maria PROTO
University of Salerno

See also in the *Berkshire Encyclopedia of Sustainability* Consumer Behavior; Global Reporting Initiative (GRI); Greenwashing; Life Cycle Assessments (LCAs); Marketing; Performance Metrics

FURTHER READING

Harrington, Lloyd, & Damnics, Melissa. (2004). Energy labelling and standard programs throughout the world. Retrieved November 13, 2009, from http://www.energyrating.gov.au/library/pubs/200404-internatlabelreview.pdf

Italian National Agency for New Technologies, Energy and Sustainable Economic Development (ENEA). (2004), *L'etichetta energetica* [Energy labeling]. Rome: Edition ENEA.

Malandrino, Ornella, & Roca, Emmanuele. (2005). L'evoluzione dell'energy labelling: Analisi delle dinamiche a livello internazionale [The evolution of energy labeling: An overview of the international trend]. *Ambiente Risorse Salute, 104*(IV), 38–56.

Nebbia, Giorgio. (1998). *Il sogno della merce* [The dream of commerce]. Rome: Zephiro Licorno Edition.

Proto, Maria. (1994). Ambiente, innov azione ed eco-management [Environment, innovation, and eco-management]. *Esperienze d'impresa, 2*(II), 7–15.

Proto, Maria, & Supino, Stefania. (1999). The quality of environmental information: A new tool in achieving customer loyalty. *Total Quality Management, 4/51*(10), 679–683.

Proto, Maria; Malandrino, Ornella; & Supino, Stefania. (2004). I sistemi di gestione per la qualità [Quality management systems]. In V. Antonelli, & R. D'Alessio (Eds.), *Casi di Controllo di Gestione, Metodi, Tecniche, Casi Aziendali di Settore*. Milan: Editions IPSOA, 41–69.

Proto, Maria; Roca, Emmanuele; & Supino, Stefania. (2005). Ecolabelling: Un'analisi critica delle recenti dinamiche evolutive [A critical analysis of recent evolutionary dynamics] *Ambiente Risorse Salute, 102*(2), 25–39.

Proto, Maria; Malandrino, Ornella; & Supino, Stefania. (2007). Ecolabels: A sustainability performance in benchmarking? *Management of Environmental Quality, 18*(6), 669–683.

Supino, Stefania. (2000). L'ecolabel: Il marchio europeo di qualità ambientale. Uno strumento per la diffusione di stili di produzione e di consumo sostenibili [Ecolabel: The EU environmental label. A tool for sustainable consumption and production diffusion]. *Esperienze d'impresa, 2*(VIII), 85–96.

United States Environmental Protection Agency (EPA). (2004). *Protecting the environment—together. Energy Star and other voluntary programs. 2003 Annual Report*. Washington, DC: Environmental Protection Agency.

Ecological Economics

An ecological economics model factors in "natural capital" and "social capital" (that is, the resource assets of our ecosystem and the value of trust in relationships among individuals) in addition to financial capital as measured by gross domestic product (GDP). It proposes we measure progress in terms that acknowledge human well-being and social fairness, ecological sustainability, and real economic efficiency.

An ideology of free-market capitalism and unlimited economic growth is based on certain assumptions about the real state of the world. The financial world serves as a set of indicators for goods, services, and risks in the real world. But when such indicators are allowed to deviate too far from reality, "adjustments" must ultimately be made; crisis and panic may ensue. Ecological economics attempts to reconnect these indicators with reality by raising two crucial questions: what are our real assets, and how valuable are they? The answers lie in acquiring a new vision of what the economy is and what it is for—the proper and comprehensive accounting of real assets—and establishing new institutions that use the market in its proper role of servant rather than master.

Present Economic Model

Our mainstream vision of the economy is based on a number of assumptions that were created during the so-called frontier period when the world was still relatively empty of humans and their built infrastructure. In this "empty-world" context, built capital was the limiting factor to economic development, while natural capital and social capital were abundant. ("Built capital" comprises the infrastructure—machines, factories, buildings, and roads, for instance—that supports a society's economy; "natural

capital" refers to the land and its stock of natural resources, including ecosystems; and "social capital" refers to the value in networks of trust among individuals, as facilitated by institutions, rules, and cultural norms.) It made sense, in that context, not to worry too much about environmental and social factors of the economy since those could be assumed to be relatively unproblematic and ultimately solvable. It made sense to focus on the growth of the market economy, measured by gross domestic product (GDP), as a primary means to improve human welfare. And it followed, therefore, to think of the economy as only marketed goods and services, and to think that increasing the amount of goods and services produced and consumed was the ultimate goal.

But the world, now relatively full of humans and their built-capital infrastructure, has changed dramatically. In this new context, many believe that the goal of the economy is to sustainably improve human well-being and quality of life—and that material consumption and GDP are merely means to that end, not ends in themselves. Indeed, ancient wisdom and new psychological research reveal that material consumption exceeding real need can actually reduce well-being. Adhering to this view requires examining what it really is that contributes to sustainable human well-being; it calls for recognizing the substantial contributions of natural and social capital, which are now the limiting factors in many countries. It asks us to distinguish between poverty assessed by a low quality of life and poverty defined merely by low monetary income. To build a sustainable economy according to these principles, we must create a new model of development, one that acknowledges the new "full-world" context and vision. This new model of development would use measures of progress that clearly acknowledge the goal of sustainable human well-being and the importance of ecological sustainability, social fairness, and real economic efficiency.

A New Economic Model

Ecological sustainability implies recognizing that built capital and human capital (knowledge and physical labor) cannot infinitely substitute for natural and social capital, and that real biophysical limits exist to the expansion of the market economy.

The concept of social fairness implies that we recognize the distribution of wealth as an important determinant of social capital and quality of life. The conventional model has brought to this concept the assumption that the best way to improve well-being is through growth in marketed consumption as measured by GDP. This focus on growth has not improved overall welfare of society, and explicit attention to distribution issues is sorely needed. As Robert Frank argued in his 2007 book, *Falling Behind: How Rising Inequality Harms the Middle Class*, economic growth beyond a certain point sets up a "positional arms race" that changes the consumption context and forces everyone to overconsume positional goods (like houses and cars) that deplete the nonmarketed, nonpositional goods and services of natural and social capital. For example, the drive to consume more positional goods led many people to reach beyond their means to purchase ever larger and more expensive houses, a situation that fueled the burst of the housing bubble in 2007. Such overarching concepts of economic growth also fuel increasing inequality of income, which actually reduces overall societal well-being, not just for the poor but across the income spectrum.

Real economic efficiency implies including all resources that affect sustainable human well-being in the allocation system, not just marketed goods and services. Our current market allocation system excludes most nonmarketed natural and social capital assets and services that are critical contributors to human well-being. A new, sustainable ecological economic model would take such factors into consideration and measure and include the contributions of natural and social capital and would thus better approximate real economic efficiency the current model lacks.

The new model would also address a complex range of property rights regimes necessary to manage adequately the full range of resources that contribute to human well-being. For example, most natural and social capital assets are public goods. Making them private property does not work well. On the other hand, neither does leaving them as open access resources (with no property rights). What is needed is a third way to "propertize" these resources without privatizing them. Several new (and old) common property rights systems have been proposed to achieve this goal, including various forms of common property trusts.

The role of government in regulating and policing the private market economy would also need to be reinvented to establish ecological economics. Government has a significant role to play in expanding the "commons sector" that can propertize and manage nonmarketed natural and social capital assets. Government is important in facilitating a developing vision of what a sustainable and desirable future for a society would look like. As Tom Prugh, Robert Costanza, and Herman Daly argued in *The Local Politics of Global Sustainability*, strong democracy, based on developing a shared vision, is an essential prerequisite to building a sustainable and desirable future.

Proposed Solution

The long-term solution to the financial crisis, as ecological economists see it, is therefore to move beyond the "growth at all costs" economic model to a model that recognizes the real costs and benefits of growth. The current addiction to fossil fuels and overconsumption supported by our current economic model must be broken; a more sustainable and desirable future that focuses on quality of life rather than quantity of consumption must be created. It will not be easy; it will require new vision, new measures, and new institutions. It will require a redesign of the entire society. But breaking this addiction does not amount to sacrificing "quality of life." Ecological economists believe quite the contrary: not breaking the addiction is the real sacrifice.

Robert COSTANZA
University of Vermont

See also in the *Berkshire Encyclopedia of Sustainability* Development, Sustainable; Ecosystem Services; Financial Services Industry; Green Gross Domestic Product (GDP); Natural Capitalism; Social Enterprise; Sustainable Value Creation; True Cost Economics

FURTHER READING

Boyd, James. (2007). Nonmarket benefits of nature: What should be counted in green GDP? *Ecological Economics, 61*(4), 716–723.

Frank, Robert H. (2007). *Falling behind: How rising inequality harms the middle class.* Berkeley: University of California Press.

Hahn, Robert W. (1989). *A primer on environmental policy design.* Chur, Switzerland: Harwood Academic Publishers.

Hawken, Paul; Lovins, Amory B.; & Lovins, L. Hunter. (1999). *Natural capitalism: Creating the next Industrial Revolution.* New York: Back Bay Books.

Prugh, Thomas; Costanza, Robert; & Daly, Herman E. (2000). *The local politics of global sustainability.* Washington, DC: Island Press.

Victor, Peter A. (2008). *Managing without growth: Slower by design, not disaster.* Cheltenham, UK: Edward Elgar.

Education, Business

In order to meet the shortage of trained managers with competence in sustainable management, business schools must design and implement programs that will prepare students to deal with the environmental and social issues they will face as managers in the twenty-first century. Business schools and associated organizations and institutions are demonstrating an increasing focus on sustainability in their courses, programs, conferences, and action plans.

Business schools were questioned and implicated during the financial crisis and global economic downturn that began in late 2007. While it has long been argued that business schools are centers of academic freedom, scholars such as Henry Mintzberg (2004) and Rakesh Khurana (2007) have pointed out how the exclusive pursuit of profit and shareholder value as the primary model of capitalism has corrupted the purpose of business. Meanwhile other scholars such as Anthony Cortese (2003) and Andrew Hoffman (2009) have highlighted the lack of connection between business school priorities, such as scientific and theoretical research, and critical, real-world issues facing managers, including an increasingly interdependent set of social and environmental issues. In the context of such critique, it is important to question the purpose of management education and examine the role of sustainability in business schools.

Sustainable Management Education

Sustainable management education is about more than changing lightbulbs or switching to recycled paper on campus. It is about rethinking what is taught and how it is taught, and reassessing the connections between what is learned in the classroom and the impact of managers'

actions in the world. It is the combination of educational context, learning processes, and content designed to prepare business students to engage in the imperative—and interconnected—management issues of the twenty-first century. Sustainable management education expands the existing paradigm of "capitalism" to include the elements, principles, and values of "natural capitalism," a concept coined by the environmentalists Paul Hawken, Amory Lovins, and L. Hunter Lovins (1999). It is ultimately about imparting the knowledge, teaching the skills, and developing the competencies and courage of managers, entrepreneurs, and leaders to create a future that is ecologically sound, socially just, and economically viable for future generations.

Responses to Sustainability Issues

More and more companies in the twenty-first century are increasingly concerned about social and environmental issues and see that there is a compelling business case for action. Many are moving rapidly to try to incorporate sustainable management theory into practice. According to the world's largest directory of company-issued sustainability reports, CorporateRegister.com (2009), more than 22,700 reports citing environmentally and socially responsible practices were registered from over 5,600 companies as of September 2009.

While this momentum is impressive, one of the fundamental barriers to effective implementation of sustainable management practices is the lack of human resources—people with the skill sets to help redesign business processes and standards, rethink systems, retrain employees, communicate with customers, and/or reevaluate finance and capital management. Simply stated, there is a shortage of trained and talented managers with knowledge of, and competence in, sustainable management. According to a McKinsey & Company survey of executives, chief executive officers (CEOs) ranked the inadequate education system and the resulting lack of talent, as well as operating in new emerging markets, at the top of future constraints in meeting the challenges of environmental and social issues (Oppenheim et al. 2007).

Higher education has lagged behind the business sector on issues of sustainability, but there has been a noticeable shift since the 1990s. Once considered a novelty in management research and teaching, one indicator of change is the number of schools that are including sustainability in courses and programs. In 1998, the World Resources Institute produced a report called *Grey Pinstripes with Green Ties* that examined the inclusion of environmental topics in thirty-seven masters of business administration (MBA) schools. Later taken over by the Business and Society Program of the Aspen Institute Center for Business Education and rebranded *Beyond Grey Pinstripes*, the benchmarking report was expanded to include teaching that was related to social-impact management. The Aspen Institute's 2008 report provided information on over 130 global MBA programs. (Although the primary focus of this article is business schools in the United States, the editors, with the guidance of the author, have commissioned articles on business education worldwide for other volumes of *The Encyclopedia of Sustainability:* volume 7, *China and India: Assessing Sustainability*; volume 8, *The Americas and Oceania: Assessing Sustainability*; and volume 9, *Afro-Eurasia: Assessing Sustainability*.)

Students are perhaps the most vocal advocates for schools and colleges to address sustainability. According to a 2009 Princeton Review survey, 68 percent of students in the United States said they would value having information on a college's commitment to the environment, and almost a third of the respondents said such information would impact their decision to apply to or attend the school "very much." This is a significant change from almost fifteen years ago when a small group of MBA students created an organization called Net Impact with a mission to educate and equip individuals to use the power of business to create a more socially and environmentally sustainable world. Today the organization has fifteen thousand members in two hundred chapters that span six continents, making it perhaps the most influential sustainability-focused network of business students, graduates, and professionals. In 2008, the members created a guide to graduate programs called *Business as Unusual* to inform prospective students who were searching for sustainable business programs. The guide has become the de facto benchmarking list and featured eighty-seven schools from around the world in its 2009 report (Net Impact 2009).

Beyond pressure from students and the corporate sector, a broader network of organizations and institutions has been instrumental in moving the case for sustainable management education forward. The Academy of Management, with almost twenty thousand members, is the oldest and largest scholarly association in the world, and it plays an important role in facilitating and disseminating knowledge about management and organizations. In 1991, a small group of faculty members created the Organizations and the Natural Environment (ONE) special interest group within the academy to facilitate and legitimize management research related to environmental issues. Today ONE is recognized as a formal division, and in 2009, the annual academy conference focused on the theme "Green Management Matters." Similarly members of the Social Issues in Management (SIM) division, which was created in the 1980s, have had an important impact on stakeholder theory, corporate citizenship, and the social dimension of sustainability. The divisions and interest groups within the academy have provided an important channel for individual faculty to share research, run specialized sessions, and build support for integrating sustainability teaching into courses and research.

Faculty and administrators have also formed networks outside of the academy. The Association for the Advancement of Sustainability in Higher Education (AASHE) works to empower schools and colleges to lead sustainability initiatives by providing resources, professional development, and support to operations, education, and research divisions. In 1990, the Association of University Leaders for a Sustainable Future (ULSF) created the Talloires Declaration, a ten-point action plan that commits institutions to sustainability and environmental literacy in teaching and practice. As of 2009, over four hundred college and university presidents and chancellors worldwide had signed the declaration. The United Nations also convened a group of scholars and leading academic organizations to articulate a set of principles for responsible management education at a summit in July 2007. By September 2009, 244 institutions had adopted the resulting six Principles for Responsible Management Education (PRME 2009).

Another hopeful sign is the recent interest in sustainability among accrediting institutions, which exist to ensure that schools adhere to high-quality standards for education. (In addition to the requirement to continuously demonstrate improvement, the US Department of Education requires accreditation in order for institutions to qualify for federal and state financial aid.) The most prestigious of the business school–focused bodies is the Association to Advance Collegiate Schools of Business (AACSB). In 2008, AACSB renamed their annual conference the Sustainability Conference. Over two hundred deans, associate deans, faculty, and administrators attend this annual event. Similarly the Western Association of Schools and Colleges (WASC), the regional accrediting body, will convene its first dialogue on sustainability at the 2010 Academic Resource Conference, which is dedicated to the topic. Both AACSB and WASC are critical players in the higher education system because they can have a profound impact on the priorities and practices of schools and colleges. Although the extent to which accrediting agencies will actually require schools to demonstrate commitment to sustainability remains to be seen, this issue is clearly on the agenda of many educators and administrators.

Other organizations that are working to create dialogue about sustainability within the university system include the following:

- Second Nature, aimed at serving and supporting college and university leaders
- Higher Education Associations Sustainability Consortium, an informal network whose Fellows Program support the work of individuals aimed at accelerating sustainability projects nationwide
- American College & University Presidents' Climate Commitment, focused on reducing greenhouse gas emissions
- US Partnership on Education for Sustainable Development, focused on developing national sustainability standards
- Disciplinary Associations Network for Sustainability, which provides resources for professional development, education, and cross-disciplinary projects, as well as access to legislative briefings about higher education and sustainability-related policies

The drivers behind these efforts are clearly diverse; however, it is evident that the stakeholders of the business school system—students, faculty, graduates, funders, vendors, utilities, government agencies, recruiters,

and accrediting bodies—are increasingly looking to see if schools "get it" with regard to the issue of sustainability.

Emerging Innovations

The depth to which sustainability is integrated into business schools is varied and inconsistent. A careful look at the *Beyond Grey Pinstripes* and *Net Impact* rankings reveals a range of approaches. MBA programs utilize five distinct approaches.

Beyond the traditional MBA, the first approach involves adding courses in sustainability as electives. The number of sustainability electives offered in MBA programs increased from 13 in 2001 to 154 in 2007 (Wankel and Stoner 2009, 345). While this is an important advancement, the optional nature of electives limits the exposure of management students to sustainability concepts.

Beyond offering electives, some programs, such as the one at the Leeds School of Business at the University of Colorado, have begun to require a course related to sustainability as part of the core MBA curriculum. The Leeds School of Business takes the same approach with respect to the issues of ethics and globalization.

The next level of curriculum design is a concentration or minor that supplements the core MBA degree with a sequence of courses in subjects related to sustainability. There are a number of progressive programs in this realm, such as those offered by Duke University, the University of Oregon, and Columbia University. A related option is to offer a dual degree. The University of Michigan is a showcase example of this strategy, where students complete a master's degree in business administration in the Ross Business School and a master's degree in science in the School of Natural Resources. A number of schools have begun experimenting with a similar model to the dual-degree category—a certificate to complement the core degree. This option is more concentrated and less formally structured than the duel-degree option. Some recent programs in this category are offered by Arizona State University, York University, and Portland State University.

Although the first three approaches are important advancements, sustainability teaching remains at the periphery of core disciplines such as operations, finance, capital management, marketing, and strategy. How can sustainability be integrated into management education? What would a model curriculum look like? How could core disciplines prepare students to

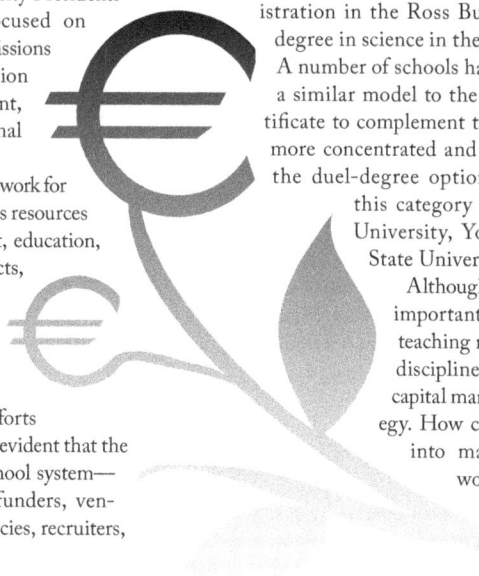

create and manage wealth while contributing to an environmentally healthy and equitable society?

A handful of institutions are experimenting with answers to these questions and providing models for sustainable management curricula. Two MBA programs blazed the trail: Bainbridge Graduate Institute launched an MBA in Sustainable Business in 2002, and Presidio Graduate School followed with an MBA in Sustainable Management in 2003. Both schools share a similar educational philosophy that is rooted in the integration of sustainability across all courses. They also share a commitment to highly relevant, practical teaching that focuses on solving real-world problems. Both schools have been recognized in the *Net Impact* and *Beyond Grey Pinstripes* reports. What is important about these examples is that they are no longer interesting experiments at the margins of higher education. In 2009, there were at least twelve similar sustainability-focused MBA programs, as well as new undergraduate and doctorate programs emerging across the United States in small, large, public, and private institutions.

Barriers to Change

It is evident that a shift is occurring in management education. While the business sector and students are the primary drivers of change, individuals, organizations, and networks are increasingly working to redefine management education and its alignment with human and natural systems. Fundamental structural issues remain for business-school educators and administrators. Perhaps the most profound is the tension between the traditional approach of management education, which focuses on rigorous research and theoretical inquiry, and the movement toward more practical, issue-based teaching, which is oriented toward meeting the challenges faced by practicing managers, including sustainability and social responsibility.

Another emerging tension is the state of the economy itself. The extent to which budget cuts to public funding in education in the United States will stall progress on sustainability remains the subject of debate in 2009. Many schools and administrators recognize that making a commitment to sustainability—if only in operations and infrastructure—is a smart thing to do. As demonstrated by the business sector, taking action on climate change reduces energy and utility costs, which could become a powerful driver for sustainability initiatives within a higher education system that faces significant budget cuts.

Outlook

While the business schools noted above deserve credit for blazing a trail and bringing change to traditional education models, the next frontier of innovation remains to be seen. In order to truly transform the economy and society, what is needed is a business school system that produces graduates who are systems thinkers and solutions-oriented problem solvers. The tipping point will be the creation of a fully integrated management education system in which the content, process, and context of learning are connected and sustainable. This vision includes:

- schools that are redesigned to function as sustainable systems; take action on issues like climate change; embody responsible consumption of energy, water, and material flow; and support sustainable development in the respective local community and region
- an approach to teaching that focuses on highly relevant, experiential, practical learning and solving real-world problems, and that creates an environment that captures and nurtures best practices that can be evaluated and replicated
- schools that function as a bridge between theory and practice by engaging business managers and leaders in dynamic learning laboratories that have real value and impact
- curriculum that goes beyond the integration of sustainability within disciplines and courses to its integration within the overarching, strategic program-level competencies—that is, management programs that are designed around, and academic excellence that is measured by, the skills, knowledge, and attributes—that management students need to have a meaningful, systems-shifting impact in the business world

Business schools have been slow to respond to the need for sustainable management education; however, the tide has begun to turn. The landscape of sustainability in business schools is best understood within a systems context, and while progress has been made with a range of innovative developments, some fundamental tensions within the larger system must be noted. Notwithstanding these tensions and the current economic outlook, the field of sustainable management continues to build momentum. Sustainability *is* the next frontier in management education where business schools will reclaim the purpose of education and produce graduates who have the courage and competence to create markets that restore ecological systems and nurture social structures.

Nicola J. ACUTT
Presidio Graduate School

Note: Information in this article regarding business school curricula and programs dates to 2009.

See also in the *Berkshire Encyclopedia of Sustainability* Corporate Citizenship; Education, Higher; Financial Services Industry; Leadership; Natural Capitalism; Stakeholder Theory

FURTHER READING

Acutt, Nicola J. (2009, July). *Alternative approaches to sustainability curriculum: The case of Presidio School of Management.* Paper presented at the AACSB Sustainability Conference, Minneapolis, MN.

American College & University Presidents' Climate Commitment. (2009). Retrieved August 18, 2009, from http://www.presidentsclimatecommitment.org/

The Aspen Institute. (2009). Retrieved August 18, 2009, from http://www.aspeninstitute.org

The Aspen Institute Center for Business Education. (2008). *Beyond grey pinstripes.* Retrieved August 18, 2009, from http://www.beyondgreypinstripes.org/index.cfm

Association for the Advancement of Sustainability in Higher Education. (2009). Retrieved August 18, 2009, from http://www.aashe.org/

Association of University Leaders for a Sustainable Future. (2001). Talloires Declaration. Retrieved August 18, 2009, from http://www.ulsf.org/programs_talloires_td.html

Association of University Leaders for a Sustainable Future. (2008). Retrieved August18, 2009, from http://www.ulsf.org/

Association to Advance Collegiate Schools of Business. (2009). Retrieved August 18, 2009, from http://www.aacsb.edu/

Barlett, Peggy F., & Chase, Geoffrey W. (Eds.). (2004). *Sustainability on campus: Stories and strategies for change.* Cambridge, MA: MIT Press.

Bielak, Debby; Bonini, Sheila M. J.; & Oppenheim, Jeremy M. (2007, October). CEOs on strategy and social issues. *McKinsey Quarterly,* 8–12.

CorporateRegister.com. (2009). Retrieved September 9, 2009, from http://corporateregister.com

Cortese, Anthony D. (2003). The critical role of higher education in creating a sustainable future. *Planning for Higher Education, 31*(3), 15–22.

Disciplinary Associations Network for Sustainability. (2008). Retrieved August 18, 2009, from http://www2.aashe.org/dans/

Environmental Association for Universities and Colleges. (2009). 2009 Green Gown Awards. Retrieved September 2, 2009, from http://www.eauc.org.uk/2009_green_gown_awards

Green, Chris. (2009, April 9). Are business schools to blame for the credit crisis? Retrieved September 2, 2009, from http://www.independent.co.uk/student/postgraduate/mbas-guide/are-business-schools-to-blame-for-the-credit-crisis-1665871.html

Hawken, Paul; Lovins, Amory; & Lovins, L. Hunter. (1999). *Natural capitalism: Creating the next industrial revolution.* Boston: Little, Brown, and Co.

Higher Education Associations Sustainability Consortium. (2007). Retrieved August 18, 2009, from http://www2.aashe.org/heasc/

Hoffman, Andrew. (2009). Deconstructing the ivory tower: Business schools' reliance on theory-driven research ignores pressing needs of real-world managers. Retrieved August 17, 2009, from http://www.thecro.com/node/786

Khurana, Rakesh. (2007). *From higher aims to hired hands: The social transformation of American business schools and the unfulfilled promise of management as a profession.* Princeton, NJ: Princeton University Press.

M'Gonigle, Michael, & Starke, Justine. (2006). *Planet U: Sustaining the world, reinventing the university.* Gabriola Island, Canada: New Society Publishers.

Mintzberg, Henry. (2004). *Managers not MBAs: A hard look at the soft practice of managing and management development.* New York: Financial Times Prentice Hall.

Net Impact. (2009). Business as unusual: 2009 student guide to graduate business programs. Retrieved September 2, 2009, from http://www.netimpact.org/displaycommon.cfm?an=1&subarticlenbr=2288

Oppenheim, Jeremy; Bonini, Sheila; Bielak, Debby; Kehm, Tarrah; & Lacy, Peter. (2007, July). *Shaping the new rules of competition: UN Global Compact participant mirror.* Washington, DC: McKinsey & Company.

Organizations and the Natural Environment: Academy of Management Division. (2009). Retrieved August 18, 2009, from http://one.aomonline.org/

Orr, David W. (1994). *Earth in mind: On education, environment and the human prospect.* Washington, DC: Island Press.

The Princeton Review. (2009, July 7). The Princeton Review gives 697 colleges "green" ratings in 2010 editions of its annual college guides and website profiles of schools. Retrieved August 17, 2009, from http://www.princetonreview.com/green/press-release.aspx

Principles for Responsible Management Education (PRME). (2009). Retrieved August 18, 2009, from http://www.unprme.org/

Rappaport, Ann, & Creighton, Sara H. (2007). *Degrees that matter: Climate change and the university.* Cambridge, MA: MIT Press.

Second Nature, Inc. (2007). Catalyzing sustainable strategies for higher education. Retrieved August 18, 2009, from http://www.secondnature.org/

Social Issues in Management Division of the Academy of Management. (2009). Retrieved August 18, 2009, from http://sim.aomonline.org/

Timpson, W. M. (2006). *147 practical tips for teaching sustainability: Connecting the environment, the economy, and society.* Madison, WI: Atwood Publishing.

US Partnership for Education for Sustainable Development. (2009). Retrieved August 18, 2009, from http://www.uspartnership.org/main/view_archive/1

Wankel, Charles, & Stoner, James A. F. (2009). *Management education for global sustainability.* Charlotte, NC: Information Age Publishing.

Western Association of Schools and Colleges. (2009). Retrieved August 18, 2009, from http://www.wascweb.org/

World Commission on Environment and Development. (1987). *Our common future.* Oxford, UK: Oxford University Press.

Facilities Management

Facilities management is a rapidly changing and diverse field that aims to seamlessly link the secondary support needs of an organization to its core business function in order to maximize business effectiveness. Much of facilities management involves planning, constructing, and maintaining built assets—sustainability and product life cycle have become important topics for the industry.

In order to understand what sustainable facilities management (FM) involves, it is first necessary to understand what FM is and, to some extent, its relatively brief history.

There is no single, definitive, and universally accepted definition of facilities management. Most explanations generally relate to a common goal. Various bodies and organizations have developed their own definitions, and they are largely concerned with what FM does, how it is done, or what difference it makes. One of the first definitions of FM was set out by the scholar Franklin Becker in 1990. He describes FM as being responsible for the coordination of all efforts relating to planning, designing, and managing buildings and their systems, including equipment and furniture. The aim is to enhance the organization's ability to compete in a world that is rapidly changing (Becker 1990, 8).

The British Institute of Facilities Management (2009) officially adopted the definition of the European Committee for Standardization, which was ratified by BSI British Standards:

> Facilities management is the integration of processes within an organisation to maintain and develop the agreed services which support and improve the effectiveness of its primary activities.

The Royal Institution of Chartered Surveyors (2006) succinctly defines FM as "the total management of all services that support the core business of an organization." And an achievement- and objective-based definition was generated in the 1990s:

> [Facilities management is] an integrated approach to maintaining, improving and adapting the buildings of an organisation in order to create an environment that strongly supports the primary objectives of that organization. (Barrett and Baldry 2003, xi)

It is tempting to assume that there is one FM industry; in reality, the FM industry is no more unified and singular than the construction industry. Both the lack of a universally accepted definition of facilities management and a lack of industry unity go hand in hand with a slightly chaotic start to the FM industry. FM as a concept originated in the early 1980s in the United States. In 1982, the term "facilities management" had not been heard in the United Kingdom, and the International Facility Management Association (IFMA) had only just formed in the United States. In 1985, a study of FM in the United Kingdom found a lack of synergy and integration among FM functions, a neglect of long-range planning, and a laissez-faire approach to space planning. It concluded, in general, that buildings were an underused resource.

As a result of a widespread lack of holistic business thinking, early FM initiatives lacked the strategic emphasis required to make FM effective. This thinking rendered FM an extension of maintenance management and too facilities oriented. Many business managers did not understand the link between primary (or core business function) and secondary (or support) business processes. More recent themes have centered on the need to simultaneously understand FM's strategic and operational aspects. Ultimately, a client is looking for effectiveness in support services (noncore activities) and facilities. The full value of FM is released when it is seamlessly integrated with the core operations of an organization; yet it needs to remain distinct enough such that it is measurable, and its value is appreciated.

A definition of sustainable facilities management should encompass the aims of sustainability and the strategic and operational importance of FM. Based on the original definition of sustainability from the UN World Commission on Environment and Development (1987), facilities management could be described as designing, constructing, and managing buildings and resources in such a way that building occupants' needs are met without the profligate use of energy and resources so that sufficient provision is left for future generations to provide for themselves.

The key to social, economic, and environmental sustainability in FM lies in a balanced approach to building design, renovation, operation, and maintenance while maximizing productivity and minimizing energy consumption, resource depletion, and waste.

FM and Sustainability

The facilities manager is well positioned within an organization to understand both the daily operational activities that keep the core business effective and the strategic implications of long-term planning decisions. He or she understands how employee satisfaction and efficiency affect productivity, as do the appropriate use of energy, materials, and resources. The subheadings that follow discuss some of the initiatives, tools, and programs that promote sustainable FM.

Environmental Management Systems

An environmental management system (EMS) is the overall framework for the actions that an enterprise takes to manage its environmental effects. Environmental management takes into account the policies, strategies, procedures, and practices that form the response of an organization to its surrounding environment.

Environmental management systems exist to ensure legislative compliance with both present constraints and anticipated future ones. Management systems and legislation were developed to minimize the risk and liability from environmental effects on the health of employees, surrounding inhabitants, and animal habitats. To this end, the reduction in the use of raw materials and primary energy will bring about increased productivity and higher resource efficiency. Decisions to improve waste-handling facilities will influence the quantity of waste produced and the associated handling costs. With higher efficiency, improved productivity, and greater environmental awareness, organizations can boost their company image and attract higher quality workers.

According to ISO14000, a global standard for environmental management systems developed by the International Organization for Standardization (2004), the environmental policy of an organization should incorporate a commitment to continual improvement in environmental performance; it should also be available for public consultation and be understood at all employee levels within the organization. ISO14000 requires a holistic approach with regard to product design, encompassing the entire life cycle to ensure that minimal environmental burdens result from new product development. Improved public image, increased asset value, improved customer satisfaction, and increased investor confidence in corporate activities can result from a well-managed EMS: increased profitability results when waste output, energy input, and resource consumption are minimized. Organizations that take responsibility for their environmental impact, and subsequently take action, are enabled to secure a more prosperous position within the global economy (Roper and Bear 2006). Five significant factors were found to support the business case for sustainability in the design and operation of buildings: resource efficiency; energy efficiency; pollution prevention; harmonization with the environment; and integrated and systemic approaches, including EMS.

Energy Use in Buildings

The built environment is the largest contributor to greenhouse gas (GHG) emissions and accounts for up to 50 percent of global carbon dioxide emissions (DTI 2002). The building construction industry consumes 40 percent of all materials entering the global economy and generates 50 percent of the global output of GHG emissions and the agents of acid rain (CEPA 2000, 2). Throughout their construction and occupation, homes in the United Kingdom are responsible for 31 percent of primary energy use (DTI 2002). From a social and economic perspective, the construction industry is the largest global industrial employer, accounting for 7 percent of total employment and 28 percent of industrial employment (Sustainable Building and Construction 2003, 5). The construction industry is responsible for a high rate of energy consumption, environmental impact, and resource depletion. In response to the Kyoto Protocol, most European governments have introduced new policy instruments to reduce the negative impacts from the building sector. The European Community's Energy Performance Directive for Buildings is one example.

Energy Performance Directive for Buildings

The European Parliament and Council's Directive 2002/91/EC on the energy performance of buildings—known as the Energy Performance Directive for Buildings, or EPDB—came into force on 4 January 2003 and aimed to increase and influence awareness of energy use in buildings. It was intended to lead to substantial increases in investments in energy-efficient measures within buildings. In December 2008, the UK government committed to an 80 percent reduction from 1990 levels of carbon dioxide emissions. Heating is the largest contributor (57 percent of domestic energy consumption; 52 percent of nondomestic energy consumption). Water heating accounts for approximately 25 percent of domestic energy consumption and 9 percent of nondomestic energy consumption; and lighting also accounts for up to one-fourth of energy consumption in commercial buildings (DTI 2002). The EPBD introduced higher standards of energy conservation for new and refurbished buildings beginning in April 2006 and requires energy performance certification for all buildings when sold or leased. In addition it introduced regular inspections for larger air-conditioning systems and made recommendations on more efficient boiler operation for commercial property.

EPCs and DECs

The EPBD has resulted in two performance certification systems within the United Kingdom. The first, Energy Performance Certificates (EPCs), gives a property an energy-efficiency rating similar to a white goods (home appliances) energy rating. They also recommend further cost-effective improvements. They are produced using standard methods and assumptions about energy usage so that the energy efficiency of one building can easily be compared with another building of the same type. This allows prospective buyers, tenants, owners, occupiers, and purchasers to see information about the energy efficiency and carbon emissions of their building so they can consider energy efficiency and fuel costs as part of their investment.

An EPC is accompanied by a recommendation report that lists cost-effective measures and other means (such as low- and zero-carbon generating systems) to improve the energy rating. A rating is also given that shows what could be achieved if all the recommendations were implemented. EPCs can be produced by accredited energy assessors only.

Since October 2008, all newly constructed and existing commercial buildings over 500 square meters require an EPC upon construction, sale, or lease. Beginning in April 2008, all public buildings over 1,000 square meters also require a Display Energy Certificate (DEC). DECs are based on actual energy consumption over a three-year period (if available). The building is given an operational rating based on its past performance, and the ratings are renewed annually. When a public building is sold or leased, an EPC is required in addition to a DEC.

BREEAM

In recognition of the fact that construction, use, and demolition of buildings account for a large share of environmental impacts arising from economic activity, the UK environmental assessment method, Building Research Establishment Environmental Assessment Method (BREEAM), was launched in 1990 and has been widely adopted there; it has inspired similar systems in the United States, Australia, and France. It offers a program for environmental labeling of buildings and sets targets for achievement in relation to a number of key performance indicators. It is a voluntary and self-funding exercise that makes assessment of global, local, and indoor impacts. BREEAM (2008) aims to:

- encourage designers, engineers, and architects to become more environmentally sensitive
- enable developers, designers, and users to respond to a demand for buildings that are friendlier to the environment and then to stimulate such a market
- raise awareness of the large impact that buildings have on the potential for global warming, acid rain, and the depletion of the ozone layer
- set targets and standards that are independently assessed and thus help to minimize false claims or distortions
- reduce the long-term impact buildings have on the environment
- reduce the use of increasingly scarce resources such as water and fossil fuels
- improve the quality of the indoor environment of buildings and hence the health and well-being of their occupants

The Scottish Natural Heritage HQ in Inverness, Scotland, is an example of a commercial project led, designed, and built by the developer yet constructed within tight budget constraints. It achieved the highest BREEAM score for offices in the United Kingdom and has an annual carbon footprint that is 30 percent below conventional best practice (26.3 kilograms of carbon dioxide per square meter) (Carbon Trust 2007). The building has been well received by its occupants, who report that they work more productively in a light and airy open-plan environment that fosters creative thinking. The internal layout is designed to stimulate casual work conversations and to allow occupants to move freely around the work space. It is a good example of how a green building can be constructed without excessive cost, while aiding productivity, supporting occupant satisfaction, and lowering carbon emissions.

LEED

The US system, Leadership in Energy and Environmental Design (LEED), is similar to the United Kingdom's BREEAM. It is based on a 0 to 100 points system and awards certificates at Certified, Silver, Gold, and Platinum levels. They can be awarded by LEED-accredited individuals only and are industry standard in the United States. Buildings constructed to LEED standards can save more than 250 percent of up-front costs over the course of a forty-year usable life cycle. The LEED rating systems can be awarded for a variety of project types including:

- new construction, designed to distinguish high performance buildings
- existing buildings, aimed at providing an operational benchmark for buildings and facilities managers
- commercial interiors, aimed at empowering tenants to make sustainable choices

Additionally there are programs for the design of core and shell systems only, schools, homes, retail and health care. The Genzyme Center in Cambridge, Massachusetts, is an example of the highest (Platinum) LEED rating for new construction, boasting a high-performance curtain-wall glazing system that allows for opening windows on each of its twelve floors. Almost one-third of its building envelope is a double-skin façade that blocks solar gains in the summer months, while trapping them in the winter. The building's central atrium allows daylight to penetrate into the heart of the building and also acts as a large return air duct. Responsible sourcing of components ensures that locally sourced and/or recycled materials have been used where possible (USGBC 2003).

Carbon Versus Cost

If the facilities manager's role is to seamlessly coordinate all activities that support the core business function and to achieve this in a sustainable manner, incorporating and embracing the initiatives set out above, then it is clear that the facilities manager's (or management team's) role should be neither position inhibited nor time bound. The facilities manager should have sufficient responsibility to endorse organizational changes that are environmentally beneficial and the authority to make decisions at the boardroom level. Often the facilities manager is uniquely positioned to understand how aspects of both the building design and operation positively or negatively influence the core business function, and how the core business requirements drive the need for built asset acquisition and disposal. At the same time the facilities manager is responsible for generating a productive and comfortable working environment. The author of a report for the Massachusetts Technology Collaborative, Gregory Kats (2003) acknowledges that the relationship between worker comfort / productivity and building design / operation is complicated, but concludes that green buildings offer better lighting quality as well as improved thermal comfort and ventilation. As a result the

report recommends that a 1 percent gain in productivity and health be attributed to LEED Silver buildings, and a 1.5 percent gain to LEED Gold and Platinum buildings. The triple bottom line (social, economic, and environmental sustainability) has been described as the mechanism that has brought sustainability to the boardroom. This highlights the economic importance of improved care of the environment. Indeed, the benefits of good environmental stewardship to an organization are numerous and include:

- reduced running costs through reduced energy consumption
- increased productivity and worker retention
- improved community standing
- increased market value
- reduced environmental impact
- reduced health liability risks

Typically the facilities manager has taken responsibility of a property at building handover, being in charge of its efficient and effective operation and management, its energy profile, maintenance, and occupancy issues. Not the least of these pressures is to achieve effectiveness at least present cost. These responsibilities are made easier when the facilities manager has input at the design and procurement stages of the building. A new facility that does not adequately satisfy a client's business needs is not capable of contributing optimally to a client's core business function.

A major controversy in the built environment and construction industries is essentially a financial one. There are two aspects to this: first is the belief that a sustainable or environmentally friendly building will cost more, and, not unrelated to the first, is an emphasis on lowest present cost rather than lowest life cycle cost.

Kats (2003) reports on the twenty-year financial net benefit of green buildings, based upon the US, Green Building Council E Analysis. When compared to conventional buildings, LEED-rated buildings consume 25–30 percent less energy, are characterized by lower peak-energy levels, are more likely to generate renewable energy on-site, and are more likely to purchase grid electricity from renewable energy sources. The twenty-year net present value (NPV) per square foot of energy savings averaged around $5.80; emissions savings, $1.20; water savings, $0.50; operations and maintenance savings, $8.50; and productivity and health benefits, $36.90 to $55.30. The associated average extra cost of building green was estimated to be between $3 and $5 per square foot. The total twenty-year NPV per square foot was $52.90 to $71.30. The direct financial benefit of improved working environments is subjective and relies on honest and objective analysis of absenteeism and employee turnover rates. There is still a clear argument,

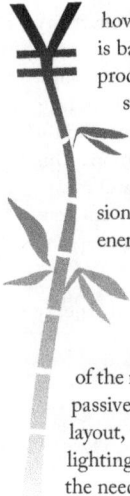

however, in support of green buildings if the analysis is based on what is truly measurable. Eliminating productivity and health benefits from the analysis still reveals a twenty-year NPV per square foot of between $11 and $13.

The overall decision to construct a sustainable building is made up of many smaller decisions that relate to issues such as occupant comfort, energy use, embodied energy, transportation, maintenance, client needs, and budgets. Raising awareness from the outset about the need for a green building with the full design team is essential in maintaining the right focus. Some of the most powerful aspects of sustainable design are passive: site selection, building orientation, internal layout, thermal mass, building fabric, solar gains, daylighting, and services. A good design team can remove the need to choose between design strategies that save energy and those that aim to boost productivity.

As an example of this teamwork, the Scottish Natural Heritage HQ has a central atrium that runs the full length of the building. It provides natural daylight, thus lowering the need for artificial lighting; it stimulates a bright and airy working environment; and it drives a passive ventilation system via heat generated in the apex. This system is operated by a stack or chimney effect whereby the velocity of escaping air increases and drives natural ventilation. The geometry and architecture of the building are designed such that the depth promotes natural cross ventilation, while a high building thermal mass limits overheating by storing heat in concrete floors and walls. The excess heat stored during the course of a day can be vented, or "night flushed" with cool air, removing the need for air conditioning. This type of "evacuated tube solar thermal system" generates 65–85 percent of the hot water requirement (Carbon Trust 2007).

The market for green products is wider than ever before: designers can specify "passive," low U-value timber windows with low-embodied energy, energy-efficient lifts or elevators, carpets with backings that don't contain polyvinyl chloride (PVC), and low–volatile organic compound (VOC) paints, to name a few. There is more competition among manufacturers, and competition has driven down the costs associated with low-energy, high-efficiency recycled goods. This widening market, which naturally contains more competition, should help to drive down the costs associated with green buildings.

Capital Versus Running Costs

Northern Europeans spend an average of 90 percent of their time indoors (Weir 1998). Compounded with the fact that most organizations attribute around 80 percent of their total costs to salaries, it is clear that life cycle issues in buildings are critical. The annual labor costs of office employees are so much greater than the those relating to the buildings they occupy that even a 25 percent saving on annual energy, maintenance, utilities, or operations are negated if the rate of absenteeism due to illness increases by one to three days per year per employee, or a loss of about two to six minutes a day of productive concentration per person (Woods 1989). It has been found that it can take about a year for an employee to reach their maximum efficiency, while the administrative costs and disruption involved in replacing a skilled employee can be as much as one-and-a-half times their annual salary (Philips 1990).

That is not to say that savings in energy, maintenance, operations, and utilities cannot be made as a result of sound management decisions and pertinent operational actions, but that it should be done with occupant comfort and productivity foremost. As legislation and initiatives regarding the office environment increase (such as EPBD, EPCs, ISO14000, BREEAM, and LEED), the wisdom of cost savings that do not consider the well-being of building occupants is questioned even further, often with the risk of litigation and accusations of professional negligence.

Achieving an effective triple bottom line therefore relies upon many factors. The use of two complimentary tools—life cycle assessment and life cycle costing—could aid in achieving this.

Life Cycle Assessment (LCA)

LCA is a methodology for evaluating the environmental impact of products, processes, and activities during their entire life cycle. The assessment includes a whole life cycle, encompassing the extraction and processing of raw materials; manufacturing, transportation, and distribution; use, reuse, maintenance, recycling; and final disposal. The facilities manager is not expected to deploy a full LCA, or any of its derivatives (such as life cycle energy analysis or life cycle carbon analysis). But an appreciation that materials and services have an embodied history attached to them, and that material and component selection is a complex combination of service life, embodied energy, carbon, efficiency of use, and possible future recycling/reuse, could significantly alter the triple bottom line of any organization.

Life Cycle Costing (LCC)

It is impossible to judge any construction project without considering its budget. LCC concerns all costs that arise from an investing decision and can be used to evaluate complete buildings, elemental parts, systems or components,

Figure 1. For most buildings, the initial capital cost is less than 25% of the total cost of ownership

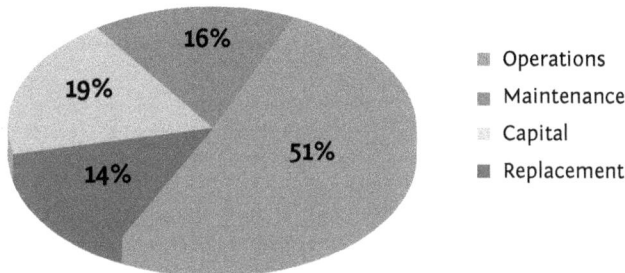

Source: RLB Building Quality Assessment, Rider Levett Bucknall, www.rlb.com/life. Retrieved 10 June, 2013, from http://rlb.com/static/2011/life/oceania/service_life-cycle-cost-and-carbon-modeling.html?nocache=22692

and materials. LCC crosses all professional boundaries and can be used by building owners, surveyors, architects, engineers, facilities managers, contractors, and material manufacturers alike. In each case, LCC is used to aid and improve the decision-making process.

LCC is defined as the present value of the total cost of an asset over its operating life, including initial capital cost, occupation costs, operating costs, and the cost or benefit of the eventual disposal at the end of its life, that is, the total cost that the project will impose throughout the whole of its life. As shown in figure 1, the initial capital cost for most buildings is less than 25 percent of the total cost of ownership. All future costs and benefits are reduced to present values by the use of discounting techniques, and therefore, the economic worth of a project can be assessed.

The facilities manager wears many hats. There is a need to satisfy energy and carbon reduction requirements, provide healthy and stimulating working environments, and to achieve these at lowest overall cost.

FM in the Twenty-First Century

The working environment is changing rapidly. Employees are increasingly becoming knowledge workers—employees whose skills are not easily transferred and whose knowledge and experience is difficult to replace, while the workplace is increasingly devoted to 24/7 activities, and a rising number of professional employees work from their own home or a mobile office. Facilities management is also evolving to keep abreast of these changes; an organization must commit to the health, safety and well-being of all its employees, regardless of work location.

The facilities manager ideally can be positioned to understand how building design and choice of materials influence the working environment, the use of energy, and the emissions of carbon; facilities managers who are responsible for the day-to-day running of built assets

need an effective understanding of how those buildings were constructed and how they operate. This understanding needs to accompany a good knowledge of building-occupant needs in relation to job function, satisfaction, communications, work-life balance, future prospects, and control of the working environment. With this mind-set, buildings are an asset that should be used efficiently and maintained effectively; the view of a building as a liability that consumes resources should diminish.

It is possible to construct low-cost, sustainable buildings that contribute to the triple bottom line of any organization. Facilities management involvement from the building conception phase through construction and operation should ensure lower environmental impact, improved productivity, better company image, and greater investment potential. The tools and methods mentioned above should guide the facilities manager to make the right decisions or even to ask the right questions. Effective FM involves being a part of a coordinated team, with influence on and direction from the boardroom.

As governments worldwide work towards satisfying the agenda set by the Kyoto agreement, the role of the facilities manager in administering buildings sustainably is likely to grow. There is a significant need for professionals who understand not only how to build new structures that are low carbon and sustainable, but who also know how to manage existing buildings more responsibly and can advise how to lessen their environmental burden.

Gillian F. MENZIES
Heriot Watt University

See also in the *Berkshire Encyclopedia of Sustainability* Accounting; Building Standards, Green; Design, Landscape; Energy Efficiency; Life Cycle Assessments (LCA); Natural Step Framework, The (TNSF); Property and Construction Industry; Smart Growth

FURTHER READING

Aronoff, Stan, & Kaplan, Audrey. (1995). *Total workplace performance: Rethinking the office environment*. Ottawa, Canada: WDL Publications.

Barrett, Peter, & Baldry, David. (2003). *Facilities management: Towards best practice* (2nd ed.). Oxford, UK: Blackwell.

Becker, Franklin. (1990). *The total workplace: Facilities management and the elastic organization*. New York: Van Nostrand Reinhold.

British Institute of Facilities Management. (2009). Facilities management introduction. Retrieved August 20, 2009, from http://www.bifm.org.uk/bifm/about/facilities

Brown, Andrew; Hinks, John; & Sneddon, John. (2001). The facilities management role in new building procurement. *Facilities, 19*(3/4), 119–130.

Building Research Establishment Environmental Assessment Method (BREEAM). (2008). BREEAM offices. Retrieved January 11, 2010, from http://www.breeam.org/page.jsp?id=17

California Environmental Protecton Agency (CEPA) Integrated Waste Management Board. (2000, July). *Designing with vision: A technical manual for material choices in sustainable construction*. Retrieved October 21, 2009, from http://www.ciwmb.ca.gov/Publications/GreenBuilding/43199009A.doc

Carbon Trust. (2007, March 31). Low carbon headquarters for Scottish Natural Heritage. Retrieved July 9, 2009, from http://www.carbontrust.co.uk/Publications/publicationdetail.htm?productid=CTS034&metaNoCache=1

Department of Trade and Industry (DTI). (2002). *Energy consumption in the United Kingdom*. Retrieved October 21, 2009, from http://www.berr.gov.uk/files/file11250.pdf

European Commission. (2006). Enterprise and industry: Construction (the European construction sector). Retrieved October 21, 2009, from http://ec.europa.eu/enterprise/construction/index_en.htm

Hodges, Christopher. (2005). A facility manager's approach to sustainability. *Journal of Facilities Management, 3*(4), 312–324.

International Organization for Standardization (ISO). (2004). ISO 14000. Retrieved on July 9, 2009, from http://www.iso.org/iso/iso_14000_essentials

Kats, Gregory H. (2003). *Green building costs and financial benefits*. Retrieved September 9, 2009, from http://www.cap-e.com/ewebeditpro/items/O59F3481.pdf

Langston, Craig, & Ding, Grace. (2001). *Sustainable practices in the built environment*. Oxford, UK: Butterworth Heinemann.

McGregor, Wes, & Then, Danny. (1999). *Facilities management and the business of space*. New York: Arnold.

Phillips, D. J. (1990). The price tag on turnover. *Personnel Journal, 69*(12), 58–61.

Rogers, Peter; Jalal, Kazi; & Boyd, John. (2008). *An introduction to sustainable development*. London: Earthscan.

Roper, Kathy O., & Bear, Jeffrey L. (2006). Justifying sustainable buildings—championing green operations. *Journal of Corporate Real Estate, 8*(2), 91–103.

Royal Institution of Chartered Surveyors. (2006). Pathway guide: Facilities management. Retrieved August 21, 2009, from http://www.rics.org/Networks/Faculties/Facilitiesmanagement/pathway_facilities_management0207.htm

Shah, Sunil. (2007). *Sustainable practices for the facilities manager*. Oxford, UK: Blackwell Publishing.

Society for Environmental Toxicology and Chemistry (SETAC). (1993). Guidelines for life-cycle assessment: A "code of practice. Woluwe, Belgium: Author.

Sustainable building and construction: Facts and figures. (2003, April–September). *UNEP Industry and Environment, 26*(2–3). Retrieved January 12, 2010, from http://www.uneptie.org/media/review/vol26no2-3/005-098.pdf

Thomas, Randall. (Ed.). (1999). *Environmental design: An introduction for architects and engineers* (2nd ed.). New York: E & FN Spon.

Von Paumgartten, Paul. (2003). The business case for high-performance green buildings: Sustainability and its financial impact. *Journal of Facilities Management, 2*(3), 26–34.

United Nations Environment Programme (UNEP). (n.d.) Sustainable building and construction. Retrieved December 21, 2009, from http://www.unep.or.jp/Ietc/Activities/Urban/sustainable_bldg_const.asp

United Nations World Commission on Environment and Development (WCED). (1987). *Our common future*. New York: Oxford University Press. Retrieved October 21, 2009, from http://www.un-documents.net/wced-ocf.htm

United States Green Building Council (USBC). (2003). Certified projects list: Genzyme Center. Retrieved September 9, 2009, from http://leedcasestudies.usgbc.org/overview.cfm?ProjectID=274

Weir, Gillian Frances. (1998). Life cycle assessment of multi-glazed windows. (Doctoral dissertation, Napier University, 2001). Retrieved October 21, 2009, from http://researchrepository.napier.ac.uk/2747/1/WeirPhDDX212540.pdf

Woods, J. E. (1989). Cost avoidance and productivity in owning and operating buildings. *Occupational Medicine, 4*(4), 753–770.

Global Reporting Initiative (GRI)

Attention to corporate social responsibility and company sustainability reporting requires a means of evaluating and monitoring an organization's business activities. Although several metrics have been developed since the late 1990s, the Global Reporting Initiative is the most widely used voluntary reporting protocol in the world. It consists of universally accepted standards that measure a business's "triple bottom line."

In an era of exposed corporate greed and resultant stakeholder demand for more comprehensive and pervasive accountability, standard concepts of business ethics and environmental stewardship have evolved into more powerful markers of corporate social responsibility and company sustainability reporting (both known as CSR). Universal guidelines have been developed and periodically updated and refined to promote increased operational transparency and to level informational reporting asymmetries. The demands and expectations of investors and other entities affected by a business's operations have served as a catalyst for the development and implementation of universally accepted standards to benchmark an organization's performance. These monitoring systems are used to measure ethical, social, and environmental performance—better known as the "triple bottom line," a form of business reporting that accounts not only for return on investment (the traditional reporting model) but also for environmental and social values. They also aid the potential investor in his or her investment decision making.

One such example of a voluntary reporting protocol—and the one most widely used internationally—is the Global Reporting Initiative (GRI) G3 Guidelines. These guidelines consist of an independent group of standards that offer a universal method of sustainability reporting. Businesses that present themselves to such scrutiny integrate their financial, environmental, and social performance reports into a single publication available to the public for open review.

Evolution of GRI Reporting

GRI was first developed in 1997—partially in response to the 1989 Exxon Valdez offshore oil spill in Alaska—by the Boston-based Coalition for Environmentally Responsible Economies (CERES) and quickly evolved into a separate division (Buchanan, Herremans, and Westwood 2008). In 2002, the United Nations Environment Programme (UNEP) bolstered the international credibility of GRI, which incorporated as a nonprofit organization and relocated its headquarters to Amsterdam. Precipitated by multistakeholder input, numerous changes to GRI measurement standards resulted in the third version of the guidelines, or G3, launched in October 2006. Currently, GRI is regarded as one of the most adopted and well-recognized methods of sustainability reporting, and it has been implemented by more than 60 percent of the Global 1000 corporations; a plethora of nongovernmental organizations (NGOs), including the United Nations; and thousands of small and medium enterprises (SMEs).

The GRI Reporting System

The GRI reporting framework consists of guidelines or queries regarding the reporting entity's operations. These measurement standards have been developed through continuous interaction with individuals representing academe, business, industry, civic organizations, labor unions, and public and governmental offices emanating from over sixty countries.

The guidelines provide core content for organizations of all sizes, geographical locations, and types. They include several terms: *indicators* measures performance; *protocols* explain the methodologies of indicators; and *sector supplements* augment the guidelines by adding content unique to certain segments of a particular industry. More specifically, the indicators contain queries pertaining to how a company's operations affect economic, environmental, human rights, labor, product responsibility, and societal issues. The protocols support each indicator by providing definitions for key terms used by each indicator and explaining the indicator's intended scope. As the "recipe" for the indicators, the protocols reflect the way in which reporting should be addressed. Sector supplements basically provide a customized version of the reporting guidelines. Several examples of industries addressed by specific sector supplements include automotive, construction and real estate, electric utilities, logistics and media, NGOs, oil and gas, and telecommunications.

G3 reporting elements are grouped into categories of economic (EC), environmental (EN), and social responsibility (SR) factors. Each of these categories is then further subdivided into individual metrics identified as "Core," or essential components, and "Additional," or supplemental components. The designation of a letter rating from *A* to *C* depends upon the number of metrics addressed and the quality and correctness of the material provided. Essentially, the measurement metrics could be identified as *how* the report is presented (for example, its clarity, level of assurances, and timeliness); *what* the report should contain as outlined by GRI's economic, environmental, and social indicators; and *whom* the submitted material affects (a designation of that entity's stakeholders). Therefore, the desired reporting outcome is to relay the extent by which company practices have impacted the Earth, people, and economies. Comprehensive, transparent reporting allows the company to reassess its strategies, provide information affecting market relations, benchmark and/or demonstrate sustainable practices, and compare its performance with other reporting companies over time. The reporting organization may self-declare its report without further assessment, elect to be audited by internal GRI personnel, or employ the assurances services of a private third-party auditor.

In addition to letter ratings, GRI offers "pluses," with *A*+ ostensibly representing the ultimate rating of integrated performance. Juxtaposed to comprehensive CSR (qualitative reporting), it is less difficult to audit financial records since numbers (quantitative reporting) are less subject to multiple interpretations. These independent audits, also known as assurance reports, must be specifically requested by the reporting company when it determines its application level. If the company indicates in its report that a third party audit was conducted, that assurance report will typically accompany the company's submission. GRI will not examine the veracity of a third-party audit. Alternatively, the reporting entity may specifically request GRI (through its network of Directors, Secretariat team, and Technical Advisory Committee) to perform this assurance process. While GRI's assessment ensures that sample research on the company's standard disclosures has been conducted and that the guidelines were used appropriately, its conclusions do not measure the quality or value of the report's content. If an independent auditor is used, GRI only checks for the presence of an external assurance statement.

Shareholder vs. Stakeholder

At a time when businesses and governments are facing conflicts that far exceed acts of internal fraud or malfeasance, and as the domestic market continues to morph internationally, there has been a transfer of focus from the individual "shareholder" to the varied and multifaceted "stakeholder." GRI has recognized this transition: the identification of a company's stakeholders is critical in achieving the highest level of transparency in reporting. In current literature, the stakeholder has been defined to include "any individual or group who can affect or is affected by the actions, decisions, policies, practices, or goals of the organization" (Carroll and Bucholtz 2006, 67). Therefore, under this broadened term, the stakeholder would represent a company's other critical constituents, including its employee pool, union representatives, the media, political units, geographic areas affected by the presence of the product manufactured or service rendered, related markets, underdeveloped and developing countries, the larger ecosystem, and ostensibly the consumer. GRI has addressed each of these stakeholders in formulating its guidelines.

Shareholders, by common definition and historical development, have encompassed persons who invest in companies, acquiring tangible evidence of their respective investments—usually in the form of stock certificates—and who expect quick, favorable financial returns. With worldwide market symbiosis, the individual concern has had to defer to more defined collective consequences. With the realities of carbon dioxide emissions threatening the ecological balance and dangerously placing all life forms in serious peril, transparent reporting and comprehensive accountability have risen to the forefront in the search for remedial answers. Therefore, the manufacture of products and creation of services must now be measured against the effects and impact upon the

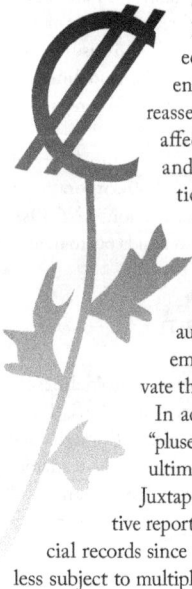

"stakeholder." GRI, through its G3 Guidelines, provides a comprehensive method of measuring such impact.

International Reporting Guidelines

The GRI sustainability guidelines are recognized as the most integrated framework for disclosure of a business's social and environmental performance, incorporating a broad range of performance metrics. Other social reporting systems include the ISO 14000 series (International Organization for Standardization), an internationally recognized environmental certification process regarded as more inclusive of all societal and environmental stakeholders that moves beyond mere compliance to developing policies of continuous improvement; ISEA Standard AA1000 (Institute of Social and Ethical Accountability), which focuses primarily on social and ethical accounting; the Copenhagen Charter, an international standard involving stakeholder communications and the commitment of key management figures to open dialogue with certain identifiable stakeholders; SAI 8000 (Social Accountability International), a system of accounting that concentrates primarily on the organization's labor practices; and EMAS (European Management Audit System), measurement indicators primarily targeted to European Union–based companies espousing environmental policies.

Inherent Deficiencies in Voluntary Reporting

Ostensibly, there will always be deficiencies in any type of reporting that involves any degree of subjectivity. And without mandatory reporting, how truly effective is reporting on a voluntary basis? Without a universal mandate for CSR, certain queries are inevitable. For instance, how truly comprehensive is a company's voluntary effort to reveal its strengths and deficiencies as well as define the overall ramifications of its business operations on its stakeholders? What are the organization's checks and balances and are they implemented on a temporary or permanent basis? What safeguards are in place to separate rhetoric from reality?

One would naturally expect there to be a certain amount of "greenwashing" and sugarcoating of facts within the report in order to lure the would-be investor and repel the investigating consumer advocate or inquiring politician. If the stakeholder is being given an increased role in dialoging with the reporting company, should not the stakeholder then participate in that business's development of its organizational program, its growth and business goals, and its particular mission? Reporting *to* or *about* nontraditional stakeholders would logically presuppose that these interested parties are in continual discourse with the reporting entity.

Self-reporting assumes that the reporter is speaking the truth, and it is not always possible to confirm the substance of the information disseminated. It is usually a chief officer who selects the information to be released, material that might be technically correct but present a distorted image of the business's operations. Trade secrets—encompassing everything from a product recipe to a customer list—are given special exemption protection, but such absence of information may undercut the goal of comprehensive transparent and sustainability reporting.

While GRI identifies detailed reporting standards, it is still the prerogative of the reporting entity to define its particular stakeholders.

The Future of GRI

GRI is a dynamic organization, continuously responding to rapidly developing technologies and feedback for additional, modified, or deleted guideline queries to respond to the needs of business and its many stakeholders. Assurance reporting, guideline categorization, and digitalizing its reporting "language" are key examples of GRI's commitment to providing the best methods of comprehensive, transparent reporting.

Sector Supplements

As all industries cannot be adequately evaluated by a "one size fits all" set of metrics, GRI has created individual categories for certain types of businesses as mentioned previously, formulating indicators unique to such industries. GRI has determined that these sectors require specialized guidance to complement, not substitute for, the Guidelines.

Matchmaker Program

The GRI organization inaugurated a "matchmaker" program with the launching of the G3 protocol to offer institutions of higher learning an opportunity to become part of a three-tiered process of reporting, verification, and critique.

Business entities voluntarily submit information concerning their operations, nature, and composition of products produced, scope of business influence and dealings, and details of labor and management interaction (the reporting element). The information disseminated is then audited by an independent entity that is allowed access to the company for verification, follow-up, and substantiation of information provided (the audit/verification element). Finally, as an affirmation of the auditing process, an institution of higher learning is invited to review and assess the reports prepared by both entities (the critique element). The findings of all three organizations are then summarized and the company is then rated. This rating and the G3 Protocol conclusions are stored online with GRI, offering the public additional details regarding stakeholder effect.

Universal Labeling

In an attempt to uniformly segregate and identify the components, characteristics, and effects of a business's operations as well as to facilitate the electronic communication of business and financial reporting, GRI is participating in the development of "eXtensible (sic) Business Reporting Language" (XBRL) and moving toward global uniform reporting and the configuration of data in a digital format compatible with financial reporting requirements. This method of organization is accomplished by placing a "tag" on certain numbers and qualitative material that can be recognized by computers and downloaded, analyzed, and stored. This process essentially filters variables and labels, helping both investors to base decisions upon sustainability information and researchers to import desired information into their data systems. For example, "GHG" would represent greenhouse gases and alert the researcher or potential investor to that particular data. In this manner, a comprehensive taxonomy list may be developed for worldwide usage.

National Annexes

As specific regions and countries pose unique features, GRI is attempting to modify its guidelines to reflect how these differences might impact the reporting process. Cultural distinctions endemic to specific countries and regions often produce a different perspective as to how the reporting entity's operations impact their respective communities. In this manner, GRI faces the challenge of identifying and labeling these indicators of community impact and assessing compliance with suggested practices.

GRI has undoubtedly pioneered the world's most extensive and widely used sustainability reporting protocol. As the framework continues to respond to changing global dynamics, GRI strives to respond accordingly through its consensus-seeking process that draws in contributors globally, representing industry, governance, labor, and professional institutions. Acknowledging the flaws of trade secret protection and potentially inaccurate self-assessment, GRI remains committed to continuous improvement to effect the highest level of transparency in sustainability reporting.

Elizabeth F. R. GINGERICH
Valparaiso University College of Business Administration

See also in the *Berkshire Encyclopedia of Sustainability* Accounting; CSR and CSR 2.0; Ecolabeling; Equator Principles; Performance Metrics; Stakeholder Theory; Transparency; Triple Bottom Line

FURTHER READING

Bartiromo, Maria. (2008, May 8). Bill Joy on going green, Google, Apple, and Microsoft. *BusinessWeek*, pp. 19–20. Retrieved September 29, 2009, from http://www.businessweek.com/magazine/content/08_20/b4084019471312.htm

Buchanan, Mark; Herremans, Irene; & Westwood, Joanne. (2008). Student engagement and sustainability reporting: The Global Reporting Initiative Matchmaker Program. Retrieved September 29, 2009, from http://www.globalreporting.org/NR/rdonlyres/C6864151-9DAC-4EC1-B8F9-96B7F8B7824C/0/GRIMatchmakerProgram_MarkBuchanan2008.pdf

Carroll, Archie B., & Bucholtz, Ann K. (2006). *Business and society: Ethics and stakeholder management* (6th ed.). Mason, OH: Thompson Southwestern Publishing.

Global Reporting Initiative. (2009). Retrieved September 29, 2009, from http://www.globalreporting.org

Habermas, Jürgen. (1990). *Moral consciousness and communicative action* (Christian Lenhardt & Shierry Weber Nicholsen, Trans.). Cambridge, MA: MIT Press. (Original work published 1983)

Ord, Gavan (2008). Major changes in the air. *Intheblack, 78*(2), 13.

Pulver, Simone. (2007). Making sense of corporate environmentalism. *Organization & Environment, 20*(1), 21–25.

Reynolds, MaryAnn, & Yuthas, Kristi. (2007). Moral discourse and corporate social responsibility reporting. *Journal of Business Ethics, 78*(1–2), 47–64.

Stern, Nicholas, (2007). *The economics of climate change: The Stern Review.* Cambridge, UK: Cambridge University Press.

XBRL could push sustainability reporting into the realm of the CFO. (2007, December 21). *The Environmental Leader.* Retrieved September 29, 2009, from http://www.environmentalleader.com/2007/12/21/xbrl-could-push-sustainability-reporting-into-the-realm-of-the-cfo/

Greenwashing

Although not always used intentionally, greenwashing refers to deceptive public relations or marketing claims about so-called environmentally friendly products. It is a prominent practice; an overwhelming majority of green goods are the focus of some type of greenwashing. These misrepresentations result in consumer distrust, which threatens the survival of the developing market for green products.

The green marketplace is an increasingly attractive one for the business world. Recent surveys indicate that over 90 percent of consumers in the United States say that they participate in the world of sustainability (Hartman Group 2007), and a large segment (37 percent) feel highly concerned about the environment (California Green Solutions 2007). US consumers are expected to increase spending on green products (products that are organic, natural, or are otherwise environmentally friendly) to $420 billion in 2010 (Mooth 2009).

Unfortunately not all signs are encouraging. Consumers in many cases still have not bought into the benefits of going green. While 49 percent say that a company's environmental record is important, only 21 percent say it has driven their choice (Wasserman 2008). Many consumers not only continue to question whether the price premium for green products is justified, but they are also skeptical of the product's environmental claims; very few—only 10 percent—trust the environmental information they get from business and the government (Futerra 2009, 1). Charges of greenwashing are consistently made by consumers, government agencies, and consumer advocacy groups.

What Is Greenwashing?

Greenwashing typically refers to advertising, public relations, or product package claims that inadvertently, or in some cases deliberately, mislead consumers about the environmental benefits of a company, product, or service. Some groups broadly apply the term to any company that promotes any aspect of environmental benefit while ignoring other damaging impacts of their company operations. For example, Shell recently withdrew its sponsorship of a wildlife exhibit after complaints that it was using this tactic to greenwash its environmental credentials. Others have tried to offer guidance by providing greenwashing categories. Notable among them is the company TerraChoice Environmental Marketing (2009), which recently found that over 98 percent of green products committed at least one of their "seven sins of greenwashing":

1. Hidden Trade-off. Seventy-three percent of companies were guilty of focusing on a narrow set of attributes while ignoring other environmental issues. A washing machine that promotes its energy savings while using large quantities of water would be an example.
2. No Proof. A paper-towel company that stated its products contained 80 percent postconsumer recycled content would be an example of this sin. Committed by

59 percent of companies, it refers to claims that "cannot be substantiated by easily accessible supporting information or by a reliable third-party certification."

3. Vagueness. *Good for the Earth and environmentally friendly* are general terms that are not easily interpreted. Fifty-six percent of products surveyed committed this sin.

4. False Labels. Many companies use legitimate third-party organizations (for example, Energy Star in the United States and European Union) to test and provide certification regarding their green claims. A company that uses its own in-house certification without additional explanation is an example of the 24 percent of companies that use false labels that mislead consumers.

5. Irrelevance. A number of claims are truthful but irrelevant. Some paper towels are advertised as 100 percent cellulose. This is true, but all paper towels are made out of cellulose. Eight percent commit this sin.

6. Lesser of Two Evils. Environmentally friendly pesticides are an example of this sin. These claims distract consumers from the potentially larger environmental impact of the product. Only 4 percent of companies committed this.

7. Fibbing. Outright deceit was committed by less than 1 percent of products. Claiming a particular certification (such as USDA organic) would be an example.

Greenwashing Versus Spin

The "seven sins" reveal that most greenwashing is not a malicious intent to deceive consumers. Particularly for new categories, consumers rely extensively on product communication to inform their decision making. Misleading communications hurt consumers and also disadvantage those companies with legitimate green attributes. Consumers may end up supporting companies with few actual green features. If consumers can't trust the green information provided, they will no longer base their purchases on this attribute, and companies no longer have an incentive to develop safe green products. The market will die before it has an opportunity to grow.

Growing consumer interest and demand for green products makes an inviting target for companies to highlight any green aspect they can find in their company or product. This has led to an increase in consumer complaints against many environmental claims; a fivefold increase has occurred in the United Kingdom since 2006 (Wilson 2008, 1). Some categories are more prone to greenwashing than others. For example, in the United Kingdom greenwashing most commonly was found in the travel and automotive industries, while in the United States it is most prevalent in toys, cleansers, and cosmetics (Futerra 2009).

Avoiding Greenwashing

Although the global standards developed by the International Organization for Standardization (ISO) provide a comprehensive list of guidelines for environmental labeling, many countries have adopted their own due to varying consumer knowledge and cultural specifics. Countries including the United Kingdom, France, and the United States are beginning to revisit guidelines that were originally developed before words such as *renewable energy, sustainability,* and *carbon offset* were introduced. Consumer advocacy groups such as Greenpeace and Co-op America consistently investigate and report corporate greenwashing instances, and websites such as greenwashingindex. com allow consumers to seek out and report greenwashing activities.

Over 60 percent of consumers view sustainability campaigns as just another marketing tool. This creates a strong barrier that companies marketing green products must overcome. Although there is no such thing as a completely green product, companies can help grow the green market by using guides such as the seven sins or the ten signs of greenwashing (Futerra 2009).

Similar to any product category, consumers need to be educated customers. They need to be wary of unsubstantiated claims and carefully examine symbols and logos. Look beyond the pretty art and lofty words. Finally, if the green product industry is to survive, consumers must be willing to support legitimate offerings through their purchasing decisions.

Norm BORIN
*Orfalea College of Business,
California Polytechnic State University*

See also in the *Berkshire Encyclopedia of Sustainability* Consumer Behavior; Ecolabeling; Marketing; Packaging

FURTHER READING

California Green Solutions. (2007, August). Green consumer research outlines the challenge. Retrieved October 12, 2009, from http://www.californiagreensolutions.com/cgi-bin/gt/tpl.h,content=688

CBS Interactive, Inc. (2008, May 18). A closer look at "green" products: Manufacturers are making more environmentally friendly products, but not all stand up to the test. Retrieved March 24, 2009, from http://www.cbsnews.com/stories/2008/05/18/eveningnews/main4105507.shtml

Futerra Sustainability Communications. (2009). *The greenwash guide.* Retrieved June 22, 2009, from http://www.futerra.co.uk/downloads/Greenwash_Guide.pdf

Hartman Group. (2007, April). *The Hartman report on sustainability: Understanding the consumer perspective.* Bellevue, WA: Author.

International Institute for Sustainable Development (IISD). (1996). *Global green standards: ISO 14000 and sustainable development.* Retrieved June 24, 2009, from http://www.iisd.org/pdf/globlgrn.pdf

Kanter, James. (April 30, 2009). Study: For consumers, green is greenwash. *New York Times.* Retrieved June 23, 2009, from http://greeninc.blogs.nytimes.com/2009/04/30/study-for-consumers-green-is-greenwash/

Mooth, Robert. (2009). Winning at green innovation. Retrieved November 2, 2009, from http://en-us.nielsen.com/main/insights/consumer_insight/issue_16/winning_at_green_innovation

TerraChoice Environmental Marketing. (2009). Seven sins of greenwashing. Retrieved June 20, 2009, from http://sinsofgreenwashing.org/

Wasserman, Todd. (2008, May 20). Mintel: "Green" products top 5,933 in 2007. Retrieved March 24, 2009, from http://www.brandweek.com/bw/news/packaged/article_display.jsp?vnu_content_id=1003805821

Wilson, Matt. (2008, June). Is green a grey area? How the Advertising Standards Authority rules on environmental marketing claims. Retrieved December 14, 2009, from http://www.warc.com/LandingPages/FeaturedContent/EnvironmentalClaims/ASAEnvironmentalClaims.pdf

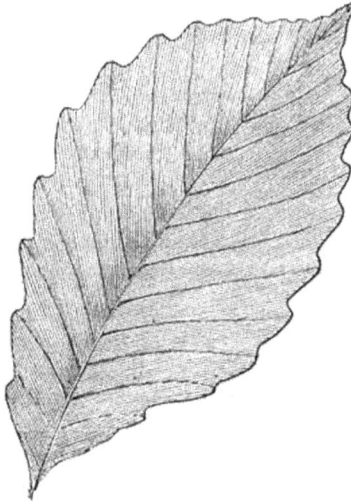

Green Gross Domestic Product (GDP)

Traditional measurements of performance, such as gross domestic product (GDP), account for economic development but do not accurately reflect human or environmental well-being. Since the 1990s several new metrics have been proposed, including green GDP, which attempts to provide a more accurate accounting that considers both the positive transactions that benefit well-being and the negative economic activities that diminish it.

The concept of "green GDP" arose in the early 1990s in reaction to the deficiencies of the traditional gross domestic product (GDP) to account for the economic costs of depleted natural resources and incurred pollution, which in turn affect human welfare. GDP is usually defined as the total market value of all final goods and services produced within a territory in a given period of time (usually a year), including exports minus imports (net exports). It has been used as a standard measure of the size of an economy in national accounting and is often mistakenly regarded as a proxy for progress in the public discourse. A closely related term is *gross national product* (GNP), which is GDP plus international income transfers. The term *gross* means the exclusion of capital depreciation from the accounting. Infrastructural wear and tear, for instance, do not make their way into the GDP. When such considerations are taken into account, *net domestic product* (NDP) and *net national product* (NNP) are used.

Limits of Traditional GDP

Ecosystem services such as climate regulation, carbon sequestration, and nutrient cycling, while indispensable for human survival, are not part of traditional economic accounting. Some have estimated the economic value of the world's ecosystem services to be US$33 trillion per year on average, mostly outside the market and almost twice as much as the global GDP total (Costanza et al. 1997). Valuing ecosystem services, however, has been controversial to some economists and ecologists for methodological and other reasons. GDP omits many of the important goods and services that we derive from nature because its scope is delimited completely by the market. Thus, despite its prominent position in economic analysis and public policy, GDP has become the target of increasing criticism in recent decades. In GDP accounting, no distinction is made between activities that contribute to well-being and those that detract from it. A classic example is an oil spill, which is counted as a positive addition to the GDP because it warrants expenditure on cleanup. In this way, many environmental damages are vindicated as contributions to economic progress. For the environmentally conscious, this is an affront to both intuition and ethics as pollution (especially of such a magnitude) is detrimental to both human and environmental health.

Also, GDP does a poor job of reflecting actual human well-being because it neither accounts for social sustainability nor future consequences of present consumptions. In fact, recent studies suggest that, for a number of countries, the positive correlation between human well-being and GDP breaks down after GDP values reach a certain threshold—known as the "threshold hypothesis" (Max-Neef 1995). A rising GDP merely signals an increasing level of market transactions, without regard for whether these activities are beneficial to humans and nature in the long run. Thus, a fixation on the temporally narrow scope of traditional economic accounting can lead to dangerously myopic policies. The absence of ecosystem services and environmental damages (known

as "externalities" in economic parlance) from monetary valuation potentiates the vicious cycle of economic shortsightedness and environmental misuse. It is widely accepted now that GDP significantly undervalues the contributions of nature to human well-being and is ill-suited for measuring sustainable development. Green GDP (also green NNP), therefore, has been proposed to explicitly estimate these missing costs by subtracting the economic penalties imposed by natural resource depletion and pollution from national accounting. As a result, the green GDP is meant to advance a more inclusive view of "natural capital" and promote more sustainable management practices.

Alternatives to GDP

The notion of "greening" GDP has gained some momentum in both academia and public policy since the early 1990s. One of the most noteworthy attempts to implement the concept was carried out by the People's Republic of China. In 2006, the Chinese government released its environmentally adjusted GDP—its green GDP, prepared jointly by the State Environmental Protection Agency and the National Bureau of Statistics (SEPA and NBS 2006). Included in the calculation were assessments of air, water, and solid-waste pollution as well as the costs of depleting various natural resources. The report concluded that the economic loss of environmental damages amounted to 3 percent of the country's GDP in 2004. Nearly as soon as the figures were released, however, it became clear that there still remained major defects in the accounting procedures. A large number of concerns were not factored into the analysis, and there were also myriad methodological obstacles that impeded a thorough economic analysis of environmental damages. For instance, only half of potentially more than twenty pollution costs were estimated in China's green GDP report. Concerns such as soil and groundwater contamination, as well as the entire categories of natural resource depletion and ecological damage, were not included in the accounting. Thus, the 3 percent diminution fell short of what many analysts believed the actual costs were. It is now evident that green GDP, for China and elsewhere, is still theoretically appealing but practically formidable.

In addition, several other development metrics similar to green GDP have also been developed as a part of a larger group of sustainable development indicators. For example, the Index of Sustainable Economic Welfare (ISEW) was developed in the late 1980s to address the flaws in GDP. ISEW accounts for both conventional economic transactions and nonmarket natural and social benefits, and its value is determined by the balance between positive transactions that benefit human well-being and negative economic activities that diminish it. Genuine Progress Indicator (GPI), developed later in 1994 by Redefining Progress (a nongovernmental organization focused on public policy), includes essentially the same measures as ISEW. The main differences between the two are related mostly to data availability and users' preferences for valuation methods. ISEW and GPI have widely been used by international organizations, governmental agencies, and academic researchers. Another common development metric is Genuine Savings (GS), proposed by the World Bank in 1999. Taking into account both natural and human capital, GS estimates the domestic savings less the value of resource depletion and environmental degradation. A relatively new metric, Happy Planet Index (HPI), was introduced by the New Economics Foundation (NEF) in 2006. HPI bypasses traditional monetary approaches and focuses on the efficiency with which countries translate natural resource use into human and societal well-being. Specifically, HPI is the ratio of happy life years (the product of life satisfaction and life expectancy) to environmental impact (measured by ecological footprint).

The Future of Green GDP

Despite the mounting criticisms of its irrelevance and the emergence of alternatives, GDP's deeply entrenched position in the mainstream discourse will likely ensure its continued prominence in both economics and public perception. It is important, therefore, to clearly understand what GDP measures and what it does not. Meanwhile, efforts for valuating the depletion of natural resources and the impacts and mitigations of pollution will continue. The environment must be part of national accounting. The United Nations has published a set of accounting guidelines in the *Handbook of National Accounting: Integrated Environmental and Economic Accounting* (known as SEEA 1993 and SEEA 2003), which provide a common framework for valuating environmental contributions to economies and economic impacts on the environment. Such efforts promote methodological standardization that in turn facilitates applications and cross-country comparisons. They also represent a continued operationalization (the process of strictly defining variables into measurable factors) of the ideas behind green GDP. Although it remains implausible that GDP will soon be displaced as the hallmark indicator of economic fitness, attempts to "green" it, despite various shortcomings, constitute a positive movement in the direction of environmental consciousness. Complementary indicators and indices are also needed if we are to adequately measure our true economic wealth and health: the sustainability of human–environmental systems.

Jianguo WU
Arizona State University

Tong WU
Northern Arizona University

See also in the *Berkshire Encyclopedia of Sustainability* Development, Sustainable; Ecological Economics; Ecosystem Services; Natural Capitalism; True Cost Economics

FURTHER READING

Abdallah, Saamah; Thompson, Sam; Michaelson, Juliet; Marks, Nic; Steuer, Nicola; & New Economics Foundation. (2009). *The happy planet index 2.0: Why good lives don't have to cost the Earth*. Retrieved October 1, 2009, from http://www.happyplanetindex.org/public-data/files/happy-planet-index-2-0.pdf

Boyd, James. (2007). Nonmarket benefits of nature: What should be counted in green GDP? *Ecological Economics 61*(4), 716–723.

Cobb, Clifford; Goodman, Gary Sue; & Wackernagel, Mathis. (1999, November). *Why bigger isn't better: The genuine progress indicator—1999 update*. Retrieved October 1, 2009, from http://www.rprogress.org/publications/1999/gpi1999.pdf

Costanza, Robert, et al. (1997). The value of the world's ecosystem services and natural capital. *Nature, 387*, 253–260.

Costanza, Robert. (2008). Stewardship for a "full" world. Current *History*, 107(705), 30–35.

Max-Neef, Manfred. (1995). Economic growth and quality of life. *Ecological Economics* 15(2), 115–118.

Qiu, Jane. (2007, August 2). China's green accounting system on shaky ground. *Nature*, 448, 518–519.

State Environmental Protection Administration of China (SEPA) and the National Bureau of Statistics of China (NBS). (2006). China's green national accounting study report 2004. Retrieved November 25, 2009, from http://www.gov.cn/english/2006-09/11/content_384596.htm

United Nations; European Commission; International Monetary Fund; Organisation for Economic Co-operation and Development; & World Bank. (2003). *Handbook of national accounting: Integrated environmental and economic accounting 2003*. Retrieved August 11, 2009, from http://unstats.un.org/unsd/envaccounting/seea2003.pdf

Investment, Socially Responsible (SRI)

Socially responsible investment (SRI) is a process that integrates environmental, social, and community concerns into a traditional financial investment framework. The SRI market's growth, especially in the developing world, depends on development of new research methods, market pressures to encourage further corporate transparency and accountability, and incorporation of SRI into national economies.

Socially responsible investing (SRI) is an investment process that considers social and environmental consequences within the context of traditional financial analysis. Investors—including individuals, institutions, and corporations—use SRI to achieve traditional financial as well as social, environmental, and community returns. They accomplish this by integrating these dimensions onto a traditional financial investment framework. An important goal of SRI is to promote corporate accountability for its social and environmental risks into mainstream financial practices and to engage a wide range of companies in improving their environmental and social responsibility practices.

Origins of Modern SRI

The origins of the modern SRI movement can be traced to the turbulent period in the 1960s when powerful social undercurrents, including environmentalism and antiwar activism, fueled a radical change in the way society viewed faith, values, and commerce. SRI funds were once primarily known as "ethical funds," and given SRI's strong Judeo-Christian roots, this is not at all surprising. The notion of an ethical business is established in Judeo-Christian traditions; examples of it exist in the book of Deuteronomy,

which dates back more than 2,500 years. But it is arguably the Quaker faith that has made the greatest impact in connecting commercial activities and ethical values in the modern age. The Quakers were the first group to practice the "negative screening" of investments when they avoided investments in the military sector by faithfully applying their peace traditions to commercial activities. One of the early examples of what we might call an SRI-like activity is an investment fund established by the Methodist Church in the 1960s that avoided investments in armaments, alcohol, gambling, and tobacco. Since the fund managed by the Methodist Church was closed to outsiders, the first modern example of what we now call an SRI fund was the US Pax World Fund, founded by two Methodist ministers in 1971. The first investment fund that specifically addressed ecological concerns was the Ecology Fund, established by Merlin/Jupiter Company in 1988 (Kreander 2001).

The political unrest in South Africa in the 1960s and 1970s set the stage for another major policy push for SRI and the important connection between ethics and business practices. The Reverend Leon H. Sullivan helped draft a code of conduct (subsequently known as the Sullivan Principles) for companies doing business in South Africa. By the early 1980s the Sullivan Principles became the rallying cry for anti-apartheid activism. In 1982 the state of Connecticut adopted the Sullivan Principles and other social criteria to guide its investment decision making. Just two years later, the California Public Employees' Retirement System (CalPERS), the largest public pension fund in the world, and the New York City Employee Retirement System developed their own investing guidelines in South Africa. In the twenty-first century, corporate divestment and boycott campaigns, addressing issues ranging from the genocide in Darfur, Sudan, to the environmental policies of ExxonMobil, got started in large part due to the success of the South Africa anti-investment campaigners (IFC 2003).

Global SRI Marketplace

The global SRI market in the wealthy countries belonging to the Organisation for Economic Co-operation and Development (OECD) was well established by 2010 and, in the case of Europe, entering a major growth phase. In the United States, US$2.7 trillion, or about 11 percent of the US$26 trillion in total investment assets, is invested in one of the three SRI strategies—screening, shareholder advocacy, and community investing. Although much smaller in size, the European SRI market has grown rapidly in recent years and is now estimated to be €2.7 trillion, accounting for as much as 17.5 percent of the asset management industry (SIF 2008). Even in Japan and the Asia-Pacific region, where awareness of social responsibility concerns lags behind North America and Europe, SRI represents one of the few financial market segments that remain vibrant in terms of market development. In addition, the SRI market in Australia grew 41 percent between 2003 and 2004 alone, twice as fast as that country's retail and wholesale investment market (Eurosif 2008).

Key Global Issues and Trends

As SRI moves to the global financial and business landscape, we can highlight three important trends. The first is the emergence of the investing community, consisting of individual and institutional investors, as a new and powerful actor in global economic and sustainability governance. The second trend attempts to determine the business and sustainability effectiveness of SRI. The third trend focuses on SRI's potential role in the mainstream of emerging and developing economies at the base of the economic development pyramid.

Investing Community's Role

The emergence of investors as important financial actors and the rise of responsible investment since the 1970s highlight the complexities of contemporary global governance. For example, the lines between the domestic and the international have blurred (as investment capital increasingly attempts to link local corporate activities with global responsibilities). Other examples are the expansion of actors from a few dedicated mutual funds (mainly in the United States) to several hundred across the world; the rise of global institutional investors involved in promoting SRI principles in their activities; the emergence of a global civil society attempting to influence financial capital; and the

variety of transnational issues motivating capital markets (from human rights–related concerns, such as apartheid in South Africa, to environmental sustainability and related concerns).

Although SRI investors can technically be anyone in society who has investment capital, institutional investors—including pension funds, investment companies, insurance companies, or those investors with money under professional management—account for the largest percentage of the total SRI market. Individual or retail investors—who owned as much as 93 percent of all US stocks in 1950 and as much as 75 percent in the 1970s—now own a record-low 34 percent of all shares. In contrast, institutional investors quickly gained greater control over the equity markets, with the percentage of their ownership shares increasing from 47 percent in 1987 to over 76 percent in 2007. In 1985, no company had institutional ownership of 60 percent or above, whereas by 2007, seventeen companies had institutional ownership of 60 percent or above, including six with institutional ownership of 70 percent or above (Conference Board 2007; 2008).

The significance of this trend, in terms of SRI, is that institutional investors are starting to have substantial economic, and albeit more subtle, business sustainability influence through the shares they own in particular companies. The equity investments allow institutional investors the right to bring forth shareholder resolutions and exert influence on companies in which they *do not* own equity shares. They can achieve this through creating standards or screens for future potential equity purchases.

Sustainable Impact and Effectiveness

One of the most commonly asked questions, if not one of the most important, is whether SRI portfolio screening and shareholder advocacy / engagement practices have a positive impact on the sustainable behavior of companies. While it is difficult to determine SRI's long-term sustainable impact and effectiveness, some preliminary evidence suggests that SRI is having a sustainability impact on business behavior. When CalPERS announced that it would start employing SRI principles in its investment management decisions in 2001, the practical results of this policy were initially unclear. A year later, after CalPERS decided that it would divest its investments in Thailand, Indonesia, and Malaysia due to unacceptably low levels of labor standards, political stability, and financial

transparency rankings, finance and stock market officials in those respective countries began scrambling to adopt policies to improve business practices in those areas (Aguilera et al. 2006).

The FTSE Group is the global index provider and the parent body of the FTSE4Good Index Series that measures corporations' SRI performances. As part of its five-year review in 2007, FTSE4Good Index Series announced that it had achieved a number of positive impacts on the corporate environmental and social responsibility practices of the companies around the world in which it invests (FTSE Group 2007). Through the enactment of various standards and protocols on supply chain management, bribery, climate change, and others, the FTSE4Good Index Series has pushed companies to adopt, or at least consider adopting, corporate environmental and social responsibility performance measures beyond basic compliance.

What is becoming clear, at least in the North American, European, Japanese, and some segments of the Asian markets, is that mainstream individual and institutional investors are starting to believe that social, environmental, and corporate governance are important factors in the investment decision-making process. Mercer Investment Consulting's 2009 review of thirty-six academic studies that examine the relationship between financial performance and environmental, social, and governance (ESG) factors reveals that twenty studies show a positive relationship (that is, financial and ESG factors are positively correlated), eight studies show a neutral relationship, and six studies show a neutral/negative relationship. Mercer's 2006 survey of 183 large financial institutional investors indicates that as much as 75 percent of the respondents (22 percent of whom were SRI investors) believe that social, environmental, and corporate governance factors can have a material impact on investment performance (Mercer 2006). The question is whether this fact—that twenty out of thirty-six academic studies find a positive relationship between financial performance and ESG factors—represents definitive evidence (Mercer 2009). It is probably safer to conclude that there is strong evidence to suggest a positive relationship between financial performance and ESG factors, albeit with the usual proviso that additional research is required.

SRI and Emerging Economies

The healthy development in the SRI markets of North America, Europe, and to a lesser degree Asia overshadows the almost complete lack of SRI activity in emerging and developing economies, where more than two-thirds of the world's population lives and works. The most recent International Finance Corporation survey (2009) of corporate executives and investment professionals' attitudes toward ESG factors in emerging markets compared their thoughts about the global financial situation before the crisis (2007) and midcrisis (2009). Forty-six percent of the investors surveyed strongly agreed with the statement that ESG issues are an important part of their research, portfolio management, and manager selection, up from 36 percent in 2007. The majority of asset owners (78 percent) also suggested that the importance of ESG factors has been amplified by the late 2007–2009 financial crisis and may result in greater use of ESG criteria over time in emerging markets (IFC 2009).

According to the International Finance Corporation, the sum of SRI assets in emerging markets is approximately US$2.7 billion, or 0.1 percent of the US$2.7 trillion global SRI market. Its most recent figure for emerging market assets held by SRI investors in industrialized countries is anywhere between US$1.5 billion and US$2 billion, while it estimates SRI assets in emerging market capitalization at the most optimistic level of 0.1 percent, or US$5 billion. While the most reliable figures on SRI assets in emerging markets come from a 2003 International Financial Corporation study, what is noteworthy is that the estimated SRI assets in emerging markets is small no matter which benchmark we use for comparison. Although the economic disparity between the wealthy, industrialized developed world and the developing world is always stark, it is nevertheless startling to see such a gap between wealthy countries and developing/emerging countries in terms of sustainable investing. This is clearly one of the many institutional hurdles SRI needs to overcome if it is to become more than just a niche market and realize its potential for sustainability at the Base of the Pyramid.

Future Development

Will SRI realize its full potential as a global sustainable business mechanism and advance sustainable strategic management? The answer to this question may depend in part on the quality and sophistication of future SRI research methodology. Smaller SRI investment companies, without their own research staff, rely on independent research providers like KLD Research and Analytics in the United States or Ethical Investment Research Service in the United Kingdom for most of their research needs. Larger SRI fund companies rely on their own internal staff to conduct research and shareholder advocacy and/or to engage with companies. While the more simplistic screening of companies from portfolios is still being used, SRI research as a whole is moving toward much more

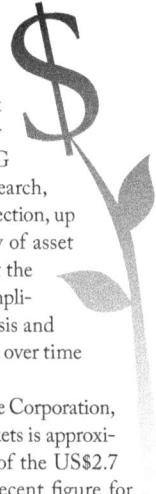

sophisticated techniques, including a myriad of quantitative analyses. Moreover, sustainability business research companies like the UK-based Trucost are starting to use sophisticated economic modeling to assess the environmental externalities that may not be captured in conventional financial accounts. The development of global sustainability indexes like the Dow Jones Sustainability Indexes and the FTSE4Good Index Series have become a much-needed investment index to the SRI capital markets and have led to greater pressure on companies to disclose relevant environmental and social indicators.

Another factor in determining the future development of SRI is the degree of market pressure, particularly from institutional investors, for corporate transparency and accountability. The financial crisis that stared in late 2007 has produced a global chorus for transparency in the financial sector, but it remains unclear if this will lead to a fundamental change in how the global financial market, including SRI, will be governed. It is clear, however, that the greater the transparency and accountability pressures, the better it will be for the future growth of the global SRI market. In 2009, a campaign began pressuring the US Securities and Exchange Commission to require companies to disclose their climate change business risks as part of their 10-K corporate filings and other reporting requirements. Similar international policy initiatives like those of the Global Reporting Initiative organization and national/ regional government programs are putting increasing regulatory pressure on strengthening disclosures of corporate environmental and social data.

Arguably the most important criterion for determining growth in SRI development worldwide is to what degree SRI becomes a mainstream investment strategy in emerging and developing economies. Just two countries (India and China) constitute 40 percent of the world's population, and China is no longer considered an emerging market. China will become the world's exporter and is expected to replace Japan as the second-largest economy in the world by 2030. Although the current total of SRI assets in emerging economies is a tiny percentage (still less than 1 percent) of the total emerging market capitalization, there are strong signs that institutional shareholder activism and tightening environmental and social regulatory pressures will become the business norm in a certain select number of emerging markets. Case in point: in 2003, the Johannesburg Securities Exchange in South Africa started requiring all companies listed with the exchange to comply

with corporate governance codes and to use the Global Reporting Initiative's guidelines for disclosing social and environmental performance. The actual dollar amount may not be as important as the development of the "right" institutional infrastructure and public–private partnerships that steer SRI toward its next phase of green business development and sustainable strategic management, in both the industrialized and emerging/developing economies.

Jacob PARK
Green Mountain College

See also in the *Berkshire Encyclopedia of Sustainability* Activism—NGOs; Base of the Pyramid; Corporate Citizenship; CSR and CSR 2.0; Equator Principles; Fair Trade; Financial Services Industry; Human Rights; Investment, CleanTech; Public–Private Partnerships; Risk Management; Supply Chain Management; Sustainable Value Creation; Transparency; Triple Bottom Line; United Nations Global Compact

FURTHER READING

Aguilera, Ruth V.; Williams, Cynthia A.; Conley, John M.; & Rupp, Deborah. (2006, May). Corporate governance and social responsibility: A comparative analysis of the UK and the US *Corporate Governance: An International Review, 14*(3), 147–158.

Conference Board. (2007). *US institutional investors continue to boost ownership of US corporations.* New York: Conference Board.

Conference Board. (2008). *Institutional investment report.* New York: Conference Board.

European Sustainable Investment Forum (Eurosif). (2008). *European SRI study 2008.* Retrieved February 3, 2010, from http://www.eurosif.org

FTSE Group. (2007). *Adding values to your investment: FTSE4Good index series—5 year review.* Retrieved February 3, 2010, from http://www.ftse.com/Indices/FTSE4Good_Index_Series/index.jsp

International Finance Corporation (IFC). (2003). *Towards sustainable and responsible investment in emerging markets.* Washington, DC: IFC.

International Finance Corporation (IFC). (2009). *Sustainable investment in emerging markets.* Washington, DC: IFC.

Kreander, N. (2001). Occasional research paper no. 33: An analysis of European ethical funds. London: Certified Accountants Educational Trust.

Mercer. (2006). *Perspectives on responsible investing.* Toronto: Mercer Investment Consulting.

Mercer. (2009). *Shedding light on responsible investment: Approaches, returns, and impacts.* Toronto: Mercer Investment Consulting.

Social Investment Forum (SIF). (2008). *2007 report on socially responsible investing trends in the United States.* Retrieved February 3, 2010, from http://www.socialinvest.org/pdf/SRI_Trends_ExecSummary_2007. pdfSocial Investment Forum (SIF). (2009). Socially responsible investing facts. Retrieved November 15, 2009, from http://www.socialinvest.org/resources/sriguide/srifacts.cfm

Leadership

The prevailing concept of leadership—one that is influenced by modern industry—must change if humanity is to succeed in establishing a more sustainable world. This new visionary paradigm of leadership will pursue higher goals that reflect common interests and values, fostering networks of collaboration more than competition. Many forms and styles of leadership, however, exercised at all levels of society, will be required to achieve sustainability.

Achieving environmental sustainability will be one of the most important leadership challenges of the twenty-first century. It will take leadership exercised at all levels of society and in many different forms and settings to effect the kinds of changes needed to reach this goal. Compared to previous large-scale challenges, sustainability is particularly daunting because rather than being able to hold out the promise of immediate and palpable gains (as with civil rights, economic prosperity, national self-determination), leaders for sustainability have a more modest, less tangible goal—averting social and biotic catastrophe. Compounding the problem is the fact that doing so will require far-reaching changes in existing behaviors and practices that may be perceived as lifestyle sacrifices in some cases. The benefits of such changes will not always be immediately evident, whereas upfront costs may be high. Environmental problems often take the form of "social dilemmas" in which individuals must forgo their own immediate interests for a wider or future social good. Whereas some individuals are naturally cooperative and/or future oriented, many others are not. Leaders will be needed who can persuade followers to act for the common good regardless of the perceived personal costs.

Furthermore, the relationship between human beings and the ecosystems that sustain them is complex and multifaceted, requiring new and more subtle forms of leadership that enable businesses and communities to interact with the natural environment in ways that nurture rather than destroy ecosystems. Command-and-control forms of leadership—which are more authoritarian or managerial—will increasingly need to be replaced by leadership that facilitates adaptation to the complex ecosystems that make up the biosphere. The sustainability challenge is so all encompassing, however, that no one leadership paradigm or approach can hope to "solve" the problem: the only certainty is that sustainability will not be achieved without the exercise of leadership at all levels of society.

For the purposes of this article, leadership is defined as an influence relationship or process aimed at achieving common goals. As such, it is more of an emergent quality than a person or position—leadership can be exercised by different individuals in the same group at different times. It can be the result of inborn traits or learned behaviors and typically involves vision and future orientation. One way to distinguish between leaders and managers is the length of the time horizon: to "manage" connotes activity in the here and now, whereas to "lead" suggests forward movement in space and time. Management typically involves short-term planning, day-to-day supervision of staff, and the implementation of existing policies. By contrast, leadership entails formulating or facilitating a common vision and influencing others to accept and act upon that vision, even if the vision itself is an essentially backward-looking one. (For example, someone might say "We need to go back to our roots of living in harmony with the Earth, as our ancestors did" and still be demonstrating leadership.)

In a world of diminishing natural resources and growing environmental degradation, leadership by definition entails environmental concern. The paramount goal of any healthy organism or group must be its own survival and flourishing, and this requires the health of the larger biosphere that sustains it. In this context, leadership will include making sure that the conditions for group survival and flourishing remain constant or are enhanced. A hunter-gatherer community that runs out of food with no alternatives will be the result of failed leadership as much as a modern business that steadily loses money and eventually goes bankrupt because its leaders were unable to foresee changes in the marketplace. Although social scientists are often uncomfortable making value judgments, from a biological standpoint "survival" and "flourishing" are not so much values as fundamental regulatory principles, the standards by which all actions are ultimately measured. As such, leaders must necessarily be attuned to them.

That we now need to be reminded of this fact is due in large part to a different—and declining—understanding of leadership that emerged in a more abundant age.

The Industrial Leadership Paradigm

Leadership models tend to reflect the concerns and ideals of the era in which they appear. Consequently the dominant leadership paradigm that emerged in the wake of the Industrial Revolution celebrates skills, behaviors, and attributes that are suited to the requirements of modern industry. As the scholar and writer Joseph Rost suggests, leadership in the industrial paradigm is understood to be "rational, management oriented, male, technocratic, quantitative, goal dominated, cost-benefit driven, personalistic, hierarchical, short term, pragmatic, and materialistic" (1991, 94). Seen from this perspective, leadership is synonymous with "good management." Also evident is the focus on the short-term economic success of the business enterprise, with little attention to the larger social and environmental costs of its activities.

Such a view of leadership became prevalent when natural resources appeared to be limitless, human populations were relatively small, and economic development promised to lift the mass of humankind out of poverty and into a "better life." It reflects the optimism of the American Dream, in which autonomous individuals can succeed if only they work hard enough, and it is based on the assumption that technological control over nature is an unalloyed good that will solve any problem. The industrial paradigm of leadership was reinforced by authoritarian assumptions

and hierarchical social structures underwritten by long-held beliefs that some individuals and/or social strata were naturally fit to rule over the rest. Thomas Carlyle's (1795–1881) "great man" theory of history expressed this mindset, as did the emphasis on identifying inborn leadership traits, which dominated the study of leadership during the first half of the twentieth century.

The industrial leadership paradigm remains common today in the business literature on leadership, which celebrates CEOs as "corporate saviors" and employs leadership as a motivational tool to enhance employee productivity and corporate profits. It is reinforced by the pressure put on business leaders to achieve short-term profitability at the expense of all else, and by the hierarchical nature of the modern corporation, in which CEOs and boards of directors can enact fundamental changes to corporate enterprises by fiat.

The scholar and writer Gayle Avery characterizes this as an unsustainable "Anglo/US shareholder value" model of leadership, in contrast to a more sustainable "Rhineland stakeholder approach." In the latter model, which is more common among continental European enterprises, leadership is more dispersed and less focused on top individuals in the corporate hierarchy, takes a longer-term view, and is more cognizant and concerned about the social and environmental impacts of its operations. It places less emphasis on maximizing short-term shareholder value and more emphasis on meeting the requirements of a wider array of stakeholders, including employees, local communities, and the natural environment. Avery suggests that "an increasing demand for sustainable leadership is driving business—willingly or unwillingly—toward leadership principles reflected in the European model" (2005, xiv).

Nevertheless, the industrial leadership paradigm remains entrenched in business as well as in the field of leadership studies. Under this model, movement toward sustainability can occur if visionary individuals in leadership positions make it a priority and are skilled at engaging followers to adopt a sustainable mindset and behaviors. Jim MacNeill, chair emeritus of the International Institute for Sustainable Development, forcefully states this perspective: "Institutionalizing sustainable development . . . will not happen, certainly not in any significant way, if the person at the top is not determined to make it happen" (MacNeill 2007, 21). Similarly, the writer Thomas Friedman argues that in an increasingly "hot, flat, and crowded" world, it is essential that leaders—from the highest levels of government and business on down to the local level—make sustainability a priority, and that the United States of America must take a global leadership role in this endeavor: "Right now, we don't have the focus and persistence to take on something really big, where the benefits play out over the long term. But I believe all that could change with the

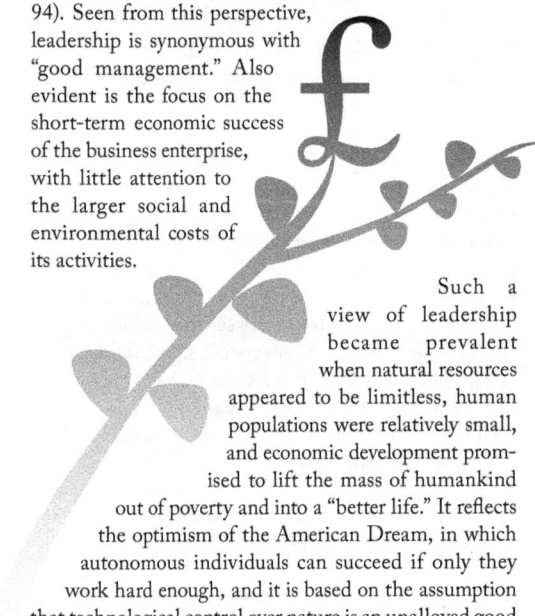

right leadership—local, state, and federal—properly framing how much we have to gain by rising to this moment and how much we have to lose by failing to do so" (Friedman 2008, 7).

Such calls acknowledge the embedded nature of power and hierarchical relationships in modern Western societies and the fact that change will not happen without the support of those who have their hands on the levers of authority. They also acknowledge the widely shared assumption among students of leadership that hierarchy and power are endemic to human (and other primate) populations and that, consequently, leadership will always entail some degree of positional power and the elevation of certain individuals into pre-eminent social roles. A unifying theme of a 1994 special issue of *Leadership Quarterly* devoted to environmental leadership was "the importance attributed to leaders' values and beliefs to initiate and implement fundamental changes in modern organizations and society" (Egri and Frost 1994, 196). Swift and massive political, social, and economic changes have typically occurred in the past under the influence of paramount leaders with considerable power, and thus it is likely that future advances toward sustainability will occur at least in part due to the efforts of top private and public sector leaders.

The Eco-Leadership Paradigm

Whether or not authoritarian forms of leadership can in themselves produce truly sustainable societies is another question, however, since they reflect mechanistic models of leadership more applicable to factories and pliable subordinates than to complex ecosystems and autonomous human beings living in postindustrial societies. Thus in contrast to the industrial paradigm of leadership, a new "eco-leadership paradigm" (in the words of the writer Simon Western) is beginning to emerge among students and practitioners of leadership. Western goes so far as to suggest that "the next [leadership] discourse will be that of the eco-leader" (2008, 184). Under this model, systems thinking and "systems intelligence"—a term coined by Peter Senge in 2006—govern leadership behaviors, which are more dispersed throughout organizations rather than residing in a single individual, and as such enable organizations to better adapt to changing environmental conditions.

The eco-leadership paradigm employs ecological models and metaphors to conceptualize leadership on the assumption that such models are better at taking into account the complexities of modern organizations and their relationship with the larger contexts and systems (including ecosystems) of which they are a part. It stresses holism (wholes are greater than the sum of their parts), connectivity (everything is connected to everything else), and interdependence (everything is dependent upon everything

else), and it assumes that achieving long-term sustainability will involve mimicking and adapting to the natural world and natural processes rather than triumphing over them. Leadership in this paradigm includes fostering networks of collaboration within and between organizations and social sectors, and building feedback loops into organizations that can help them learn and adapt to changes in the various external systems (including the biosphere) of which they are a part.

If earlier leadership researchers looked to primate communities as evidence for the "naturalness" of leadership, thinkers working in the eco-leader paradigm take organic and evolutionary processes as "natural" touchstones for conceptualizing leadership. In this model, leadership involves facilitating the operation of autonomous systems more than controlling them from above. It seeks to serve the greatest possible number of stakeholders in any one process or system, based on the recognition that failures in any of the parts can cause failures in the whole system. In this paradigm, centralized planning is replaced with empowerment of local leaders to make changes as needed at the periphery. Paramount leaders in this paradigm must look for "patterns of interdependency" and should be capable of "seeing into the future" (Senge 2006, 40). That is, they must keep an eye on the organization as a complex living being that must be kept in right relationship with its surroundings in order to thrive, and to be cognizant of larger systemic changes on the horizon. To use a nautical metaphor, such a leader is more of a lookout who surveys the functioning of the ship and the wider horizon from above the deck, calling out signals as needed, than an imperious captain who stands on the bridge (or sits in the cabin) barking orders to the crew.

The emerging eco-leader paradigm is not only a response to the growing ecological crisis but to deep and ongoing social and economic changes as well. The notion of a rising "postindustrial society" has become increasingly prevalent since the 1970s and signifies the broad shift away from heavy industry and manufacturing and toward the provision of goods and services and the rise of information technologies and the "knowledge economy." This shift has occurred at the same time as populations and pollution levels have dramatically increased, and as natural resources and nonhuman biotic communities have been forced into severe decline. Democratization and anti-authoritarianism have simultaneously been on the rise (with important exceptions) around the world, along with increasing emphasis on individual rights and the values of equality and diversity. Thus just as modern industry gave rise to an "industrial paradigm" of leadership, postindustrial society is giving rise to a postindustrial model. In each case, a concatenation of factors has combined to produce a vision of leadership deemed appropriate to its time and place.

Transformational Leadership

An influential leadership model that is applicable to leadership for sustainability is transformational leadership. Originally proposed in 1978 by James MacGregor Burns as "transforming" leadership, the model has been subsequently revised and expanded by Bernard Bass since the 1980s and has become one of the more well-researched theories in the field of leadership studies. Much evidence has been marshaled that demonstrates its effectiveness in fostering deep changes in organizations and societies and increasing follower satisfaction. As originally stated by Burns, transforming leaders engage in a teaching role, uniting followers in the pursuit of higher goals that reflect the common interests of leaders and followers and end values like liberty, justice, and equality. Transforming leaders raise their followers to higher levels of morality, and "the test of their leadership function is their contribution to change, measured by purpose drawn from collective motives and values" (Burns 1978, 426).

Building on Burns's theory, Bass and Ronald Riggio distinguish four components of transformational leadership: idealized influence, inspirational motivation, intellectual stimulation, and individualized consideration. In the first instance, transformational leaders serve as admired and respected role models. Secondly, they "behave in ways that motivate and inspire those around them by providing meaning and challenge to their followers' work" (Bass and Riggio 2006, 6). Thirdly, transformational leaders stimulate followers to think and act in new and creative ways "by questioning assumptions, reframing problems, and approaching old situations in new ways" (Bass and Riggio 2006, 7). Finally, transformational leaders pay close attention to the individual needs of followers, adapting their leadership behaviors accordingly; as such, transformational leaders act as mentors or coaches.

Given that the survival and flourishing of all living creatures is a fundamental end value, transformational leadership is a powerful and proven form of leadership for sustainability. It focuses on enacting fundamental changes that engage the highest ideals of both leaders and followers, and it prescribes particular behaviors that can be developed by those interested in showing leadership on this issue. Achieving sustainability will require deep and lasting changes to how we think and act,

and transformational leadership is in essence a theory of how leaders can help bring about such changes. Burns's model of transforming leadership is aimed more at broad social and political change, while Bass's adumbration of the theory makes it more applicable to particular organizations (including businesses). As such, the model is applicable to a wide range of settings in which sustainability is a goal.

Other Perspectives

Given the fact that achieving sustainability will require far-reaching social, cultural, psychological, economic, technological, and even spiritual changes in the fabric of our lives, there is ample room for a variety of approaches to leadership for sustainability. Recent research on this topic, including perspectives from the fields of history, sociology, religious studies / spirituality, business, literature, communication, psychology, political science, and the arts, was published in the volume *Leadership for Environmental Sustainability*, by Benjamin Redekop and Steven Olson (2010). Research on the narrative aspects of leadership suggests, for example, that leaders interested in sustainability are well advised to develop their storytelling abilities, since stories are one of the most powerful and engaging forms of human communication. We must imagine a sustainable future as a precondition for acting on it, and it is through stories that leaders can help constituents envision the way things can be.

Others argue that moving toward sustainability will require a spiritual transformation from materialism and consumerism to a more profoundly spiritual relationship with each other and the biosphere. Leadership for sustainability from this perspective involves the facilitation of spiritualities that help to transform behaviors in ways that are both more sustainable and more spiritually satisfying. Historians for their part have much to tell us about the successes and failures of past environmental leaders, while sociologists provide analyses of the social forces that impede or foster sustainable behaviors and the social constraints under which leaders operate. One of the bugbears of leadership studies is "attribution error," in which successes or failures are wrongly attributed to leaders instead of other social, economic, and contextual factors. A sociological perspective helps to clarify social factors that are beyond the control of leaders while also providing insights into the ways that leaders can help set the social conditions for sustainability.

Environmental psychology is a growing field of study that has much to offer those interested in leading for sustainability. For example, self-determination theory suggests that internal motivation is one of the best ways to

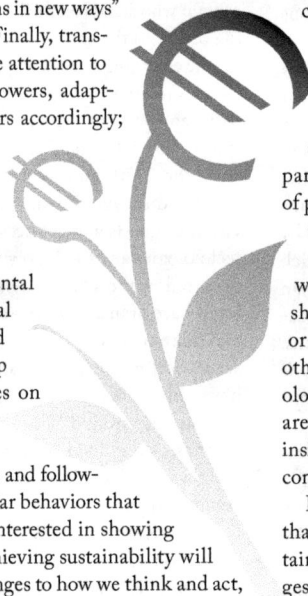

promote pro-environmental behaviors, in part because it results in a cascading effect in which such behaviors are willingly spread to others. Autonomy supportive requests—in which leaders acknowledge the perspective of followers, allow choices (where possible) in how such requests will be fulfilled, and provide a rationale for such requests—are more likely to be effective than more coercive measures. Research has likewise shown that if fear appeals are to be effective, they must be accompanied by expressions of hope and a sense of how constituents can productively respond to the problem. Researchers have identified a personality variable termed "consideration of future consequences" (CFC) that predicts pro-environmental behaviors; they also have provided evidence that populations differ according to their willingness to cooperate in solving social dilemmas. According to this research, about 20 percent of the population are "cooperators," about 60 percent are "individualists," and 20 percent are "competitors." Cooperators and individualists can be convinced to engage in sustainable behaviors, whereas competitors may never willingly cooperate since they measure success in terms of gaining an advantage over others. Much work remains to be done to refine such data and incorporate it into our understanding of leadership for sustainability (Joireman 2005; Osbaldiston and Sheldon 2002).

Outlook for Sustainable Business Leadership

Many business leaders have begun to make their influence felt on this issue. Scholars suggest that—in addition to leaders themselves modeling sustainable behaviors—successful business leadership for sustainability requires embedding sustainable perspectives, processes, and behaviors into every level of an organization. An important first step is the formulation of a corporate vision and mission statement that reflects deep-seated concern for the natural environment and sustainability. Also crucial are the creation of education initiatives that provide employees with the skills and resources to act on the organizational vision, and the formulation of a strong business case for environmental responsibility. Significant savings can result from increased efficiencies, and forward-looking business leaders devote such savings to further measures aimed at achieving sustainability. Among the many business leaders that could be mentioned, Ray Anderson of Interface Inc. (the world's largest producer of commercial floor coverings and carpets) stands out as one of the most prominent and influential business leaders on this issue, and his book *Mid-Course Correction* has been widely recognized as one of the more compelling personal testaments

written by a business leader on the topic of environmental sustainability.

An "environmental leadership model" (ELM), originally proposed in 1994 by the scholars Brenda Flannery and Douglas May, specifies four important antecedents to an organization's environmental strategy formulation process, including the existence of moral norms and values for environmental responsibility, the environmental attitudes of top organizational leaders, stakeholder influences, and the perceived degree of control over regulatory, financial, and technological constraints on pro-environmental behaviors. Such models help to conceptualize how businesses and other organizations chart a strategic path toward sustainability, and they highlight the fact that business leaders operate in a larger system that both encourages and constrains pro-environmental behaviors—that is, that leadership is a necessary but not sufficient condition for the achievement of environmental sustainability. They also help to convey the scale and complexity of the leadership task, and the need for both industrial and postindustrial forms of leadership to confront the multifaceted sustainability challenge. Leaders in business and other fields will need to draw from many disciplines and perspectives in order to effectively lead on this issue. Scholars of leadership, for their part, must move the study of environmental leadership beyond its current "fledgling stage" (Egri and Herman 2000, 599) if they wish to play a productive role in the increasingly urgent quest for sustainability.

Benjamin W. REDEKOP
Christopher Newport University

See also in the *Berkshire Encyclopedia of Sustainability* Corporate Citizenship; Education, Business; Education, Higher; Stakeholder Theory

FURTHER READING

Allen, Kathleen E.; Stelzner, Stephen P.; & Wielkiewicz, Richard M. (1998). The ecology of leadership: Adapting to the challenges of a changing world. *The Journal of Leadership Studies, 5*(2), 62–82.

Anderson, Ray C. (1998). *Mid-course correction: Toward a sustainable enterprise: The interface model.* Atlanta: Peregrinzilla Press.

Avery, Gayle C. (2005). *Leadership for sustainable futures: Achieving success in a competitive world.* Cheltenham, UK: Edward Elgar.

Bass, Bernard M., & Riggio, Ronald E. (2006). *Transformational leadership.* Mahwah, NJ: Lawrence Erlbaum.

Berry, Joyce K., & Gordon, John C. (1993). *Environmental leadership: Developing effective skills and styles.* Washington, DC: Island Press.

Burns, James M. (1978). *Leadership.* New York: Harper Perennial.

Carlopio, James. (1994). Holism: A philosophy of organizational leadership for the future. *Leadership Quarterly, 5*(3/4), 297–307.

Egri, Carolyn P., & Frost, Peter J. (1994). Leadership for environmental and social change. *Leadership Quarterly, 5*(3/4), 195–200.

Egri, Carolyn P., & Herman, Susan. (2000). Leadership in the North American environmental sector: Values, leadership styles, and contexts of environmental leaders and their organizations. *Academy of Management Journal, 43*(4), 571–604.

Flannery, Brenda, & May, Douglas. (1994). Prominent factors influencing environmental activities: Application of the environmental leadership model (ELM). *Leadership Quarterly, 5*(3/4), 201–221.

Friedman, Thomas. (2008). *Hot, flat, and crowded: Why we need a green revolution—and how it can renew America.* New York: Farrar, Straus and Giroux.

Gordon, John C., & Berry, Joyce K. (2006). *Environmental leadership equals essential leadership: Redefining who leads and how.* New Haven, CT: Yale University Press.

Hazlitt, Maril. (2004). Rachel Carson. In George R. Goethals; Georgia J. Sorenson; & James MacGregor Burns (Eds.), *Encyclopedia of Leadership* (Vol. 1, pp. 146–149). Great Barrington, MA: Berkshire/Sage Reference.

Heifetz, Ronald. (2006). Anchoring leadership in the work of adaptive progress. In Frances Hesselbein & Marshall Goldsmith (Eds.), *The leader of the future 2: Visions, strategies, and practices for the new era* (pp. 73–84). San Francisco: Jossey-Bass.

Joireman, Jeff. (2005). Environmental problems as social dilemmas: The temporal dimension. In Alan Strathman & Jeff Joireman (Eds.), *Understanding behavior in the context of time: Theory, research, and application* (pp. 289–304). Mahwah, NJ: Lawrence Erlbaum.

MacNeill, Jim. (2007). Leadership for sustainable development. In *Institutionalising sustainable development* (pp. 19–23). OECD Sustainable Development Studies. Paris: Organisation for Economic Co-operation and Development.

Osbaldiston, Richard, & Sheldon, Kenneth M. (2002). Social dilemmas and sustainability: Promoting peoples' motivation to "cooperate with the future." In Peter Schmuck & Wesley P. Schultz (Eds.), *Psychology of sustainable development* (pp. 37–57). Boston: Kluwer Academic Publishers.

Redekop, Benjamin W., & Olson, Steven. (2010). *Leadership for environmental sustainability.* New York: Routledge.

Rost, Joseph C. (1991). *Leadership for the twenty-first century.* New York: Praeger.

Senge, Peter. (2006). Systems citizenship: The leadership mandate for this millennium. In Frances Hesselbein & Marshall Goldsmith (Eds.), *The leader of the future 2: Visions, strategies, and practices for the new era* (pp. 31–46). San Francisco: Jossey-Bass.

Shrivastava, Paul. (1994). Ecocentric leadership in the 21st century. *Leadership Quarterly, 5*(3/4), 223–226.

Steinberg, Paul F. (2001). *Environmental leadership in developing countries: Transnational relations and biodiversity policy in Costa Rica and Bolivia.* Cambridge, MA: The MIT Press.

Western, Simon. (2008). *Leadership: A critical text.* Thousand Oaks, CA: Sage Publications.

Wielkiewicz, Richard M., & Stelzner, Stephen P. (2005). An ecological perspective on leadership theory, research, and practice. *Review of General Psychology, 9*(4), 326–341.

Life Cycle Assessments (LCAs)

Life cycle assessment, together with life cycle thinking and life cycle management, are systems approaches for addressing the environmental consequences of an entire product chain, from resource extraction to waste management. Life cycle assessments are used in business and policy making to promote sustainable consumption and production. They offer alternatives to point-source strategies, which only reduce pollution at its source.

Life cycle assessment (LCA) is a method of analyzing the environmental impacts associated with a product or service. The method studies the material and energy flows throughout the product or service system, from raw materials extraction, through production and use, to disposal.

An LCA study is defined both by the product system it covers and the procedure used to study it. The procedure consists of several steps. Researchers start by developing the goal and scope definition, which specifies the product to be studied and the purpose of the LCA study. In the inventory analysis step, they construct the life cycle model of the product system and calculate the amounts of emissions produced and the resources used in the product system, such as raw materials and energy. During the impact assessment step, the researchers relate emissions and resource use to potential environmental problems (e.g., resource depletion and global warming) by classifying and characterizing the environmental impacts. In the weighting step, they add up the different environmental impacts by applying factors that indicate their relative significance, and then they calculate the total environmental impact of the studied product system. The interpretation step is an iterative process of evaluating the modeling of the product system. During this step, the researchers adjust the methodological choices to suit the purpose and the stakeholders of the study and to evaluate the quality of the results.

Some formalized definitions of LCA are found in publications such as the Society of Environmental Toxicology and Chemistry (SETAC) guidelines (Consoli et al. 1993) and the International Organization for Standardization standards on LCA (ISO 2006). A comprehensive description of the development, methodology, and the application of LCA appears in the textbook by professors Henrikke Baumann and Anne-Marie Tillman (2004) and in the operative guidelines to the ISO standard on LCA (Guinée 2002).

When the results are presented as the amount of emissions and resources used per functional unit, they are called an LCI, or life cycle inventory, study. Usually LCIs identify a large number of pollutants and resources, sometimes more than two hundred parameters, making it difficult to summarize the results. Results can also be presented at different levels of aggregation: as inventory results that identify the gases and chemicals emitted during production; as characterization results that identify environmental impacts such as acidification, eutrophication, and global warming; or as results weighted together into a one-dimensional indicator, or one number that indicates the total environmental impact according to various methods. By grouping inventory results into impact categories, researchers can calculate the characterization results, leading to fewer parameters (Guinée 2002). It is possible to further aggregate results through various formalized weighting methods. Different weighting methods express different ways of prioritizing environmental problems. For example, priorities can set through political policies with environmental goals, recommendations by Delphi panels (experts who work together to forecast and revise results), or economic policies that encourage a "willingness to pay" to avoid environmental problems.

Methodologies

LCA is principally a methodology for comparing equivalent product systems, although a stand-alone LCA comparison is also possible. In a stand-alone LCA, researchers compare different parts of one product system. In all types of LCAs, they make a comparison by relating environmental impact to a unit that expresses the function of the product system. For example, beverage-packaging systems can be compared on the environmental impact per liter of packaged drink. The unit of comparison is called the functional unit, and its definition is essential for conducting a fair comparison. Other methodologies that influence the quality of a comparison include the system boundary definition (e.g., deciding whether to include in the system items such as the production of capital equipment), the types of environmental impacts being considered (e.g., aiming at a comprehensive evaluation of environmental impacts versus limiting the study to one or two impact categories), and the level of detail in the study (e.g., deciding whether to use site-specific data or average data over a number of production sites).

Different types of LCA are possible, depending on how the comparison is made. In quantitative LCA studies, researchers calculate the environmental impacts for the product systems, whereas in qualitative LCAs, they identify and evaluate the environmental impacts through reasoning supported by, for example, checklists. Another distinction concerns whether the comparison is prospective or retrospective. In a prospective study, researchers investigate the environmental consequences of the proposed changes to an existing product system. An example is a study of the significance of possible waste-management alternatives (e.g., recycling and incineration) to an existing packaging system. Prospective studies are also called change-oriented LCAs or consequential LCAs. In a retrospective LCA, often called an accounting LCA, researchers compare existing product systems. The comparison of ecolabeled products typically builds on an accounting LCA. (Ecolabeling is a voluntary program in which manufacturers and service providers certify the environmental performance of their products and services.)

The distinction between the change-oriented / consequential LCA and the accounting/retrospective LCA is a difference in focus: in one, the existing situation is compared to an alternative future situation (change-oriented / consequential LCA), and in the other, two existing alternatives are compared (perspective/accounting LCA). In addition, system boundary definition and data choices differ substantively between these two types of LCA study. Studying the consequences of change typically leads to a focus on modeling the parts of the system that are affected by change and to the use of marginal data. But comparing the existing products typically leads to a focus on how complete the model of the product systems is and to the use of average data.

Cradle to grave, cradle to gate, and *gate to gate* are other terms for LCA. They indicate the extent to which the product system is modeled in an LCA, from raw materials extraction to waste management, to the factory gate, or between factory gates, respectively.

LCA is also associated with the philosophy of life cycle thinking (LCT) and the practices of life cycle management (LCM). Expressions of life cycle thinking can be found in, for example, corporate environmental policies. Life cycle management is the managerial practices and organizational arrangements that result from life cycle thinking. LCM's goal is to coordinate environmental concerns and work among actors within the product system, rather than develop independent measures in each company (cf. Remmen, Jensen, and Frydendal 2007).

History

The development of early LCA between 1969 and 1989 is distinct from its development afterward. Since 1990, systematic description and the development of the methodology has come to the fore, making it a subject of academic study. It was not until the early 1990s that the term *life cycle assessment* came into general use—earlier studies were called ecobalances, resource and environmental profile analyses, or cradle-to-grave studies.

A study conducted in the United States for Coca-Cola by the Midwest Research Institute from 1969 to 1970 is generally considered the first LCA study. Early independent studies were also conducted both in the United Kingdom (for Schweppes by Ian Boustead) and in Sweden (for Tetra Pak by Gustav Sundström). All the early LCAs between 1969 and 1972 studied packaging and waste management. They coincided with the environmental debate concerning wasteful resource use and disposable packaging in throwaway societies (Meadows et al. 1972). What identifies these studies as LCAs is their simultaneous attention to material and energy flows, from raw materials extraction to the waste disposal of a product system and the pollution and resource use associated with it. This distinguishes them from the systems studies focusing on energy that became common after the oil crisis in 1973. Nevertheless, the oil crisis fueled interest in LCA, and a handful of consultants in the world carried out small-scale LCA studies.

Between 1970 and 1989, the consultants William Franklin and Robert Hunt conducted some two hundred studies in the United States, and consultant Gustav Sundström conducted about one hundred studies in Sweden, many of them for private companies. LCA resurfaced in the public debate with the surge of environmental interest during the mid-1980s, again in relation to packaging. In 1984, the Swiss environmental agency conducted a large packaging study (Bundesamt für Umweltschutz 1984) that was widely criticized. The study was updated five years later (Bundesamt für Umwelt, Wald und Landschaft 1989). Its criticism paradoxically increased attention toward the possibilities of LCA and inspired packaging studies in other European countries (e.g., in Denmark in 1990, in Sweden in 1991, and in the Netherlands in 1992). The many packaging studies showed diverging results and partly differing methodologies, starting a new era of methodological discussion and development.

The increased interest in LCA can be explained by industry's shift in focus toward environmental work. Since the early 1990s, manufacturers have increasingly supported the idea that environmental protection should go beyond "end-of-pipes" strategies that deal with pollution after it happens. Many of those in industry see the environmental optimization (identifying where reductions like waste minimization and material substitution can be most efficient) of products as an effective path toward sustainability. LCA's appeal is that it deals with environmental issues in a systematic and comprehensive way, handling several environmental problems at a time and extending the environmental analysis beyond controlling emissions at their point source. In doing so, LCA helps avoid suboptimization, or settling for a lesser outcome, in the environmental management of industrial systems.

Guidelines, Standards, and Developments

The Society of Environmental Toxicology and Chemistry (SETAC) provides a forum for discussing LCA experiences and developing an international consensus on a "harmonized LCA methodology" (Consoli et al. 1993). After sponsoring seven international workshops and conferences between 1990 and 1993, it published the first international guidelines in its code of practice (Consoli et al. 1993). It also established a number of working groups to speed up the process of developing a standardized methodology. The first international standard for LCA, providing its main principles and framework, was issued in 1997 by the International Organization for Standardization.

Since then a series of LCA standards have been issued and updated. Other organized efforts to promote LCA take place, for example, through the Life Cycle Initiative, a collaboration between the United Nations Environment Programme (UNEP) and SETAC. This initiative's goals include disseminating widely accepted methods for the reliable and easy use of LCAs, first to developing countries and later more widely (Life Cycle Initiative n.d.). The European Commission also supports the dissemination of LCA through policy and business practices (European Commission—Joint Research Centre 2009).

The core of LCA—flow modeling—has remained much the same since the beginning, while impact assessment methodologies saw the most advances during the 1990s. Since 2000, methods have been developed that include the social aspects in life cycle impact assessment and the economic cost-benefit analysis along the product chain. These developments better align LCA with the discourse of sustainable development and make LCA more attractive to the business community. But much work remains before such methods become common practice. Much work also went into the development of software, databases, and standardized formats for data exchange: simple data management is crucial to facilitating calculation and data availability since any LCA study requires much data. The exploration of alternative data sources, such as economic input-output tables, led to new types of LCA: IO-LCA (input-output LCA) (Hendrickson, Lave, and Matthews 2006) and hybrid LCA, which combines standard LCA with IO-LCA (Suh et al. 2004). These methods enable researchers to conduct new types of studies (cf. Tukker and Jansen 2006) that explore the consumption activities that have the most-polluting product flows in society (typically transportation, housing, and food). Since these studies include the impacts of production that is outsourced to developing countries, they contribute to the debate on the role of consumption and global industry in sustainability (cf. Hertwich 2005).

A scholarly journal for developments in the field of LCA, *The International Journal of Life Cycle Assessment*, began publishing in 1996. The first conference on life cycle management was held in 2001, and the European network on IO-LCA also held it first meeting in 2001. In short, research related to LCA, LCT, and LCM is mainly prescriptive, dealing with methodology development. Consequently research exploring the practices of LCA and LCM is less common.

Applications

LCA and LCT attract interest both in business and policy making. Policy makers use LCA in studies to guide policy development away from point-source control and into

product-oriented policy making. For example, the packaging studies that were discussed above in the history section were often used to identify which materials should have recycling policies. LCT gave rise to the notion of extended producer responsibility, in which a consortium of companies is responsible for the environmental costs of their products through the end of the products' life cycles. The result is producer take-back policies that require the manufacturer to pay for the collection, disposal, and recycling of their products. Other life cycle-influenced policies include ecolabeling, which was discussed along with methodology. The application of LCT to policy making is, however, a challenge: the global nature of business spreads material and energy flows outside the reach of governmental policy makers.

Since the 1990s, LCA has been applied to nearly all sectors of business and society. In the transportation sector, LCA studies are often called well-to-wheel studies. LCA's focus on products has made it particularly applicable to product development and ecodesign as well as ecolabeling. The prescriptive use of LCT in the sustainable design of products and services, for example, appears in cradle-to-cradle design model (McDonough and Braungart 2002). LCA-based ecolabeling programs have been put forward both by governmental organizations (as in the European Union's "Flower" ecolabel) and by industrial coalitions (as in the International EPD Consortium's Environmental Product Declaration program). LCA has also been applied to "greening" the control methods of manufacturing and production systems. Upstream application areas, which occur in the manufacturing and production stages, include greening supply-chain management and procurement. Downstream application areas, which occur around the sale of the product, include waste and recycling management. Several LCA tools are specially adapted to the requirements of the various fields of application.

Despite its widespread use and application, LCA's use in business is relatively limited. Surveys on businesses' adoption of LCA are rare. In 2002, almost 10 percent of the largest corporations in Europe worked with LCA in some way. Compare this with the percentage of corporations that adopted environmental management systems: almost two-thirds in the same survey (Hibbitt and Kamp-Roelands 2002). One reason for this difference is that LCA reaches outside a company's normal boundaries of responsibility. This makes LCA irrelevant or overambitious in the eyes of

some; alternatively, others believe it offers a novel and useful perspective on business operations. Most LCA studies done for companies are conducted by consultants or through collaborations with research institutes, sector organizations, or academia. In companies where the LCA process has been internalized, it is typically an experimental activity performed by the environmental or research and development department (cf. Frankl and Rubik 2000; Rex and Baumann 2007). Analysis shows that LCA studies often lead to organizational learning, a new and widened perspective on business operations, and, often, surprising insights. In just one such example, people in a paper mill were about to reduce their point-source emissions by investing in more state-of-the-art, end-of-pipe technology, but they realized through an LCA that they could save money and reduce their emissions tenfold through simple changes in the logistics from forest to mill (Baumann and Tillman 2004).

Little is known about the business rationales for LCA since proponents inside the company drive much of the LCA work. But studies show that, in companies where LCA practices are institutionalized, risk aversion or trust-building with actors in the supply chain are the business rationales for LCA (Rex and Baumann 2007). In these companies, specially adapted LCA tools and considerations were implemented in the business process, for example, in product development or procurement. The same studies also show that LCA practices differ greatly among businesses, even between similar, same-sector companies. For example, LCA practices in product development in European truck companies range from using simple LCA-based guidelines to combining extensive LCA studies with strategic planning.

Implications

There are many controversies over LCA methodology. Concerns about the inappropriate use of LCAs in the United States led a coalition of state attorneys general to decide that "the results of LCAs should not be used to advertise or promote specific products until uniform methods . . . are developed" (ENDS 1991). Such concerns are strong reasons for standardization efforts. Because LCA is quantitative and describes physical flows with scientific methods, it is often thought of as an objective method that produces general scientific results. But this is far from the case. Many methodological choices depend on the purpose and the type of LCA. Methodological alternatives are also a matter of choice. Eventually gaps and unresolved ambiguities develop in the methodology. Together, these issues lead to the possibility that similar LCA studies would have divergent results. Such results pose special problems for the ISO standard on LCA, since it aims to be a comprehensive standard for all types of LCA.

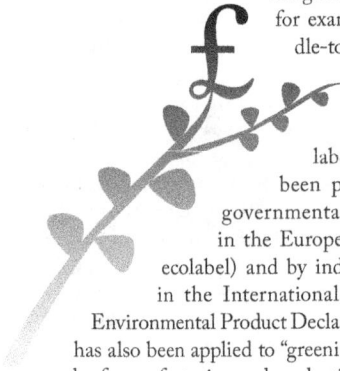

Debate is particularly intense and enduring over two issues: how to allocate environmental loads across several products, and how to conduct impact assessment. Since LCA focuses on a single product at a time, the material flows of different products being connected to each other can complicate the inventory analysis. Whenever more than one product is produced in a process, an allocation problem occurs in the LCA. It also arises when many products are collectively treated in the same waste-treatment process and when a product's material is recycled into another product. The allocation problem concerns how the environmental loads of a process are divided among the process's different products. Several methods exist for dealing with this, including applying various principles to partition the environmental loads onto the products based on physical relationship, weight, volume, or economic value. Another approach is system expansion, which includes the parts of the surrounding industrial system that are affected by changes related to the object of study. Some people argue for strict recommendations for partitioning the environmental loads, and some argue for more-open recommendations that allow researchers to choose the method depending on the purpose of the study. The ISO standard is contradictory because it acknowledges both the need to choose the method based on the goal and prescribes an allocation procedure that ignores the goal-dependant method.

Many debates about impact assessment concern what counts as an environmental impact and where to model the impact in the cause-effect chain between emissions and their effects. Methodology is being developed to cover additional types of impacts, including some social and economic impacts. Some impacts are difficult to describe; for example, the effects of eco-toxicity and land use on biodiversity result in LCA studies that emphasize easily modeled impacts. Some researchers debate whether to describe impacts through end-point or midpoint assessment, that is, whether the methodology should describe real or potential impacts. The significance is that real impacts depend on the location of the impact, which adds geographical complexities to modeling. As a result, several impact assessment methods exist. Many of these methods conflict with work on potential impacts, thereby rendering them generally applicable but inaccurate.

The time and resources it takes to carry out an LCA study have always been a contentious issue, and many claim that the costs of performing the life cycle inventory are too high. Efforts to simplify the execution of LCA studies take various paths. One path develops screening and streamlining methodologies that drastically reduce the amount of data needed. An alternative path increases the availability of data by setting up and maintaining databases for researchers to use.

Research activities also reflect different perspectives on how to further the use of LCA. The dominant approach intended to resolve the methodological problems in LCA, and it led to many prescriptive, relatively realistic recommendations concerning LCA's application. A small but growing body of knowledge aims to develop an understanding of practices related to LCA, LCT, and LCM in business and policy making. This more descriptive research indicates that many of the prescriptive recommendations for LCA application are too general to fit a diverse business community.

Many find LCA complicated and time consuming, but this is more a case of LCA reflecting the complexities of our world. LCA offers a systematic way to describe the environmental consequences of production and consumption in a comprehensive way that enables communication about large, complex environmental issues. LCA development has mostly taken place in the engineering community, but cross-disciplinary integration with the social, economic, and management sciences is increasing. Such integration can modify the technical LCA approach to be more useful for business and other actors in society.

Henrikke BAUMANN
Chalmers University of Technology

See also in the *Berkshire Encyclopedia of Sustainability* Biomimicry; Cradle to Cradle; Design, Industrial; Ecolabeling; Energy Efficiency; Integrated Product Development (IPD); Manufacturing Practices; Natural Step Framework, The (TNSF); Product-Service Systems (PSSs); Remanufacturing; Zero Waste

FURTHER READING

Baumann, Henrikke, & Tillman, Anne-Marie. (2004). *The hitch hiker's guide to LCA: An orientation in life cycle assessment methodology and application*. Lund, Sweden: Studentlitteratur.

Bundesamt für Umweltschutz. (1984). Eco-balances of packaging. In *Report series environment (No. 24)*. Bern, Switzerland: Bundesamt für Umweltschutz.

Bundesamt für Umwelt, Wald und Landschaft. (1991). Eco-balances of packaging: Status 1990. In *Report series environment (No. 132)*. Bern, Switzerland: Bundesamt für Umwelt, Wald und Landschaft.

Consoli, F., et al. (1993). *Guidelines for life-cycle assessment: A "code of practice."* Brussels: Society of Environmental Toxicology and Chemistry (SETAC).

Environmental Data Services (ENDS). (1991). Curbs urged on use of life cycle analysis in product marketing. ENDS report 198. London: Environmental Data Services.

Environmental Product Declaration (EPD). (n.d.) The international EPD system: A communication tool for international markets. Retrieved July 9, 2009, from http://www.environdec.com

European Commission—Joint Research Centre. (2009). Life cycle thinking. Retrieved July 9, 2009, from http://lct.jrc.ec.europa.eu

Frankl, Paolo, & Rubik, Frieder. (Eds.). (2000). *Life cycle assessment in industry and business: Adoption patterns, applications and implications.* Berlin: Springer-Verlag.

Guinée, Jeroen B. (Ed.). (2002). *Handbook on life cycle assessment: Operational guide to the ISO standard.* Dordrecht, The Netherlands: Kluwer.

Hendrickson, Chris T.; Lave, Lester B.; & Matthews, H. Scott. (2006). *Environmental life cycle assessment of goods and services: An input-output approach.* Washington, DC: Resources for the Future.

Hertwich, Edgar G. (2005). Life cycle approaches to sustainable consumption: A critical review. *Environmental Science and Technology, 39*(13), 4673–4684.

Hibbitt, Chris, & Kamp-Roelands, Nancy. (2002). Europe's (mild) greening of corporate environmental management. *Corporate Environmental Strategy, 9*(2), 172–182.

Hunt, Robert G., & Franklin, William E. (1996). LCA—how it came about: Personal reflections on the origin and the development of LCA in the USA. *International Journal of LCA, 1*(1), 4–7.

International Organization for Standardization (ISO). (2006). *ISO 14040:2006: Environmental management—life cycle assessment—principles and framework.* Geneva: ISO.

The Life Cycle Initiative. (n.d.) The Life Cycle Initiative: International life cycle partnership for a sustainable world. Retrieved July 9, 2009, from http://lcinitiative.unep.fr

McDonough, William, & Braungart, Michael. (2002). *Cradle to cradle: Remaking the way we make things.* New York: North Point Press.

Meadows, Donella H.; Meadows, Dennis L.; Randers, Jørgen; & Behrens, William W., III. (1972). *The limits to growth.* New York: Universe Books.

Remmen, Arne; Jensen, Allan Astrup; & Frydendal, Jeppe. (2007). *Life cycle management: A business guide to sustainability.* Retrieved July 9, 2009, from http://www.unep.fr/shared/docs/publications/LCM_guide.pdf?site=lcinit&page_id=F14E0563-6C63-4372-B82F-6F6B5786CCE3

Rex, Emma L. C., & Baumann, Henrikke. (2007). Individual adaptation of industry LCA practice: Results from two case studies in the Swedish forest products industry. *International Journal of Life Cycle Assessment, 12*(4), 266–271.

Suh, Sangwon; Lenzen, Manfred; Treloar, Graham J.; Hondo, Hiroki; Horvath, Arpad; Huppes, Gjalt; et al. (2004). System boundary selection in life-cycle inventories using hybrid approaches. *Environmental Science and Technology, 38*(3), 657–664.

Tukker, Arnold, & Jansen, Bart. (2006). Environmental impacts of products: A detailed review of studies. *Journal of Industrial Ecology, 10*(3), 159–182.

Manufacturing Practices

Since the 1980s, some of the manufacturing industry has adopted practices that emphasize sustainable manufacturing, and integral to this concept is a decrease in or elimination of waste. Reducing energy and water use is often the first step, but sustainable manufacturing also involves standards and performance frameworks. Sustainable manufacturing must address social and economic sustainability in addition to the environment.

Sustainable manufacturing practices are mainly based on the concept of resource productivity, which promotes increasing the efficiency of resources to reduce waste. These practices seek to create goods while using fewer resources (energy, water, and materials); because of these practices, the materials used in the supply chain should have low embedded energy and water (energy and water used in the chain to prepare the material). These practices favor renewable energy and materials with recycled content. Companies are modifying manufacturing practices to lower the volume of wastes going to all environmental media (air, water, and land). While many companies have some waste reduction programs in place, the judicious use of resource productivity is increasingly important.

A number of independent events occurred in the late 1980s to trigger a directed movement that helped shape what we know as sustainable manufacturing practice. From these five events many companies developed separate sustainability methods; the combination or integration of these methods, however, is the heart of sustainable manufacturing.

In 1987 the US Congress amended the Stevenson-Wydler Technology Innovation Act of 1980 to establish the Malcolm Baldrige National Quality Award, which promotes awareness and recognition of performance excellence. At the time, foreign competition challenged the country's manufacturing quality and costs, and for two decades US manufacturing productivity growth had improved less than that of other countries. Congress believed poor quality was costing companies up to 20 percent of their sales revenues and that improved quality of manufactured goods and services would be accompanied by improved productivity, lower costs, and increased profitability. The award provides a process management category that calls out best practices for manufacturing processes. Sustainability and corporate social responsibility are specifically included in later versions of this important business-excellence guide.

The World Commission on Environment and Development published its findings in the 1987 book *Our Common Future*. This book is widely referenced as the source of the original definition of sustainable development—a marriage of economy and ecology—that encourages governments and their people to take responsibility for environmental damage and the policies causing that damage. The United Nations established the commission in 1983 to reexamine the critical environmental and development problems that were being recognized all over the world. The UN sought realistic proposals to solve these problems and to ensure that human progress would be sustained through development, without bankrupting the resources of future generations. Companies that have been practicing sustainability pay particular attention to the term *eco-efficiency*. It is the forerunner of the term *resource productivity* described above.

Also in 1987, the International Organization for Standardization issued a three-part quality management system (ISO 9000) for manufacturing companies:

1. The model for quality assurance in design, development, production, installation, and servicing applies to companies whose activities include the creation of new products.

2. The model for quality assurance in production, installation, and servicing is basically the same as number 1 but does not cover the creation of new products.
3. The model for quality assurance in final inspection and testing covers only the final inspection of finished products.

Even though the standard emphasizes conformance with procedures rather than the overall management process, it was an important step for manufacturing to better control processes. In 2000, the related ISO 9001 was changed to emphasize a process focus and a systems approach to management. It is a foundation for companies involved in making resource productivity part of a sustainable manufacturing practice.

The US Environmental Protection Agency released a draft of the *Waste Minimization Opportunity Assessment Manual* in 1988. The manual derived from a set of manufacturing sector reports produced by the state of California. The manual discussed "source reduction" and examined both product and process change as a means for promoting the judicious use of resources, energy efficiency, reuse of input materials during production, and reduced energy and water consumption. Such changes would include these benefits:

• reduced risk of criminal and civil liability
• reduction of operating costs
• improved employee morale and participation
• enhancement of the company's image in the community
• protection of public health and the environment

The manual proposed a hierarchy of waste management that favored waste elimination over waste reuse and recycling. Waste treatment and disposal would be considered as a last resort. This was a major shift in thinking for the manufacturing industry.

Finally, people recognized the link between the growing interest in total quality management (TQM) and the interest in pollution prevention (Pojasek 1987). Quality management tools (e.g., root cause analysis, process mapping, brainwriting, bubble sorting, and action planning) could be used to involve employees and suppliers in systematically reducing or eliminating all wastes from all manufacturing processes. This was the birth of the "systems approach to process improvement." Widespread deployment of manufacturing methodologies such as Lean and the Six Sigma process improvement followed.

Different professionals in the industrial and environmental engineering communities used these efforts independently. Ultimately people would integrate performance frameworks with management systems and use process improvement to drive the continual upgrading necessary to achieve sustainable manufacturing practice.

When Is Sustainable Manufacturing Sustainable?

The term *sustainable manufacturing* means different things to different people. Many of these differences come from the discipline and bias of the manufacturing professional. People often are needlessly sidetracked by definitional disputes. Nevertheless, the achievement of sustainable manufacturing in any business is a journey, not a static state. Sustainable manufacturing is a key component of operating a sustainable business that creates value for its constituents. Manufacturing industry sectors are very interested in sustainable manufacturing, and the world has experienced a major shift in philosophy, acceptance, and emphasis on it since its humble beginnings.

Becoming sustainable often starts when a company adopts a formal program to drive resource productivity. Many companies use the ISO 9001:2008 standard as a foundation. They integrate elements of ISO 14001, risk management (draft ISO 31000), social responsibility (draft ISO 26000), and a business excellence framework (the Baldrige Performance Excellence Program). These integrated management systems help make sustainable manufacturing practices part of the companies' day-to-day operations. Products made in this manner can be certified to sustainable product standards issued by the American National Standards Institute (ANSI) and similar standard-setting bodies.

The manufacturing process then must operate in an eco-efficient manner. Companies analyze the direct and indirect use of all resources (energy, water, and materials) and the loss of resources from each activity in the manufacturing process. The indirect use and loss of resources comes from supporting processes and facility infrastructure (air compressors, air and water pollution control equipment, boilers, chillers, and heating ventilation and air conditioning). Companies use process mapping and resource accounting to ensure they follow what ISO 9000:20000 calls a process focus and a systems approach to management (Pojasek 2005).

An interest in sustainable manufacturing does not automatically translate into a commitment to change the product process. Many businesses worry about the cost and benefit of this path. Many manufacturing executives view this as a choice between being more environmentally responsible and allowing employees to keep their jobs. But such executives are slowly realizing that business opportunities that gain positive feedback

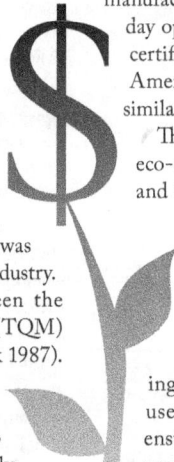

from environmentally conscious customers can result in an increase in sales.

Reducing energy and water use are the most common and simplest places to start converting to a sustainable manufacturing process. Eliminating all waste from all business practices is an important midpoint goal. In the long term, the business can develop sustainable manufacturing technology and products that raise the sustainability level. Environmental and social responsibility in manufacturing includes both contributing to the company's sustainability and being able to manufacture supplies that will facilitate other sectors' ability to become sustainable. This involves life cycle management, which is based on the interconnectedness of materials and processes.

Successfully transitioning to sustainable manufacturing requires a company to align its manufacturing program with its vision, mission, and core values (Pojasek 2007). The management support necessary for the business to complete the process can only be gained by fully integrating the sustainable manufacturing effort with the core business. Employees and stakeholders need to be involved in the program's planning and implementation. Employees are a key source of knowledge for the transition. Mutually beneficial relationships with suppliers, customers, and key stakeholders are also important. Success usually depends on the integrated use of performance frameworks, management systems, and process improvement. Sustainable manufacturing uses these proven methods to meet customer and market needs, while providing eco-efficient processes and their benefits to the environment, key stakeholders, and the community. Sustainability comes from the value to the business's top line (branding) and the bottom line as it helps create a robust local economy. This may be the best argument to use when seeking senior management's support for sustainable manufacturing processes.

Innovative Practices

Vigilance and discipline lead to initial improvements in resource productivity. Employee involvement programs bring about many suggestions for using and losing fewer resources. Occasional innovations occur simply by altering machinery. For example, if an industrial laundry places its incoming city water pipe inside the wastewater discharge pipe, the heat from the discharged wastewater heats the incoming water. This lowers the amount of fuel the boiler needs to heat the wash water. To a low-tech company, this is innovation. (Later the company can invest in a more-efficient heat exchanger.)

The coatings area has seen many innovations. New and more effective technologies have improved the application of coatings and adhesives. Painting went from the spraying of liquid paints, which contain many volatile solvents, to the application of high solids paints, which have much fewer volatile organic solvents to carry the pigments onto the surface to be painted. The move to powder paints, which have no carrying agent at all and thus no volatile organics, followed.

Even something as mundane as cleaning mixing vessels has improved with spray-ball technology. Previously technicians cleaned a vessel by filling the tanks with cleaning solvent, turning on the mixer, draining the tank, and repeating the process. Now a "ball" with many small holes shoots a high-pressure spray through holes, using a fraction of the cleaning fluid. Other cleaning applications employ air knives—high-pressure air that blows material off a surface—before using a liquid to remove the remaining contaminants.

Some innovations follow a new approach called "servicizing," where a business or supplier refocuses from selling products to providing services. For example, carpet companies lease carpeting and service it instead of replacing it. Because of legislation in Europe, companies take back their products and reuse portions in new products. Recyclable and reusable toner cartridges are one example, and plastic housings from old cathode ray tube (CRT) computer monitors are converted into roofing shingles.

The design of a product and the design of its manufacturing process influence the use and loss of resources. Some companies require their design professionals to work on the plant floor to learn how to increase resource productivity with new products. Similarly, designers are beginning to use biomimicry to develop new products. Biomimicry seeks sustainable solutions by emulating nature's designs and processes. For example, the tubercles on a humpback whale's flippers, which allow it to move quickly in the water, inspired WhalePower Corporation's tubercle technology. Products using tubercle technology, such as wind turbines, fans, and compressors, are often at least 20 percent more energy efficient than conventional technology (WhalePower 2009).

Innovation does not happen by accident or good intentions. It can be sparked by the challenge of improving resource productivity after the easy solutions are taken. A

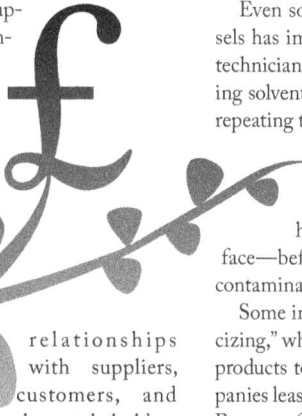

sustainable manufacturing company can involve employees and suppliers in a culture that develops processes and methodologies and encourages innovations. The drive to increase resource productivity can create impassioned internal champions, or employees focused on making the program successful (compared with managers, who must juggle many responsibilities). By evangelizing innovative means for extending resource productivity and regularly communicating the efforts of those involved, champions lay the groundwork for further innovation. The company that uses sustainable manufacturing processes, no matter their source, and keeps a process focus in all of its efforts is positioned to be highly innovative.

Controversies

A number of controversies come up in discussions of sustainable manufacturing processes. Some are addressed below.

Green versus Sustainable Manufacturing

The term *green* is usually restricted to manufacturing that has substantially lowered it energy use or waste production, or that uses materials with high recycled content. But sustainable manufacturing seeks to move beyond green. We must examine three types of outcomes—environmental, social, and economic—to consider whether practices are sustainable. This is controversial because many manufacturers limit their so-called sustainability efforts to what they call "environmental sustainability." Other manufacturers refer to their work as green manufacturing or "lean to green" manufacturing. If we apply the three outcomes for sustainable manufacturing, then green and lean-to-green efforts do not fit the definition.

Stakeholder Engagement

Many sustainable manufacturing companies show their various stakeholders detailed information about the core processes responsible for their activities, products, and services. Such knowledge takes away some of the stakeholders' concerns and provides transparency and accountability. Often they have good comments that can lead to further innovation.

As noted above, stakeholder engagement includes increasing employee involvement in the process and asking suppliers how they make their products and how others use them. Stakeholders in the surrounding community can discuss their "interest" in the manufacturing process. Some stakeholder engagement tools are easily available (AccountAbility 2007); these tools can be used over the long term once companies become familiar with them and see their value in adding sustainability to manufacturing processes.

Management Systems

A management system is defined as making quality, sustainability, and environmental and social responsibility part of a company's operation. Companies using management systems are usually required by their clients to use ISO standards, which many manufacturing managers are uncomfortable with. So they implement minimally responsible programs to meet the request and consequently realize little benefit from them. The argument that ISO standards are inflexible and bury companies with useless procedures and paperwork is no longer true, although older ISO versions had these problems. ISO revises its standards: ISO 9001:2000 recognized process focus and a systems approach to management; ISO 9001:2008 made the standard easier to integrate with ISO 14001; ISO 14001:1997 was updated to ISO 14001:2004; and ISO 26000 (on social responsibility) will be issued in 2010. These standards help many companies move to sustainable manufacturing. Even the minimally responsible versions can be improved to accomplish what is needed to progress to this goal.

Operating in Silos

Many manufacturing companies operate their process improvement programs and management initiatives independently of one another. Independent programs are referred to as "silos" (Pojasek 2008). Each silo is often run by a champion whose value to the company is determined, to some extent, by the success of the initiative's (or silo's) activities. Champions are often reluctant to consider integrating programs (e.g., management systems, business excellence frameworks, risk management, and process improvement techniques like Six Sigma); they find it threatening. Employees become confused by many initiatives and the competition between them for attention, and the initiative champions will not be able to help employees do their jobs more effectively. But if the integration focuses on equipping employees with a single, integrated approach to their work, some threats can be mitigated. In this way, the silos are not destroyed—they are harmonized to help employees move to sustainable manufacturing processes.

Ecolabels and Green Marketing Claims

If a company has developed sustainable manufacturing practices, marketing professionals will try to differentiate the resulting products in the marketplace. The ISO standard on ecolabels (ISO 2009a) recognizes three claims by manufacturers:

- seals of approval that are received for meeting the ISO standard
- specific claims that add terms like *biodegradable* or *organic* to the product promotion material
- labels that constitute a grade, such as "USDA choice beef" or "five-star hotel"

The most-effective labels are sector specific, accurate, and third-party verified. There is still much controversy over labeling. The US Federal Trade Commission has been reviewing its ecolabel guidelines to help companies avoid "greenwashing," defined as "the act of misleading consumers regarding the environmental practices of a company or the environmental benefits of a product or service" (TerraChoice Environmental Marketing 2009). A company that exaggerates claims and does not link them to demonstrable sustainability advantages will likely be contacted by consumer watchdog groups looking for greenwashing.

Successes and Impacts

Despite the controversies associated with sustainable manufacturing practices, many large companies have operated successful programs. Many smaller and medium-sized companies have benefited from their examples.

DuPont

For years, DuPont's "goal of zero" has maintained its core direction toward sustainable growth. Its website defines the goal as "the creation of shareholder and societal value while we reduce our environmental footprint along the value chains in which we operate." It further explains: "We will conduct our business with respect and care for the environment; we will implement those strategies that build successful businesses and achieve the greatest benefit for all our stakeholders without compromising the ability of future generations to meet their needs." DuPont (2009) states clearly that all injuries, occupational illnesses, and safety and environmental incidents are preventable, and its goal for them is zero.

DuPont also drives toward zero waste generation by looking at the source of each type of waste and by preventing waste in the first place through process change. It has even stated its desire to drive toward zero emissions. It looks at efficiently using fossil fuels and feedstock, land, water, minerals, and other natural resources: "We will seek to conserve and protect natural resource biodiversity and will manage our land to enhance habitats for wildlife." DuPont (2009) also extends its commitment to its products: "We will continuously analyze and improve

our practices, processes and products to reduce their risk and impact throughout the product life cycle." DuPont's Responsible Care Management System helps implement these claims and make them part of how it does business.

Xerox Corporation

Xerox (2009) has long been committed to producing "waste-free products in waste-free facilities.... [Its] aim is to design products, packaging and supplies that make efficient use of resources, minimize waste, reuse material where feasible and recycle what can't be reused." Since this program started in 1991, it has prevented over 2 billion pounds of potential waste from entering the disposal stream to landfills and incinerators. Xerox uses ISO 14001 to incorporate this program into its business unit operations. Through employee involvement, it enjoys a 92 percent recycling rate for all nonhazardous materials that are not used in its products. Its annual nonfinancial reports provide the program's progress.

Subaru of Indiana

Subaru of Indiana's improvements in its manufacturing processes allowed it to virtually eliminate the waste sent to landfills—while making over 110,000 vehicles per year (Subaru 2009). Some of the recycle systems (e.g., the paint solvent recovery system) were expensive to implement, and paybacks took over seven years. But Subaru management agrees the money was well spent and they have moved toward their goal of sustainable manufacturing. Many ideas came from enthusiastic employees. Subaru shares its ideas with other automobile manufacturers, other manufacturing industry facilities, and a host of zero-waste groups.

Outlook for the Twenty-First Century

It may be easy to understand the many varied elements that constitute sustainable manufacturing practice. But it takes focus and persistence to set up these elements and begin the continual improvement process that ultimately leads to sustainable manufacturing. Some have said that this is nothing but "good business," but it seems that many manufacturing companies have little time for such good business. When manufacturing volume is high, many companies are too busy to work on these processes and programs. When manufacturing volume is low, they cut the resources necessary to plan and implement them. In contrast, the examples cited in the previous section have been maintained in both bull and bear markets. If we review the annual sustainability reports of the three companies above, we see that they provide accounting of their gains *every* year on their websites. These companies also present papers at large sustainability conferences and demonstrate how persistence leads to sizable savings.

Regulation has increased the cost of waste management, including air and water pollution costs. With less waste, less money is spent managing waste. But every time something is reworked, more resources are used. Thus companies will continue to be interested in accounting for the "embedded costs" associated with energy use, carbon footprints, reuse, and remanufacturing. Their motivation is the need to include the true cost of producing goods in their products' costs, from resource extraction to end of life and reuse or recycling. This true cost is more than the "value added" through these stages; it is also the environmental and social costs associated with product life cycles. But determining true cost is not easy since we often do not have good data. The American National Standards Institute (ANSI), however, has sustainable product standards that require measuring these values for carpets.

The state of California may require bidders to incorporate costs for all the embedded energy, materials and other resources, labor, and environmental impacts and accompanying social requirements and impacts in the price of their products. The state (2007) already mandates that a carpet must score at the "platinum" level (ANSI NSF 140 Sustainable Carpet Standard) in order to be sold to state agencies. Walmart asks its 65,000 suppliers to answer fifteen questions and submit to a sustainability index for everything they sell to it.

Whether the United States implements a carbon tax or a cap-and-trade system, experts expect a $1 trillion impact on the economy. Companies that begin to incorporate "environmental economics" in the design and production of their products are likely to be ahead of their competition. Once they recognize these costs, they will stop at nothing to eliminate them. This is what sustainable manufacturing will be about in the twenty-first century. While Walmart will drive this practice for retail goods, others will drive it for other manufactured goods.

Robert B. POJASEK
Harvard University

See also in the *Berkshire Encyclopedia of Sustainability* Biomimicry; Chemistry, Green; Design, Industrial; Ecolabeling; Energy Efficiency; Integrated Product Development (IPD); Life Cycle Assessments (LCAs); Product-Service Systems (PSSs); Remanufacturing; Stakeholder Theory; Supply Chain Management; Zero Waste

FURTHER READING

AccountAbility. (2007). *Stakeholder engagement and facilitation.* Retrieved September 19, 2009, from http://www.accountability21.net/default.aspx?id=256

Baldrige National Quality Program. (2009). *The Malcolm Baldrige National Quality Improvement Act of 1987—Public Law 100-107.* Retrieved September 3, 2009, from http://www.quality.nist.gov/Improvement_Act.htm

Benyus, Janine. (1997). *Biomimicry: Innovation inspired by nature.* New York: William Morrow.

Biomimicry Institute. (2009). Retrieved September 3, 2009, from http://biomimicryinstitute.org

DuPont. (2009). *The DuPont commitment.* Retrieved September 3, 2009, from http://www2.dupont.com/Sustainability/en_US/Performance_Reporting/commitment.html

International Organization for Standardization (ISO). (2009a). *ICS 13.020.050: Ecolabelling.* Retrieved September 3, 2009, from http://www.iso.org/iso/products/standards/catalogue_ics_browse.htm?ICS1=13&ICS2=020&ICS3=50&

International Organization for Standardization (ISO). (2009b). *ISO 9000 and ISO 14000.* Retrieved September 3, 2009, from http://www.iso.org/iso/iso_catalogue/management_standards/iso_9000_iso_14000.htm

Pojasek, Robert B. (1987, January). Improving operations through waste minimization. *Journal of the American Institute of Plant Engineers,* 11–15.

Pojasek, Robert B. (2005). Understanding processes with hierarchical process mapping. *Environmental Quality Management, 15*(2), 79–86.

Pojasek, Robert B. (2007, Winter). A framework for business sustainability. *Environmental Quality Management, 17*(2), 81–88.

Pojasek, Robert B. (2008). Energy and water management systems: Building more silos? *Environmental Quality Management, 18*(2), 79–87.

State of California/Green California. 2007. Standards & specifications. Retrieved February 1, 2010, from http://www.green.ca.gov/EPP/standards.htm

Subaru. (2009). *Environmental policy.* Retrieved September 3, 2009, from http://www.subaru.com/company/environmental-policy.html

TerraChoice Environmental Marketing Inc. (2009). *The seven sins of greenwashing.* Retrieved September 3, 2009, from http://sinsofgreenwashing.org/

WhalePower. (2009, May 22). *WhalePower finalist for major international award.* Retrieved September 21, 2009, from http://www.whalepower.com/drupal/

Xerox. (2009). *Prevent and manage waste.* Retrieved September 3, 2009, from http://www.xerox.com/about-xerox/environment/recycling/enus.html

Marketing

Marketing's four components—pricing, product, place, and promotion—play a key role in sustainable business practice. Sustainable marketers consider the needs of the environmental consumer and study product impact from resource use and production to product use and disposal. They face the challenges of assessing consumption, improving consumers' perception of the quality of green products, and making accurate, substantiated claims in labeling and advertising.

The role of marketing in business sustainability has a long, rich history. It has developed in both breadth and depth since the early 1960s in response to changes in consumer attitudes and behaviors, internal corporate strategies, and governmental regulations. Dramatic environmental impacts that have taken place in countries throughout the world—China's move toward adopting the practices of Western industrialized and consumption-oriented societies, for example—have driven many of these changes. Early green marketing was essentially a fringe strategy that a limited number of individuals or small companies used to target a small group of environmentally active consumers with products that typically did not appeal to the mainstream customer. These products were often priced high, did not work well, and had to live up to exaggerated claims about performance. For example, early green detergents often did not produce adequate suds and failed to clean products sufficiently. The Hefty brand of biodegradable bags (made by Mobil) provides another example of a green product that did not meet expectations because they can only degrade under open-air conditions that are not common at landfills.

The phrase "sustainable marketing" has been used interchangeably with "ecological," "environmental," or "green" marketing, but, according to the 2009 *Dictionary of Sustainable Management*, it is generally defined as a marketing approach that highlights "products and production methods that improve environmental performance, further ecological causes, or solve environmental problems" (Presidio n.d.). The researchers Jagdish N. Sheth and Atul Parvatiyar describe sustainable marketing as a way to reconcile economic and ecological objectives through a new understanding of products and systems (Fuller 1999). Others argue that social impacts must be part of any decision-making process dealing with sustainability.

As an activity responsible for creating, communicating, delivering, and exchanging products or services that provide value for customers, marketing has a key role in sustainable business practice. Heightened societal interest in environmental impact has created opportunities for companies to develop new strategies that focus on sustainability using the traditional "4 Ps" of marketing—pricing, product, place, and promotion. In order to develop effective strategies, marketers have spent considerable time researching consumer needs and wants in these areas.

The Green Consumer

A number of studies have been conducted to describe the environmental consumer. The main objective of these analyses is to develop separate groups that can be uniquely targeted by a company. These groups can also be tracked over time to determine any changes in their needs to which companies must respond. One of the most commonly referred-to segmentation studies is the Green Gauge Study developed by GfK Roper Consulting. This report is the only nationwide, long-term syndicated study of consumer attitudes and behaviors toward the environment. It breaks consumers into the following segments (GfK 2007):

- *Apathetics:* This group is the least interested in environmental issues and not likely to respond to them. This segment decreased in size from 28 percent of US consumers in 2000 to 18 percent in 2007. "Apathetics" tend to have lower incomes, be less educated, and have lower interpersonal influence than other consumers.

- *Grousers:* These consumers represented 15 percent of US consumers in 2007, down from 20 percent in 2000. They are generally uninterested in green issues and tend to view them as too complicated and large to do anything about.
- *Sprouts:* They are the classic fence-sitters and represented 26 percent of US consumers in 2007, down from 34 percent in 2000. They will buy green products but evaluate the issues one by one and only purchase a green product if its value exceeds its costs.
- *Greenback Greens:* This category has grown from 5 percent of US consumers in 2000 to 10 percent in 2007. They are interested in green issues, but they will only buy if their comfort and convenience are not jeopardized.
- *True-Blue Green:* This group has jumped the most dramatically from 12 percent of US consumers in 2000 to 30 percent in 2007. They are extremely interested in environmental issues. In comparison to other consumers, they are highly educated, have higher incomes, and are more likely to influence others.

Marketers are often interested in investigating the reasons why consumers purchase green products. They can use this information to develop strategies to appeal to consumer needs and wants. For some consumers, such as the "True-Blue Green," the primary motivation to purchase a green product is the reduced environmental impact—irrespective of the price and quality. For example, these consumers would be willing to pay a premium for an environmentally safe detergent even if it did not do a good job at cleaning. Other green products may be sought because they are truly better on a key attribute that significantly impacts the environment. The hybrid electric Toyota Prius is generally acknowledged as a "better car" because it outperforms other vehicles on miles per gallon; consumers not only save money on gas but also lessen their impact on the environment. Marketers have also found that consumers may purchase green products based on their differences in reducing risk. The Hartman Group (2007) analyzed 1,500 consumers and found that risk reduction is a key motivator behind consumption of sustainable products. Different levels of risk were identified for consumers in this study beginning with personal and family risk, then community-based risks, and finally global risks. The results showed that 52 percent of consumers looked for environmental information to protect their personal or family health. Thus consumers often purchase organic foods not for their green factor but because they reduce the perceived health risk of pesticides and fertilizers. Similarly, a Toyota Prius might

be purchased not only because of the greater gas mileage but because it reduces the risk of global warming.

Marketing Strategies and Innovations

The "4 Ps" of marketing—pricing, product, place, and promotion—provide a useful framework to describe company initiatives in the area of sustainable marketing. Although these will be discussed as discrete activities, it is important to note that true sustainable marketing considers all aspects of a company's strategies and also factors in their impact throughout a product/service life cycle. Thus, marketers must think about the extraction of raw materials, production of goods, transportation, consumption, and final disposal. The elimination of waste produced at each stage must also be part of a true sustainable plan.

Product

There are many approaches to developing sustainable products. The product's key attributes can be developed with the environment in mind, or other aspects of the product can be designed to reduce environmental impact. Companies have researched ways to build products that can be recycled or refurbished or that require less material.

As described above, marketers must understand the relative importance consumers place on product features to help define what features to attempt to make sustainable and whether to focus on these features as a communication strategy. Some products, such as Clorox's Green Works natural cleaners, have focused all key attributes and communications on sustainability. The Toyota Prius hybrid is fuel efficient relative to most automobiles, but the initial appeal of the product was based as much on the technology as it was on the green aspects. Consumers interested in driving the latest technology were attracted to the Prius's ability to take the energy created when braking and store it in a battery. Displaying the car's miles per gallon on the dashboard only added to the "cool" factor; the increased gas mileage was an added benefit. Finally, there are products that contain green aspects, but these are not key consumer decision criteria. An example would be bottled water or sodas—the bottles are typically made from recycled material, but people are motivated more by convenience than conservation.

Electronics, paper, glass, and metals are examples of products that are recycled and can therefore reduce waste and resource demands. (The universal triangle symbol on many products indicates that they may be recycled.) Sometimes these products can be recycled into the same products (for example, glass containers), while other times they must be transformed into products of lower quality.

Each time paper is recycled, for instance, its quality is reduced.

Refurbished or remanufactured products are those that customers may have returned and, in some cases, that the manufacturer must repair. This strategy extends the life of the product. A Motorola refurbished cell phone is an example. Some products are designed for reuse, such as Welch's jam and jelly jars that may be used as drinking glasses.

Companies have successfully developed methods to reduce materials usage in their products. For example, beverage companies have significantly reduced the amount of plastic used in water and soda containers. Arrowhead's "Eco-Shape" bottle uses 30 percent less plastic than comparable bottles. Extending the useful life of a product is another way to reduce materials. Another is to allow the product to be upgraded or simply to make it more durable. Although it may seem disadvantageous to develop a product that lasts a long time, consumers have been willing to pay more for these types of products (for example, Honda automobiles).

Today's innovative sustainable marketers consider product impact from resource use through production, utilization, and disposal. The goal is to design products or processes that minimize these impacts. This process is referred to as Design for Environment, or DFE. Hitachi used this approach in its washing machine: the final design for the machine required only six screws, which led to a decrease in manufacturing time of 33 percent and a reduction in the amount of inventory. Less servicing and higher customer reliability were also benefits of this approach (Esty and Winston 2006). The automotive industry provides another example—this time driven by social and governmental demands as well as limits on available land for product disposal. European automakers must demonstrate reusability and/or recyclability of at least 85 percent, and reusability and/or recoverability of at least 95 percent by weight. Many of these automakers incorporate these rules in aspects of their product design, disassembly, and disposal.

Promotion

With nearly half of the US marketplace stating that they do not have enough information to increase their green behavior, communication needs to play a critical role in the sustainable marketplace. Marketers use advertising, public relations, personal selling, and sales promotions to inform the marketplace. One of the primary decisions sustainable marketers must make is how much their communication strategy should focus on the environmental aspects of the product. Despite the increased interest in low environmental-impact products, consumers are still primarily interested in specific attributes of the product. For example, the fact that a printer is made from 100 percent postconsumer

waste is likely to be less important to a consumer than the paper capacity or speed of printing. If the product is already viewed positively against competitors on key attributes, there may be an opportunity to highlight the positive environmental aspects; otherwise, the product needs to primarily focus on traditional buyer decision criteria.

Another important part of a product's communication is the package label. Although there are a variety of words, symbols, emblems, and logos used in labeling, the International Standards Organization (ISO) identifies three types of "ecolabels":

- Type I is the most common type of label. Although Type I labels are typically voluntary, they may be mandatory if toxic ingredients exist. These labels are provided by third-party organizations that allow the use of their symbol if the product meets either specific or multiple criteria. Examples include Germany's Blue Angel, Canada's Environment Choice Program, and the US Forest Stewardship Council. Type I labels do not require disclosure of the detail used to establish the criteria.
- Type II labels do not require third-party verification and include any type of environmental declaration made by any level of a distribution channel. The terms *eco-safe* or *biodegradable* fall under this label type. The confidence in these types of labels can be improved if set definitions can be agreed upon.
- Type III labels are similar to nutritional labels and require an analysis of a product's environmental impact throughout its life cycle. An open consultation process is required for these labels, and the final products should be easily compared by consumers.

Due to the effects of "greenwashing," which focuses on positive claims made about green products and downplays their negative impacts, there is a growing body of guidelines for communicating the environmental features of a product on package labels. Specific wording is important. Instead of claiming that the product "includes recycled content," labels should state that the "package includes 20 percent postconsumer content." Marketers should ensure that consumers understand whether the claim refers to the product, package, process, or company. Vague, unsubstantiated terms should be avoided. "Environmentally safe," "eco-friendly," and "practically nontoxic" are deceptive descriptors, especially if not followed by clear and prominent qualifying language that limits the safety representation to a particular product attribute that can be substantiated (and provided that no other misleading implications are created by the context). Marketers should also focus on relevant benefits that have significant impact. Many companies still promote the fact that their products do not contain chlorofluorocarbons. This ingredient was banned more than two decades ago, and thus it is no longer a feature that needs to be communicated. Labels also need to include more information. Recent studies, such as the GfK Roper Yale Survey on Environmental Issues (2008, 12), indicate that consumers want labels that describe the environmental impacts of the product's manufacturing process (73 percent of respondents), its use (73 percent of respondents) and the impact of its disposal (79 percent of respondents). Patagonia is an example of a company that presents detailed environmental impact information about its various products.

Legislation to regulate green marketing claims has had difficulty keeping up with the large number of new green products and claims constantly being introduced. Many countries are revisiting their initial guidelines. For example, the US Federal Trade Commission (FTC) is currently revising their list to include the concepts of carbon trading and the general term *sustainability*. Current guidelines provide advice on the use of terms such as *compostable*, *recyclable*, *degradable*, *source reduction*, and *refillable*. Although the guidelines are developed for voluntary compliance, the commission may take action if the conduct is unlawful. For example, the FTC alleged that Kmart Corporation, Tender Corporation, and Dyna-E International each made false and unsubstantiated claims that their products—disposable plates, wipes, and towels, respectively—were biodegradable. According to the FTC, the products would not decompose in nature under conditions of normal disposal practices (most are placed in landfills or are incinerated or recycled). As of late 2009, Kmart and Tender Inc. have agreed to settle their claims while the case against Dyna-E is proceeding to trial.

Price

Similar to any other product, marketers need to consider costs, consumers, and competition when setting the price of environmental products.

One key pricing issue that is constantly debated is the idea of using life cycle analysis to arrive at the final costs of products. Many advocates of green products do not feel that these products are overpriced but rather that the prices of conventional products do not reflect their true environmental costs. Thus, if the price of a factory-produced bottle of water had to account for the environmental impact of resource extraction (for example, water use and all raw materials), the emission of toxic chemicals during production, the visual impact of trash in the environment, and finally the landfill disposal or incineration costs, then the price would be substantially higher and the price of competitive products would be relatively lower. If consumers in the colder climates of the United States want to eat fruit grown in South America during winter months, then the product should actually reflect the true environmental costs of this product. As software becomes available, the use of

life cycle analysis is increasing to set prices and evaluate alternative production and distribution strategies.

The price of competitive products may be used as a good benchmark for a price bottom or ceiling. But marketers must also consider the varying levels of importance consumers place on environmental versus conventional attributes. If conventional attributes are considered more important, then environmental price premiums may not be warranted.

Customer value must be assessed when deciding the final price. There is somewhat conflicting information on whether consumers are willing to pay a premium for sustainable products. Although the Green Gauge report (GfK 2007) found that 40 percent of consumers are willing to pay a premium for a product that is better for the environment, 74 percent thought green products were too expensive. Home Depot found that consumers were only willing to pay 2 percent more for its line of environmental wood. A number of academic studies have also investigated this topic. One found that consumers were willing to pay 2 to 16 percent more for tables that were labeled as environmentally friendly versus those that were not (Veisten 2007). The type of consumer also plays a role. Another study (Vlosky, Ozanne, and Fontenot 1999) found that consumers with higher levels of environmental consciousness were willing to pay more for environmentally friendly products. The consumer segments of the Green Gauge study also varied in their willingness to pay extra, with the "Greenback Greens" and "True-Blue Greens" willing to pay more. Country of origin also affects a consumer's willingness to pay a price premium. For example, people in Canada are more willing to pay a price premium for green products than are people in the United States. Sixty-five percent of Canadians will pay a premium for ecofriendly detergent compared to 51 percent of people in the US; 56 percent of Canadians versus 40 percent of people in the US will pay more for ecological computer paper (GfK 2008).

Place

Key place or distribution-channel decisions a marketer must make are (1) where the product is available for consumer or business purchase, (2) how it arrives at its location, and (3) where it is manufactured or produced. Sustainable marketing distribution constantly examines the amount of waste created in the channel as the product moves from the extraction of materials to final disposal.

Historically, only retailers that focused on social and green issues carried or promoted environmentally friendly products or communicated other green aspects of their operations (for example, The Body Shop, Whole Foods, Patagonia). But due to increased consumer awareness and interest, anticipated government regulation, and new competition, a number of historically nongreen companies have turned green. This could involve changes in their building and operations or in their product assortment. Home Depot carries over 2,500 products that earn their Eco Options label, including all-natural insect repellents, compact fluorescent lightbulbs, cellulose insulation, front-load washing machines, and certified sustainable forestry products. By 2009, Home Depot expected the Eco Options label to grow to 6,000 products. Walmart's website lists many sustainable initiatives, but in simple terms, Walmart wants its stores to be supplied 100 percent by renewable energy, to create zero waste, and to sell products that sustain resources and the environment. UPS (United Parcel Service) reduced greenhouse gas emissions by purchasing close to 3 million kilowatt-hours of green power for its California facilities; it also has the largest alternative-fuel and low-emission fleet in the industry (19,647 such vehicles worldwide) and streamlined its delivery routes and eliminated close to 30 million miles of driving (Galehouse 2007).

Some methods of transportation are more environmentally damaging than others. Patagonia found that using ground transportation was less damaging than airfreight. (Their website displays the environmental impact of some of their products that are sourced throughout the world). Companies can also improve their sustainability by minimizing the number of delivery trips and mistakes.

Many advocates of sustainable marketing have promoted the advantages of purchasing locally grown and produced products. Advocates claim that locally grown produce has fewer chemicals and uses less fuel. Others argue that efficient distribution and delivery systems have reduced chemical needs and actually use less fuel than the many local trucks used to deliver local products.

Controversies in Sustainable Marketing

Marketers must consider how to integrate sustainability and consumption. How can marketing and sustainability be congruent if the main purpose of marketing is to create consumption that drains the planet's resources and leads to global warming, increasing environmental toxins, and water depletion? A complicating factor in this discussion is that not all groups believe consumption is wrong. Some have argued that marketing-generated consumption accelerates economic development and raises the quality of life of all people—particularly those in impoverished societies. Research on ecological footprints has shown that current consumption is beyond Earth's capacity to provide the continued resources to support it. Fuller (1999) argued that marketers need to focus on a production-consumption system that regenerates itself. Products are designed that minimize resource utilization and can be fed back into this

system over and over. Strategies and innovations that consider products from cradle to grave or cradle to cradle will help maintain consumption levels without degrading the environment. Buildings are now being designed that are net producers of energy; utensils are being produced that add nutrients back into the ground as they decompose.

The quality of environmental products poses another challenge. As of 2007, 61 percent of US consumers believed that green products did not do as well as conventional ones (Bonini and Oppenhelm 2007). This may be due to bad press coverage or the consumers' own experiences. Unfortunately, early green products did not perform well or as advertised when they first entered the marketplace. The original compact fluorescent bulbs had a harsh glare and irritating noise when they were on. Even the much-heralded Toyota Prius suffered from an image of poor acceleration and lack of power. Marketers can help improve the perception of quality by delivering on their promises and ensuring that their product performs well on all key conventional attributes.

The term *greenwashing* has a number of definitions but generally refers to advertising, public relations, or packaging information that highlights the positive environmental aspects of a company, product, or service while ignoring its negative environmental impacts. A washing machine that promotes its reduced energy usage but ignores its high water consumption is one example. A dishwashing detergent that claims it is free from phosphates that create algae in streams but in small print lists the toxic chemical chlorine as a key ingredient is guilty of greenwashing as well. The energy producers BP and Shell have engaged in many green activities such as investing in alternative energy and building service stations that have vegetation on their roofs. The fact that the majority of their energy production still focuses on fossil fuels, however, has opened them up to corporate greenwashing charges. Companies can reduce greenwashing incidents by using guidelines provided by governmental agencies such as those provided by the United Kingdom's Department for Environment, Food, and Rural Affairs and Department of Trade and Industry, the United States' Federal Trade Commission, or private consulting groups in environmental marketing such as TerraChoice or Futerra Sustainability Communications.

The Future of Sustainable Marketing

The sustainable market from the 1960s to the1990s did not expand beyond a few companies and a limited number of consumer segments due to poor product quality, limited product choices and availability, bad media coverage, and consumer disinterest. As of 2009, the market has attracted a significantly larger number of companies and consumers. In 2009, consumers are expected to double their spending on green products to $500 billion. The number of self-styled green products released in the United States more than doubled between 2005 and 2007 from 2,607 products to 5,933 (Wasserman 2008).

One study (Esty and Winston 2006) identified a number of critical natural issues that may significantly impact a company, including climate change, energy, water, biodiversity and land use, chemicals, toxics, and heavy metals. Successful sustainable marketers will closely examine how issues such as these can impact the industry in which they operate and develop plans that take advantage of opportunities and minimize problems created from these types of forces. For example, the Dutch government blocked sales of Sony's PlayStation because of a small amount of the illegal toxic element cadmium in the cables. This problem cost them $130 million (Esty and Winston 2006, 1). On the other hand, BP identified ways to reduce greenhouse gas emissions and has saved over $1.5 billion in expenses (Esty and Winston 2006, 2).

As the number of sustainable products proliferates, marketers will have an increasingly challenging time differentiating products. Some experts believe that it will not be long before "green" will no longer be the primary sales pitch for a product. Sustainable marketers, however, will always play a pivotal role in identifying consumer needs and wants in the area of sustainable products and services, and in helping to design green products that are valued at an appropriate price and quality level, communicated without greenwashing, and easily available to the target market.

Norm BORIN
*Orfalea College of Business, California
Polytechnic State University*

See also in the *Berkshire Encyclopedia of Sustainability* Consumer Behavior; Ecolabeling; Greenwashing; Packaging; Telecommunications Industry

FURTHER READING

Bonini, Sheila M., & Oppenhelm, Jeremy M. (2007). Helping "green" products grow. Retrieved July 6, 2009, from http://www.mckinsey.com/clientservice/ccsi/pdf/helping_green_products_grow.pdf

Davis, Joel J. (1993). Strategies for environmental advertising. *Journal of Consumer Marketing, 10*(2), 19–36.

Department for Environment, Food, and Rural Affairs. (2003). Green claims—Practical guidance: How to make a good environmental claim. Retrieved June 1, 2009, from http://www.defra.gov.uk/environment/business/marketing/glc/pdf/genericguide.pdf

Esty, Dale C., & Winston, Andrew S. (2006). *Green to gold: How smart companies use environmental strategy to innovate, create value, and build competitive advantage.* New Haven, CT: Yale University Press.

Federal Trade Commission. (1998). Guides for the use of environmental marketing claims. Retrieved February 1, 2009, from http://www.ftc.gov/bcp/grnrule/guides980427.htm

Fuller, Donald A. (1999). *Sustainable marketing: Managerial-ecological issues.* Thousand Oaks, CA: SAGE Publications.

Futerra Sustainability Communications. (n.d.). The greenwash guide. Retrieved June 1, 2009, from http://www.futerra.co.uk/downloads/Greenwash_Guide.pdf

Galehouse, Maggie. (2007, November 29). Top 10 green retailers. Retrieved January 6, 2010, from http://blogs.chron.com/livinggreen/

GfK Custom Research North America. (2007, August 21). Americans reach environmental turning point: Companies need to catch up according to Gfk Roper Green Gauge(R) study. Retrieved May 22, 2008, from http://www.csrwire.com/News/9473.html

GfK Roper Yale Survey on Environmental Issues. (2008). *The GfK Roper Yale survey on environmental issues: Summer, 2008: Consumer attitudes toward environmentally-friendly products and eco-labeling.* Retrieved August 27, 2009 from http://environment.research.yale.edu/documents/downloads/a-g/GfK-Roper-Yale-Survey.pdf

The Hartman Group Inc. (2007). *The Hartman report on sustainability: Understanding the consumer perspective.* Bellevue, WA: Hartman Group.

McDonough, William, & Braungart, Michael. (2002). *Cradle to cradle.* New York: North Point Press.

Ottman, Jacquelyn A. (2004). *Green marketing: Opportunity for innovation.* Charleston, SC: BookSurge Publishing.

Patagonia Inc. (2009). The footprint chronicles. Retrieved March 1, 2009, from http://www.patagonia.com/web/us/patagonia.go?assetid=23429&ln=66

Peattie, Ken, & Crane, Andrew. (2005). Green marketing: Legend, myth, farce or prophesy? *Qualitative Market Research, 8*(4), 357–370.

Polonsky, Michael Jay, & Mintu-Wimsatt, Alma T. (1995). *Environmental marketing: Strategies, practice, theory, and research.* New York: Haworth Press.

Presidio Graduate School. (n.d.). The dictionary of sustainable management. Retrieved July 3, 2009, from http://www.sustainabilitydictionary.com/e/ecological_marketing.php

Schaefer, Anja, & Crane, Andrew. (2005). Addressing sustainability and consumption. *Journal of Macromarketing, 25*(1), 76–92.

TerraChoice Environmental Marketing Inc. (2009). The seven sins of greenwashing. Retrieved June 1, 2009, from http://sinsofgreenwashing.org

Veisten, Knut. (2007). Willingness to pay for eco-labelled wood furniture: Choice-based conjoint analysis versus open-ended contingent valuation. *Journal of Forest Economics, 13*(1), 29–48.

Vlosky, Richard P.; Ozanne, Lucie K.; & Fontenot, Renee J. (1999). A conceptual model of US consumer willingness-to-pay for environmentally certified wood products. *The Journal of Consumer Marketing, 16*(2), 122–140.

Wasserman, Todd. (2008, May 20). Mintel: "Green" products top 5,933 in 2007. *Brandweek.* Retrieved March 24, 2009, from http://www.brandweek.com/bw/news/packaged/article_display.jsp?vnu_content_id=1003805821

Natural Capitalism

Capitalism as practiced today does not value the intact ecosystems that make all life, and thus economics, possible. A new approach—natural capitalism—shows businesses how to increase profitability through resource efficiency, conduct business the way nature does, and manage business so that it is restorative of both human and natural capital.

The prominent environmentalist David Brower (1912–2000) once said you cannot do business on a dead planet. The way that business is now conducted is testing this dictum.

The challenges facing humankind are daunting: every major ecosystem on the planet is in decline; the global climate crisis is immediate; energy prices are soaring, perhaps because the world has reached peak oil production; populations continues to rise; water shortages may prove even harder to solve than energy shortages; and China—with India right behind—has entered the world market for essentially everything. At the same time, companies, communities, and countries are facing the "sustainability imperative." Clearly a new approach to economics is needed.

Loss of Ecosystem Services

Industrial capitalism, as it is now practiced, does not value but liquidates the most important forms of capital, especially natural capital—the living world whose resources and ecosystem services make all life possible. As headlines report food crises, water shortages, soaring energy prices, wars driven by climate change (like the one in Darfur), and the rapacious appetites of China, India, and the United States, among others, for the world's resources, it is becoming ever

clearer that deteriorating living systems cannot sustain a growing human population. The limits to economic growth are being set by the scarcities of natural capital.

In 2001 the United Nations commissioned the Millennium Ecosystem Assessment, a comprehensive study of the consequences of human activity on the world's ecosystems. The work of 1,360 experts in ninety-five nations from twenty-two national science academies and published in 2005, the findings reported that over the past fifty years a rising human population has polluted or overexploited 60 percent of the ecological systems on which life depends (MEA 2005a, 1).

At the heart of this assessment is a stark warning: "Human activity is putting such strain on the natural functions of Earth that the ability of the planet's ecosystems to sustain future generations can no longer be taken for granted" (MEA 2005b, 5). Former UN secretary-general Kofi Annan said the report demonstrates how "the very basis for life on earth…is declining at an alarming rate" (Doyle 2005).

Sometimes the value of intact ecosystem services becomes apparent only when lost. In China's Yangzi basin in 1998, for example, upstream deforestation triggered flooding that killed 3,700 people, dislocated 223 million, and inundated 60 million acres of cropland. That $30 billion disaster forced a logging moratorium and a $12 billion crash program of reforestation.

The 2007 release of the Fourth Assessment Report by the Intergovernmental Panel on Climate Change (IPCC) represented the agreement by essentially all of the world's climate scientists that humans have altered the world's climate and that greenhouse gases must be reduced by at least 90 percent by 2050, with more immediate action taken within the next few years. Worldwide economic losses due to extreme weather have risen since the 1950s, a decade that saw twenty "great catastrophes" (those requiring international or interregional assistance), and they have continued to do so more steeply since the 1970s, when there were forty-seven such disasters. In the 1990s an expenditure of $608 billion was required to cope with eighty-seven weather-related disasters. In 2008, weather-related damage cost insurers over $200 billion, compared to $82 billion in 2007 (Environmental Leader 2009). Claims from weather-related disasters are now rising twice as fast as those from all other mishaps. Insurers at Munich Re, which now takes climate change into account in its projections, state that the loss statistics fit the pattern of their climate models, with atmospheric warming causing weather to "run in top gear" (Environmental Leader 2009).

Natural Capitalism

As companies and communities struggle to find ways to meet their needs in the face of challenges, an increasing number are turning to an approach outlined in the 1999 book *Natural Capitalism: Creating the Next Industrial Revolution*. It set forth a way of doing business that is more profitable, but that reverses the planetary destruction now underway.

- There are three principles of natural capitalism:
- Buy time to address the challenges facing the world by radically increasing resource efficiency.
- Redesign how the economy makes and delivers all products and services by doing business in the way that nature does.
- Manage all institutions to be restorative of natural capital in ways that reverse the loss of ecosystem services.

Increasing Resource Efficiency

It is relatively easy today to profit by using resources more efficiently because current resource use is incredibly wasteful. Globally the economy mobilizes a resource flow of half a trillion tons per year. Of that, only about 1 percent becomes embodied in a product that is still in use six months after sale. The other 99 percent is waste. Cutting such waste represents a vast business opportunity.

The architect William McDonough criticizes efficiency as simply doing less bad and, therefore, still bad (McDonough and Braungart 2002). Clearly, eco-efficiency alone will not deliver a sustainable society, but the criticism misses the significance of using resources more efficiently. The foundation of a building is obviously not a complete house, but without solid underpinnings, no structure can stand for long. Without eco-efficiency, sustainability is unachievable. More important, using fewer resources buys critical time necessary to solve increasingly severe challenges, like climate change and loss of ecosystems, and to develop and implement more systematically sustainable

practices. Eco-efficiency is the easiest component of the transition to sustainability to implement. It is usually profitable and is familiar to industrial engineers.

Building greener buildings and designing better communities is key to increasing efficiency. State-of-the-shelf technologies can make old buildings three to four times more energy efficient and new ones ten times more efficient at similar cost and with better performance. The US Green Building Council's Leadership in Energy and Environmental Design (LEED) standards are being adopted by many communities, incorporated into codes, and embodied in government mandates. It is no longer uncommon to have buildings that produce all the energy they need to operate and even export power back to the grid and that treat their wastewater on site using such biological treatment systems as Eco-Machines (devices that use algae, bacteria, etc., to break down organic pollutants). Typical US tract-home developments drain storm water away in costly underground pipes. Village Homes, an early solar housing development near Sacramento, California, instead installed natural water-catchment channels that allowed rainwater to soak in, recharging groundwater. Eliminating storm drains saved $800 per house, enabling investment in edible landscaping and people-centered site planning (pedestrian/bike greenways in front of the houses, tree-shaded streets), saving more land and money. These features cooled the area around the houses, yielding better comfort with little or no air-conditioning, and created a safe and child-friendly neighborhood that cut crime by 90 percent. The development was simply a better place to live. The same integrative design that improved environmental, resource, and human performance also improved market and financial performance. Market values averaged nine dollars per square foot above normal, and houses sold three times faster than average (Rocky Mountain Institute et al. 1998).

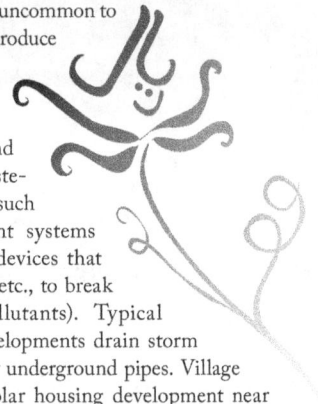

Redesigning the Economy

Resource efficiency is natural capitalism's cornerstone, but only its beginning. Natural capitalism means not only reducing inefficiency, but eliminating the entire concept of waste by adopting biological patterns, processes, and often materials. Essentially every product of today's industrial world is produced in unsustainable ways that require fossil fuels, toxic chemicals, brute force, and nonrenewable resources.

Biomimicry, the conscious emulation of life's genius, is a profound approach to sustainability. Janine Benyus, author of *Biomimicry: Innovation Inspired by Nature*, asks a simple question: "How would nature do business?" Nature, for example, runs on sunlight, not high flows of fossil energy. It manufactures everything at room temperature. Nature does make dangerous substances, but nothing like nuclear waste that remains deadly for millennia. It creates no waste, using the output of all processes as the input to some other process. Nature shops locally and creates beauty.

Biomimicry, though, is only half of what is required to redesign the economy. The other half is called cradle-to-cradle production—remanufacturing, reusing, and returning products to use rather than to landfills. In 1976 Walter Stahel, director of the Swiss Product Life Institute (widely recognized in Europe as one of the founders of the sustainability movement), proposed extending the life of products as a way to deliver better value and substitute the use of people for resources such as energy. Stahel analyzed cars and buildings and concluded that every product-life extension saved enormous amounts of resources while generating jobs.

Stahel described how in 1993, as US companies faced hard times, the corporate world made heroes of such restructurers as Al Dunlap and Jack Welch. Dunlap, in the name of "creating shareholder value" gained the name "Chainsaw Al," when in twenty months as CEO of Scott Paper he devastated the 115-year-old company by terminating 11,000 people, or 35 percent of the labor force, including 71 percent of the staff at corporate headquarters. His counterpart at General Electric (GE), dubbed "Neutron" Jack Welch, cut GE employment from 380,000 to 208,000.

Stahel also described how, in contrast, in the early 1990s Honda used its workers to maintain and repair its own machines rather than suffer layoffs that would damage worker morale and lead to work stoppages. Moving toward eco-efficiency, European and Japanese policy makers are increasingly considering tax shifting—eliminating taxes on employment and income and substituting taxes on pollution and depletion of resources. For example, taxes on heavy metal emissions in the Netherlands have reduced water pollution in the county while paving the way for cuts to income and wage taxes (Worldwatch Institute 1997).

The logic of capitalism, the greatest known system in human history for the creation of wealth, hasn't changed: economize on your scarce resources. But with 10,000 more people arriving on Earth every hour, and every ecosystem in decline, today's recipe for prosperity is to restructure the economy, as Stahel outlined, to encourage the use of people and to penalize the waste of resources.

Managing for Restoration

The third principle of natural capitalism is to manage all institutions to reverse the planetwide destruction of ecosystems by reinvesting profits from eliminating waste to restore natural and human capital. For example, wildlife biologist Allan Savory's Holistic Management has shown how to use more ecologically intelligent grazing practices that increase the size of herds while improving even arid and degraded rangelands and increasing ranchers' profits. (Savory and Butterfield 1999). The California Rice Industry Association partnered with environmental groups to switch from burning rice straw to flooding 30 percent of California's rice acreage after harvest. The business model is a far more profitable mix of lucrative hunting licenses, free cultivation, and fertilization by millions of wild ducks and geese, high-silica straw, and groundwater recharge, all with rice as a profitable by-product (personal communication with Ralph Cavanagh, National Resources Defense Council, 1999).

This approach is clearly essential in industries like forestry, farming, and fishing, whose success depends on the health of the natural systems from which they draw, but it is spreading rapidly to other industries as well.

Perhaps the tipping point in the corporate movement toward greener production came when GE announced "ecomagination." As part of the initiative, GE chairman Jeffrey Immelt promised to double GE's investment in environmental technologies to $1.5 billion by 2010. Immelt also announced that GE would reduce the company's greenhouse gas emissions 1 percent by 2012; without action, emissions would have risen 40 percent. Immelt stated at a speech at George Washington University: "We believe we can help improve the environment and make money doing it" (Bustillo 2005).

Critics charged that GE was "greenwashing," badging some of its existing products as green and changing little else. Hypocrisy, however, is often the first step to real change. Less than a year after his first announcement, Immelt announced that his green-badged products had doubled in sales volume over the prior two years, with back orders for $50 billion more, far surpassing his initial prediction of $12 billion in sales by 2010. Over the same time frame, the rest of GE's products had only increased 20 percent in sales. GE also announced that it had reduced greenhouse gas emissions by 4 percent in 2006, dwarfing its 2012 target of 1 percent.

Companies that increase resource productivity and implement such sustainable strategies as biomimicry and cradle to cradle, especially in the context of a broader

whole-system corporate sustainability strategy, enhance every aspect of shareholder value.

More recently, a company's profits and stock value have had to increase over each quarter or a company was considered to be on shaky ground. This highly questionable metric is so incompatible with managing an enterprise for long-term value that even the Financial Accounting Standards Board (FASB) has undertaken to rewrite financial reporting to encourage alternatives to such short-sighted behavior.

Sustainability advocates have urged that companies instead manage to a "triple bottom line": achieve profit, but also protect people and planet. While a tempting formulation, this has had the effect of forcing companies to care about the environment and social well-being in ways that increase costs, which reduces the traditional measure of profit.

A much more useful approach is that of the "integrated bottom line," which recognizes that profit is a valid metric but only one of many that gives a company enduring value. Done smartly, behaving responsibly increases profitability. When the other aspects of shareholder value are included, the business case for sustainability is overwhelming. The integrated bottom line measures three major criteria:

- Enhanced financial performance from energy and materials cost savings in
  - industrial processes
  - facilities design and management
  - fleet management
  - operations
- Enhanced core business value by
  - sector performance leadership
  - greater access to capital
  - "first mover advantage," that is, the advantage gained by the first entity in a market segment
  - improved corporate governance
  - the ability to drive innovation and retain competitive advantage
  - enhanced reputation and brand development
  - increased market share and product differentiation
  - ability to attract and retain the best talent
  - increased employee productivity and health
  - improved communication, creativity, and morale in the workplace
  - improved value chain management
  - better stakeholder relations
- Reduced risk by
  - insurance access and cost containment
  - legal compliance
  - reduced exposure to increased carbon regulations and price
  - reduced shareholder activism

Business success in a time of technological transformation demands innovation. Since the first Industrial Revolution, there have been at least six waves of innovation, each shifting which technologies underpinned economic prosperity. In the late 1700s, textiles, iron mongering, waterpower, and mechanization enabled modern commerce to develop. The second wave introduced steam power, trains, and steel. In the 1900s, electricity, chemicals, and cars began to dominate. By the middle of the twentieth century, it was petrochemicals and the space race, along with electronics. The most recent wave of innovation brought computers and ushered in the digital or information age. As we enter "the next Industrial Revolution" and economies move beyond iPods, older industries will suffer dislocations unless they join the increasing number of companies implementing the array of sustainable technologies that make up this next wave of innovation. This is the "sustainability imperative."

L. Hunter LOVINS
Natural Capital Solutions

This article is adapted from the article "Natural capitalism: Path to sustainability?" by L. Hunter Lovins. Retrieved October 23, 2009 from http://www.natcapsolutions.org/publications_files/PathToNatCap.txt

See also in the *Berkshire Encyclopedia of Sustainability* Biomimicry; Climate Change Disclosure; Cradle to Cradle; Development, Sustainable; Ecosystem Services; Energy Efficiency; Energy Industries—Overview of Renewables; Energy Industries—Solar; Facilities Management; Green-Collar Jobs; Investment, CleanTech; Investment, Socially Responsible (SRI); Remanufacturing; Social Enterprise; Transparency; True Cost Economics

FURTHER READING

Benyus, Janine M. (2002). *Biomimicry: Innovation inspired by nature.* New York: Harper Perennial.

Brown, Lester. (2009). *Plan B 4.0: Mobilizing to save civilization* (Rev. ed.). New York: W. W. Norton.

Bustillo, Miguel. (2005, July 3). Turning warming into cash. Retrieved October 29, 2009, from http://seattletimes.nwsource.com/html/businesstechnology/2002356266_warming03.html

Doyle, Alister. (2005, March 30). Human damage to Earth worsening fast—Report. Retrieved January 29, 2010, from http://www.planetark.com/dailynewsstory.cfm/newsid/30136/story.htm

Environmental Leader. (2009, January 6). Weather-related catastrophes push insurance losses to new heights. Retrieved February 4, 2010, from http://www.environmentalleader.com/2009/01/06/weather-related-catastrophes-push-insurance-losses-to-new-heights/

Hawken, Paul; Lovins, Amory B.; & Lovins, L. Hunter. (1999). *Natural capitalism: Creating the next Industrial Revolution.* New York: Back Bay Books.

Intergovernmental Panel on Climate Change (IPCC). (2007). *Fourth assessment report (AR4): Climate change 2007. Synthesis Report.* Retrieved January 29, 2009, from http://www.ipcc.ch/pdf/assessment-report/ar4/syr/ar4_syr.pdf

Laszlo, Chris. (2008). *Sustainable value: How the world's business leaders are doing well by doing good.* Stanford, CA: Stanford Business Books.

Lockwood, Charles. (2006, May). Building the green way. Retrieved on April 25, 2009, from http://summits.ncat.org/docs/HBR_building_green_way.pdf

Lovins, Amory B.; Lovins, L. Hunter; Krause, Florentin; & Bach, Wilfrid. (1982). *Least-cost energy: Solving the CO2 problem.* Amherst, NH: Brick House.

McDonough, William, & Braungart, Michael. (2002). *Cradle to cradle: Remaking the way we make things.* New York: North Point Press.

Millennium Ecosystem Assessment (MEA). (2005a). *Ecosystems and human well-being: Synthesis.* Retrieved January 29, 2010, from http://www.millenniumassessment.org/documents/document.356.aspx.pdf

Millennium Ecosystem Assessment (MEA). (2005b). *Living beyond our means: Natural assets and human well-being. Statement from the board.* Retrieved January 29, 2010, from http://www.maweb.org/documents/document.429.aspx.pdf

Rocky Mountain Institute; Wilson, Alex; Uncapher, Jenifer L.; McManigal, Lisa; Lovins, L. Hunter; Cureton, Maureen; & Browning, William D. (1998). *Green development: Integrating ecology and real estate.* New York: John Wiley & Sons.

Sant, Roger W. (1980, May). Cutting energy costs: The least-cost strategy. *Environment, 22*(4), pp. 14–20, 42.

Savory, Allan, & Butterfield, Jody. (1999). *Holistic management: A new framework for decision-making.* Washington, DC: Island Press.

Weizsäcker, Ernest U. von; Lovins, Amory B.; & Lovins, L. Hunter. (1997). *Factor four: Doubling wealth, halving resource use.* London: Earthscan.

Wilhelm, Kevin. (2009). *Return on sustainability: How business can increase profitability & address climate change in an uncertain economy.* Indianapolis, IN: Dog Ear Publishing.

Winston, Andrew. (2009). *Green recovery: Get lean, get smart, and emerge from the downturn on top.* Cambridge, MA: Harvard Business Press.

Worldwatch Institute. (1997, May 8). Shifting tax burden to polluters could cut taxes on wages and profits by 15 percent. Retrieved February 4, 2010, from http://www.worldwatch.org/node/1609

Packaging

Because product packaging is a highly visible symbol of the impacts of economic development, it has been a frequent target of environmentalists. Whether undertaken voluntarily or regulated by governments, the ways that packaging is designed, used, and managed throughout its life cycle are changing; it is expected to utilize energy efficiently, avoid hazardous and toxic substances, and be recoverable at end-of-life.

It is worth addressing the question of why we package products in the first place: to protect the product, to increase the shelf life, and to ensure the integrity of the product contained within are all important considerations. Products are also packaged for marketing reasons. The presentation of a product is often the key reason for its success or failure; therefore packaging is integral to modern systems of production and consumption.

The packaging industry has been under pressure for more than twenty years to reduce the environmental impacts of its products. Over that time the emphasis has shifted from a simple concern regarding landfill to the twenty-first century's emphasis on reducing carbon dioxide emissions. Packaging has maintained its high profile in the public discussions on environmental issues because it is a visible symbol of the impacts of industrial development on the environment. This has resulted in government responses varying from strict regulations to voluntary agreements between stakeholders. Most of these measures are developed around the traditional waste management hierarchy: reduction, reuse, recycling, and recovery.

Environmental Regulations

The environmental impacts of packaging are subject to an increasing number of international government regulations and co-regulatory agreements. Because these regulations are extremely varied, companies that manufacture or use packaging need to stay up-to-date on these regulatory trends; indeed these regulations are driving changes in the way that packaging is designed, used, and managed at end-of-life and, of course, in the legal obligations pertaining to that.

One of the key changes is a shift to "product stewardship," or the idea that companies need to share responsibility for reducing the impact of products on the environment over their total life cycle. Companies are required to look at the impacts of their supply chain and to work closely with suppliers to implement environmental improvement programs. They are also required to design products that use materials and energy as efficiently as possible, as well as avoiding the use of toxic or hazardous substances in the products. Companies must also design products that are recoverable at end-of-life.

In the United States and Australia, among others, the "shared responsibility" regulatory model is preferred. There is no federal legislation in the United States specifically targeting packaging and its environmental impact, but state and local government concerns about packaging waste continue to grow. As of 2009, some US states have established minimum recycled content standards for plastic (California, Oregon, Wisconsin), glass containers (California, Oregon), plastic trash bags (California), and newspapers (twenty-seven states). Cities such as Seattle, Washington, and thirty municipalities in California (including San Francisco) have recently banned or restricted the use of expanded polystyrene (EPS, more commonly known as Styrofoam) in "to-go" containers.

The National Packaging Covenant (NPC) in Australia promotes product stewardship in the packaging supply chain through voluntary agreements and action plans. The new draft Australian Covenant focuses more on design for sustainability, incorporating the concepts of cradle to cradle and life cycle analysis to ensure that sustainable practices are implemented by the supply chain.

The extended producer responsibility (EPR) approach is more commonplace in Europe, where physical or financial responsibility for waste management is placed on producers. EPR makes the brand owner or importer primarily responsible for the recovery of packaging. From the late 1980s to early 1990s, various European countries started developing EPR regulations. To harmonize the approach, the European Union (EU) introduced the Packaging and Packaging Waste Directive in 1994 (amended 2004). The Directive sets standards known as the Essential Requirements (ERs). All companies who sell products in EU member states must comply with the five areas outlined below:

- Source Reduction: Companies must demonstrate that they have reduced their packaging as much as possible and then identify the critical area (such as product protection, safety, consumer acceptance, and so on) that prevents further reduction in weight or volume of a packaging component.
- Recovery Standards: Packaging components must be recoverable by at least one of three recovery routes (energy, organic, or material recovery) and must meet certain requirements specific to that recovery route.
- Reuse: Optional, but a package must meet the requirements of the reuse standard if it is claimed as reusable.
- Heavy Metals Content: Sets a concentration limit for lead, cadmium, mercury, and hexavalent chromium in packaging; standards are similar to those in effect in nineteen US states.
- Reduction of Hazardous Substances in Packaging: Substances classified as noxious (for example, zinc) must be minimized if they could be released in emissions, ash, or leachate when packaging is landfilled or burned.

All packaging placed on the EU market must be in compliance with the ERs, and products that do not comply may be removed from the market. Companies must incorporate the ERs into their packaging design systems and document how each standard was considered into its packaging design protocol. The assessment process to prove compliance with the ERs is similar to ISO14000 requirements in that it establishes a framework for evaluating the attributes of a packaging system (and identifying areas for improvement) with respect to the requirements of the law. The European standards have been developed to provide a common procedure for assessing and documenting compliance.

A range of packaging regulations have been introduced in parts of Asia including China, Japan, South Korea, and Taiwan. Japan has chosen the EPR option with its Packaging Source and Separation Law (1995), which makes manufacturers responsible for recycling plastic containers, glass, paper cartons, and paperboard boxes. Many Chinese municipalities have adopted recycling mandates or bans for certain food packaging materials.

Various regulations also attempt to prevent excessive packaging through specific requirements, in addition to the incentives that result from fee structures. Several countries have implemented regulations regarding empty space and the permissible number of layers in a packaging system. Many countries, such as Australia, Belgium, the Netherlands, Greece, Slovakia, Spain, and South Korea, require companies to submit a detailed packaging reduction plan. These plans must outline the long-term goals of the manufacturers to reduce their packaging.

Regulations relating to misleading advertising of products as "environmentally friendly," deceptive environmental labeling, and proper material coding have been adopted by many countries. Since 2005, more than thirty countries have introduced environmental packaging design requirements including regulations on toxics in packaging, empty space and source reduction, recycled content, environmental labeling, and packaging prevention planning.

What Is Sustainable Packaging?

The high visibility of packaging married with its importance as an essential facilitator for the distribution, marketing, and safe use of consumer and other products creates significant challenges for advancing sustainable development in packaging. Consumer behavior and spending trends, market segmentation, and developments in distribution are examples of motivators for new packaging formats and technologies, which are often contrary to the principles of sustainable development (James, Fitzpatrick, Lewis, and Sonneveld 2005).

Even though packaging and the relevant environmental regulations are found worldwide, there is no clear international understanding about what constitutes sustainable packaging. The Sustainable Packaging Alliance (SPA) has identified this as one of the most pressing and overarching challenges in advancing sustainable development in the packaging domain.

Various packaging organizations, including the SPA in Australia and the Sustainable Packaging Coalition (SPC) in the United States, have tried to define "sustainable packaging" by establishing sets of principles or strategies that could guide decision making by businesses.

Four Principles of Sustainable Packaging

As defined through research by Australia's Sustainable Packaging Alliance, there are four principles that can be integrated into business systems to guide their packaging practices and product stewardship (Lewis, Fitzpatrick, Varghese, Sonneveld, and Jordan 2007, 16–18). Each of these characteristics needs to be adapted to the specific requirements of the company, and not every action will be addressed or relevant to every business.

Effective: Social and Economic Benefit

Packaging systems add value to society by effectively enclosing and safeguarding products as they travel through the supply chain. Packaging should also encourage educated and responsible utilization. In order to achieve this benefit, businesses must:

- eliminate any excessive packaging
- guarantee that the packaging satisfies supply chain requirements for product protection, containment, distribution, retailing, and use
- design the packaging system to reduce total life cycle environmental impact
- reduce overall supply chain expenses
- present information to consumers on environmental qualities of the packaging
- provide guidance to the consumer on correct disposal of the packaging

Efficient: Doing More with Less

Packaging systems are designed to use materials and energy efficiently throughout the product life cycle. Efficiency should be defined through reference to best practice at each stage of the packaging life cycle, including steps such as:

- reducing packaging volume and weight to only what is needed for product protection, safety, hygiene, and acceptance by the consumer
- increasing the efficiency of the product-packaging system by changing the product
- reducing product waste
- raising energy and water efficiency during manufacturing and recovery systems
- improving transport efficiency

Cyclic: Optimizing Recovery

Recycling of packaging materials used in the system should occur through natural or industrial systems with nominal material degradation. Recovery rates should be improved to ensure that they achieve optimum energy and greenhouse

gas reductions. There are many opportunities that businesses can pursue to implement this principle:

- guarantee that the packaging can be collected and processed within identified cyclic loops
- employ reusable packaging to reduce environmental impacts by increasing return rates
- use only one material whenever possible, or use materials that are easy for the consumer to separate and that do not contaminate recycling systems
- identify compostable rather than oxo-degradable materials and ensure that a system is available for collection and processing. ("Oxo-degradable" refers to plastics that have been manufactured in such a way that the degrading process is sped up, ideally to the point that the plastic disintegrates into its component minerals. The process is controversial, with some critics saying that the technology is worse for the environment than ordinary plastic; critics also say the process is unregulated [Smith 2009].)
- specify renewable materials that provide the lowest environmental impact
- utilize renewable energy (both stationary and transport types) with the least environmental impact
- use cleaner production techniques for manufacturing, best practice materials, and energy consumption technologies

Safe: Nonpolluting and Nontoxic

Packaging components used in the system—including materials, finishes, inks, pigments, and other additives—should not pose any risks to humans or ecosystems. Safety includes complete avoidance or minimization of:

- heavy metal–based additives
- any material or additive that can migrate into food and be harmful to the health of living organisms
- materials or additives that may endanger humans or ecosystems during recovery or disposal
- the environmental impacts of transport (considering distance, mode of transport and fuel type) to the greatest extent possible

Outlook for the Twenty-First Century

Associating sustainability with product packaging systems is an abstract and complex concept, and one that is very much open to interpretation. To be able to advance sustainable development in packaging, stakeholders need specific guidance as to how they can implement it into their daily business practice. A collaborative, multidisciplinary approach is required for sustainable packaging because the process involves many professionals, including designers, technologists, marketers, and environmental managers.

Individual large brands and organizations are developing or have developed useful frameworks to support sustainable packaging strategies. Walmart's goal is to reduce packaging used by suppliers by 5 percent by 2013. In an effort to achieve this target, the retail introduced a scorecard system that will allow manufacturers to rank their current use of packaging. Scores will be given on several relevant categories including: greenhouse gas emissions produced per ton of packaging, raw material use, packaging size, recycled content, material recovery value, renewable energy use, transportation impacts, and innovation. Since the beginning of 2008, Walmart has made purchasing decisions based on the scorecard results.

New tools have been developed to evaluate the life cycle environmental impacts of packaging, while the global warming debate has encouraged some companies to focus on the carbon footprint of packaging as a relevant and simple way of communicating environmental impact.

The issue of sustainable packaging requires ongoing debate with the objective of achieving consensus among stakeholder groups on definitions and key indicators. For example, the sector will need to reconcile the sometimes conflicting lifestyle expectations of consumers, (such as the greater convenience, safety, and shelf life of products) with the sustainable packaging expectations of many of these same citizens (Sonneveld, James, Fitzpatrick, and Lewis 2005).

Anne CHICK
University of Lincoln (formerly of Kingston University)

See also in the *Berkshire Encyclopedia of Sustainability* Consumer Behavior; Cradle to Cradle; Design, Industrial; Ecolabeling; Life Cycle Assessments (LCAs); Manufacturing Practices; Marketing; Supply Chain Management; Zero Waste

FURTHER READING

European Organization for Packaging and the Environment. (2009). Retrieved October 1, 2009, from http://www.europen.be/

Industry Council for Packaging and the Environment (INCPEN). (2009). Retrieved October 1, 2009, from http://www.incpen.org/

International Association of Packaging Research Institutes. (2009). Retrieved October 1, 2009, from http://www.iapriweb.org/

James, Karli; Fitzpatrick, Leanne; Lewis, Helen; & Sonneveld, Kees. (2005). Sustainable packaging system development. In William Leal Filho (Ed.), *Handbook of sustainability research*. Frankfurt: Peter Lang Scientific Publishing.

Lewis, Helen; Fitzpatrick, Leanne; Varghese, Karli; Sonneveld, Kees; & Jordan, Robert. (2007). Sustainable packaging redefined. Retrieved September 17, 2009, from http://http://www.sustainablepack.org/default.aspx/database/files/newsfiles/Sustainable%20Packaging%20Redefined%20Nov%20%202007.pdf

PIRA International. (2009). Retrieved October 1, 2009, from http://www.pira-international.com/

Smith, Chris. (22 July 2009). Bioplastics industry joins oxo-degradable debate. *European Plastic News*. Retrieved 28 December 2009, from http://plasticsnews.com/headlines2.html?id=1248283104

Sonneveld, Kees; James, Karli; Fitzpatrick, Leanne; & Lewis, Helen. (2005, April). *Sustainable packaging: How do we define and measure it?* Paper presented at the 22nd International Association of Packaging Research Institutes (IAPRI) Symposium, Campinas, St. Paul, Brazil. Retrieved October 2, 2009, from http://http://www.sustainablepack.org/default.aspx/database/files/SPA%20paper%2022nd%20IAPRI%20Symposium%202005.pdf

Sustainable Packaging Alliance. (2007). Retrieved October 1, 2009, from http://www.sustainablepack.org/default.aspx

Sustainable Packaging Coalition. (2007). Retrieved October 1, 2009, from http://www.sustainablepackaging.org/

SustainPack. (n.d.). Retrieved October 1, 2009, from http://www.sustainpack.com/index.php

World Packaging Organisation. (2007). Retrieved October 2, 2009, from http://www.worldpackaging.org/default.asp

Performance Metrics

Due largely to pressure from stakeholders, "performance metrics" now analyze not only the economic value of a business or organization but its environmental and social impacts as well. Increasing numbers of organizations report this information, but the quality of data varies widely. It is critical for organizations to improve the quality of reporting for the sake of both internal and external decision making.

For organizations, a sustainability performance framework—metrics to measure and manage social, environmental, and economic impacts—enables management to create enduring value for multiple stakeholders. Leading companies increasingly are examining the impacts of their products, services, processes, and other activities more broadly. They are looking at a more comprehensive set of social, environmental, and economic consequences and identifying and measuring impacts on a broader set of stakeholders. The size of corporate social and environmental expenditures is increasing rapidly, and the necessity of improved identification and management of these impacts has become critical.

But, at the same time, creating and implementing this framework challenges managers to understand the complex interrelationships between economic, environmental, and social performance, as well as the interconnectedness of diverse stakeholder groups. Much of this information is not routinely captured by the financial or cost-accounting systems of the firm; however, by incorporating sustainability metrics into internal decision-making tools and external reporting, managers are increasing their accountability for the firm's sustainability initiatives.

Internal Accountability and Decision-Making Tools

As outlined in *Making Sustainability Work* (Epstein 2008, 127), measures that send the right signals and elicit appropriate decisions within the organization should:

- connect to the strategic objectives
- focus on core cross-functional processes
- identify critical success variables
- act like early warning signals of potential problems
- identify critical factors going awry
- link to rewards

A corporate sustainability performance model consists of a mix of input, process, output, and outcome measures. There are cause-and-effect linkages between these four components of the model (see table 1 on the following page). Metrics must be developed to measure the impact that the inputs have on the processes and to translate the impact of the processes on goals and objectives of the organization.

Many firms have implemented the "balanced scorecard" as a strategic management system, in which typical performance measures are grouped into four dimensions: financial, customer, internal business processes, and learning and growth. Each of these indicators is considered in determining overall progress toward a company's strategic goals. Table 1 shows an example of sustainability measures that could be included in the various dimensions of the balanced scorecard.

Certification and External Reporting Tools

The demand for both environmental and social accountability and reporting is growing, and as frameworks for

TABLE I. **Examples of Balanced Scorecard Measures for Sustainability**

Financial		Customer	
Environmental	**Social**	**Environmental**	**Social**
Percentage of sales from "green" products	Philanthropic contributions	Cost of cause-related marketing (for charitable or other worthwhile causes)	Customer perceptions
Recycling revenues	Workers' compensation costs		Number of cause-related events supported (e.g., breast cancer, AIDS)
Cost of fines and/or penalties	Employee benefits	Number of "green" products	
Environmental health and safety costs (percentage of sales)	Costs of legal actions	Product safety	Contributions to community
	Training budgets	Number of recalls	Number of community meetings
Capital investments	Percentage of sales from socially-positioned products (products affiliated with a cause)	Customer returns	Customer satisfaction
Energy costs		Percentage of products reclaimed after use	Social report requests
Disposal costs	Increased sales from improved reputation	Product life	Number of product recalls
Cost avoidance from environmental actions			Customer group demographics
		Functional product eco-efficiency (e.g., energy costs of a washing machine)	Promotion of healthy activities
Internal Business Processes		**Learning and Growth**	
Environmental	**Social**	**Environmental**	**Social**
Percentage of materials recycled	Number of employee accidents	Number of of employees trained	Workforce diversity (age, gender, race)
Percentage of waste to landfill	Number of lost workdays	Number of training programs and/or hours	
Percentage of suppliers certified	Hours of overtime work		Number of internal promotions
Number of accidents and/or spills	Cost of warranty claims	Reputation per surveys	Employee volunteer hours
Energy consumption	Cost of minority business purchases	Number of employee complaints	Number of involuntary discharges
Percentage of facilities certified		Number of community complaints	
Percentage of products remanufactured	Number of suppliers certified	Number of shareholder complaints	Pay ratios (highest/lowest)
Energy savings	Environmental quality of facilities	Unfavorable press coverage	Cost of employee education
Packaging volume	Observance of international labor standards	Number of employees with incentives linked to environmental goals	Cost of employee benefits
Non-product output	Number of safety-improvement projects		Employee satisfaction "Quality of life" programs (e.g., career counseling, stress management, substance counseling)
Number of supplier audits per year	Local sourcing of inputs	Number of functions with environmental responsibilities	Unfavorable press coverage
Natural resource consumption		Number of employees using car pools	Number of employee grievances
Emissions reduction			
Hazardous material output			
Vehicle fuel use			
Habitat changes due to operations		Workforce equity	
		Job training	

Source: authors

The "balanced scorecard" is a tool to help a businesses analyze its performance in reaching certain goals, in this case environmental sustainability. Identifying areas of relative weakness and strength is the first step in solving problems.

reporting become better developed and distributed, the number of companies issuing environmental and social reports is expected to increase. The demand for this accountability comes from numerous stakeholders, in particular investors and shareholders, government agencies, public interest groups, the local community, and consumers.

Two primary standards have been developed for environmental management systems certification: the International Organization for Standardization's (ISO) 14000 series and the European Union's Eco-Management and Audit Scheme (EMAS). The ISO 14000 series of standards quickly has become the primary international standard for environmental certification; ISO 14000 certifications have increased over tenfold in the past decade, with 154,572 facilities certified as of 2007 (ISO 2009). The European Union (EU) introduced the EMAS standards in 1993 as a voluntary set of environmental performance measures for facilities operating in the EU. While ISO 14000 are process-oriented standards, the EMAS standards emphasize performance measurement by focusing more on significant environmental impacts or outcomes. Released in 2010, the ISO 26000 standard will focus on broader issues of corporate responsibility.

Social Accountability 8000 (SA8000) is a standard that focuses on workplace values and specifies baseline requirements regarding child labor, forced labor, health and safety, freedom of association, discrimination, disciplinary practices, working hours, compensation, and management systems. As of 31 March 2009, 1,942 factories located in sixty-five countries and representing sixty-six industries have been SA 8000 certified (SAAS 2009).

The Institute for Social and Ethical Accountability (ISEA) has published the Accountability 1000 series of standards. These standards are focused on accountability principles, assurance, and stakeholder engagement.

During the past decade, there has been an explosion in the number of companies producing external reports for environmental and social responsibility. Thousands of companies are now issuing corporate environmental reports, or in some cases, corporate sustainability reports that contain additional social and economic measures of performance. Among the companies that do issue social and environmental reports, there is wide variation in both the reporting frequency and in the breadth and depth of information reported. Many companies only center their reports on data that is required by regulatory agencies and include almost no insights into the company's social and environmental

strategies, how those strategies are being carried out, and the effectiveness of their efforts.

There is a growing consensus that external social and environmental reports should contain more comprehensive information than just that required by regulatory agencies. Information typically reported by leadership companies includes:

- management systems and policies, including goals, targets, and accountability systems
- inputs such as material, energy, and other natural resource use
- outputs such as waste and emissions
- process management such as risk management methods, accident and safety data, and stewardship practices
- product data such as life cycle analyses, product packaging changes, and remanufactured products
- financial data related to reactive versus proactive spending, capital and operational expenditures, charitable contributions, and costs avoided
- stakeholder identification and concerns

The Global Reporting Initiative (GRI) Sustainability Reporting Guidelines are designed to help companies articulate and evaluate the alignment between corporate environmental strategy and operational goals and measurements, while providing a framework for communicating with external stakeholders. The GRI guidelines identify six primary areas of sustainability performance reporting: economic, environmental, labor practices and decent work indicators, human rights, society, and product responsibility (GRI 2007).

Implementing Performance Metrics

The practices that have been described are being used successfully by many organizations to better measure and manage social and environmental impacts of corporate decisions. For example, Wisconsin Energy measures employee turnover rates and also employee turnover by diversity classification, to help evaluate corporate human resource practices. The United Kingdom's Cooperative Bank measures accessibility of its branches and services to the overall community to help evaluate community involvement of the bank. Implementing a strategy to improve performance by measuring and managing sustainability impacts can be accomplished through following, in whole or in part, these following eight steps:

- Develop a social and environmental strategy and then organize the corporate structure to effectively implement and measure the success of that strategy.
- Identify and measure social and environmental benefits and costs. Think broadly and consider current and future

impacts on both the company and society through a total stakeholder analysis.

- Prepare an inventory of current social and environmental activities and track and accumulate costs and benefits related to social and environmental impacts.
- Integrate all current and future social and environmental costs and benefits into corporate decisions, including those on product design, product costing, and capital investments.
- Integrate accounting and financial analysis techniques, including risk assessment, into evaluating the social and environmental impacts of corporate decisions. This will help improve analyses of choices between product improvement, process improvements, and capital improvements, as well as better analysis of uncertainties related to changing regulations and technologies.
- Integrate corporate social and environmental performance into performance evaluation systems. Consider sustainability performance as a variable in evaluating the total corporation as well as of divisions and individuals.
- Collect and provide feedback throughout the firm on the effects of various decisions so that the social and environmental strategy can be continuously updated and decision making can be better informed. Use practices to verify and standardize the information collected.
- Institute a reporting strategy for both internal and external stakeholders and decision makers.

Marc J. EPSTEIN
Rice University

Priscilla S. WISNER
Montana State University

See also in the *Berkshire Encyclopedia of Sustainability* Accounting; CSR and CSR 2.0; Equator Principles; Facilities Management; Financial Services Industry; Global Reporting Initiative (GRI); Green Gross Domestic Product (GDP); Integrated Product Development (IPD); Manufacturing Practices; Stakeholder Theory; Supply Chain Management; Sustainable Value Creation; Transparency; Triple Bottom Line

FURTHER READING

Epstein, Marc J. (1996). *Measuring corporate environmental performance: Best practices for costing and managing an effective environmental strategy.* Chicago: Irwin Professional Publishing.

Epstein, Marc J. (2008a). Implementing corporate sustainability: Measuring and managing social and environmental impacts. *Strategic Finance, 89*(7), 24–31.

Epstein, Marc J. (2008b). *Making sustainability work: Best practices in managing and measuring corporate social, environmental and economic impacts.* Sheffield, UK: Greenleaf Publishing.

Epstein, Marc J., & Hanson, Kirk O. (Eds.). (2006). *The accountable corporation* (Vols. 1–4). Westport, CT: Praeger Publishing.

Epstein, Marc J., & Roy, Marie-Josée. (2001). Sustainability in action: Identifying and measuring the key performance drivers. *Long Range Planning, 34*(5), 585–604.

Epstein, Marc J., & Wisner, Priscilla S. (2001a). Good neighbors: Implementing social and environmental strategies with the balanced scorecard. *The Balanced Scorecard Report, 3*(3), 3–6.

Epstein, Marc J., & Wisner, Priscilla S. (2001b). Increasing corporate accountability: The external disclosure of balanced scorecard measures, part 2. *The Balanced Scorecard Report, 3*(4), 10–13.

Epstein, Marc J., & Wisner, Priscilla S. (2001c). Using a balanced scorecard to implement sustainability. *Environmental Quality Management, 11*(2), 1–10.

Epstein, Marc J., & Wisner, Priscilla S. (2006). Actions and measures to improve sustainability. In Marc J. Epstein & Kirk O. Hanson (Eds.), *The accountable corporation* (Vol. 3, pp. 207–234). Westport, CT: Praeger Publishing.

Global Reporting Initiative (GRI). (2007). Reporting framework overview. Retrieved on July 30, 2009, from http://www.globalreporting.org/ReportingFramework/ReportingFrameworkOverview/

Institute for Social and Ethical Accountability. (2007). Retrieved on July 30, 2009, from http://www.accountability.org.uk

Institute of Management Accountants. (2008). Statements on management accounting 67: The evolution of accountability—Sustainability reporting for accountants. Retrieved November 3, 2009, from http://www.eduvision.ca/uploadfiles/SMA_Sustainability_062708.pdf

International Organization for Standardization (ISO). (2009). Retrieved on July 30, 2009, from http://www.iso.org

Social Accountability Accreditation Services (SAAS). (2009, March 31). Certified facilities list. Retrieved August 19, 2009, from http://www.saasaccreditation.org/certfacilitieslist.htm

Social Accountability International. (n.d.). Retrieved on July 30, 2009, from http://www.sa-intl.org

World Business Council for Sustainable Development. (2009). Retrieved on July 30, 2009, from http://www.wbcsd.org

Public–Private Partnerships

The public sector—government—has not always been successful in providing adequate services, especially in poorer, more remote areas. Since the 1990s, the private sector has been used to deliver financing opportunities and improve services in conjunction with the public sector through public–private partnerships. Water and sanitation has been one sector addressed globally through different types of these contractual agreements.

Throughout the world, the public sector is principally responsible for water and sanitation services, operating more than 90 percent of the piped networks in developing countries. On the whole, however, the public sector has not succeeded in improving water and sanitation access and quality in many parts of the world, especially for poorer people, and in more remote areas. Such operators typically suffer from various problems, including low service coverage and quality of service, artificially low tariffs, billing and collection difficulties, lack of capacity, lack of capital investment, lack of operation and maintenance and poor consumer relations. In the 1990s, public–private partnerships (PPPs) began to be promoted as a means to deliver financing for investments and efficiency improvements. Infrastructure (telecommunications; electricity generation, transmission, and distribution; natural gas transmission and distribution; transport; and water) accounted for half of privatization/PPP proceeds in developing countries in 1990–2003 (ADB 2008). By 2000, private operators were serving 93 million people in developing countries (Marin 2009); high profile projects were undertaken in Latin America as well as in megacities including Buenos Aires, Argentina; Manila, the Philippines; and Jakarta, Indonesia.

What Is a Public–Private Partnership?

While there is a large volume of literature relating to public–private partnerships, there appears to be no hard and fast definition. The predominant understanding of public–private partnerships is a general one: public–private partnerships serve to implement projects in which there is some form of collaboration between the public and private sectors; they finance or otherwise increase resources for the sector (resources include people, skills, expertise, knowledge, technology, equipment, facilities, and spare capacity) in order to expand capabilities.

In general, public–private partnerships have a number of common features:

- A formal or informal agreement. The majority of PPPs are governed by a formal contract, which is generally understood to be a legally binding written agreement. But public–private partnership is also used to describe other types of less formal agreements between governments and private organizations. These "agreements" spell out the responsibilities of each party but stop short of being legally binding arrangements.
- A public- and a private-sector entity. There is a lack of consensus over the definition of what constitutes the private sector in the context of PPP arrangements. For example, a private partner might be a private company (international or local), an informal service provider (international or local), a nongovernmental organization (NGO), or a community-based organization (CBO). The partnership may be a bilateral contractual arrangement or a multiparty arrangement.
- An outcome. PPPs are intended to ensure that services are provided in the most efficient and effective ways possible and usually through joint realization. For

example, the private sector typically contributes design, construction, operation, maintenance, finance, and risk management skills while the government is responsible for strategic planning, regulation, and so on. This sets PPPs apart from other forms of public–private interaction, such as when a private-sector operator or an NGO has essentially been subcontracted to provide a service (or services) independently.

• A degree of risk borne by the private-sector entity. Most definitions of PPPs usually refer to the degree of risk borne by the private sector. There is a distinction between models of PPP with low private-sector risk, such as service and lease contracts, and those with significant private-sector risk, such as concession contracts (Sohail 2003).

PPP Models

There are a number of different types of PPPs in existence. The following is a typical categorization of different contractual arrangements for private-sector participation, but several hybrid arrangements are also possible.

Service Contracts

Under a service contract, the government pays a private entity to perform specific tasks. Service contracts are a long-established practice used for routine operations (meter reading or leak detection), engineering works, and the laying of pipelines.

Management Contracts

Management contracts are contractual agreements between the government and a private partner under which the private partner is given the responsibility for day-to-day management of an enterprise in exchange for a fee; the government, however, retains financial and legal responsibility for delivery of services. These are arrangements in which a municipality or local government purchases management services from a company.

Leasing or Affermage

Under this model, the government delegates management of a public service to a company in return for a specified fee, commonly based on the volume of water sold, while ownership of assets remains with a holding company operating for the government.

Concessions

This arrangement usually gives the concessionaire (the owner or operator) a monopoly service provision for a fixed period of time, during which the concessionaire also assumes any significant investment risk. The model of large concessions has worked in some places, but its suitability to most developing countries has been questioned.

Why Use PPPs?

Public–private partnerships are pursued as a way to leverage knowledge, resources, and capabilities to achieve public goals. PPPs are often used to address non-revenue water reduction (reducing the amount of water "lost" before it reaches the customer and is paid for), billing collection, and labor productivity. While the early models of partnerships focused on the gains from private financing, the most successful PPPs in the water and sanitation sector have largely been based on public financing (leases or hybrid programs) combined with private-sector efficiency. Thus rather than improve access to private financing, PPPs have been used to improve the financial viability of the water and sanitation operators through service quality, access expansion, and increasing cash flow for investment and creditworthiness. In the long term these improvements should translate into broader, more equitable, efficient, affordable, and effective delivery of services. Nevertheless, PPPs may not be selected as an option to improve service delivery on ideological grounds or the basis of public service ethos (Sohail 2002a).

Innovative Solutions

Access has improved by expanding the water network to poor neighborhoods that were previously unserved, as in Queenstown, South Africa; La Paz–El Alto, Bolivia; Manila; and Buenos Aires. In Queenstown, a much smaller PPP covering a population of 22,000 was amended to include an extra 170,000 inhabitants of predominantly low-income areas (Sohail 2005). The renegotiation of existing concession contracts operated in Manila and Buenos Aires led to affordable connection charges for lower-income consumers—benefiting 400,000 in Manila and 260,000 in Buenos Aires. Connection-fee cross-subsidies were used in Buenos Aires; reduced connection costs through distant meter locations and the use of community labor led to 90 percent cost reductions in water tariffs for the poor in Manila (Nickson and Franceys 2001). Nonetheless, there is little evidence of coverage extended to the urban poor as a result of

larger scale, formal private-sector companies in PPPs, at least in the initial stages of the contract (Sohail 2004).

In 2000, 80 percent of the water PPP market in developing countries was dominated by five international water companies. Since 2001, however, most new contracts have been signed by private operators from developing countries (these account for 90 percent of the growth in the number of people served by PPP projects). By 2007, local private water operators served more than 67 million people; some international operators have also transferred their existing contracts to local investors (Marin 2009, 9).

Water operator partnerships (WOP) have been promoted by the UN since 2006 as a way to strengthen local water and sanitation services by sharing expertise through training and technical assistance. WOPS are defined as "cooperation between water operators," on a "not-for-profit" basis (UNSGAB 2006, 3). Some may not classify them as PPPs, but they are partnering arrangements: the receiving partners are always public undertakings (water and sanitation utilities, drainage and sewerage companies, or wastewater organizations), but their collaboration partners may be well-performing public (foreign public utilities or local public utilities) or private operators (international private operators or local private operators), small-scale water and sanitation service providers, or community-based organizations.

Small, often informal service providers play a significant role by filling in the gaps in service delivery. These service providers, however, are often not officially recognized or involved in PPPs. The potential for these small service providers in PPPs has not been accurately assessed.

Controversies

In developing countries, PPPs haven't met initial expectations: there have been a series of highly publicized contract cancellations, mostly in Sub-Saharan Africa, and in Latin America among concession programs. Doubts still remain over the suitability of PPPs both for improving the performance of water utilities and extending access to water and sanitation to the unserved in developing countries.

Cherry-picking is a particular danger with PPPs, that is, the sites that are most attractive to private investors—large cities in countries with large economies and a large middle class—will be selected rather than areas with the greatest

need. Poor areas and people are often seen as unprofitable and difficult to serve, which means that connections and extension of services are typically not made to residents with insufficient funds, insecure tenure, and those living in difficult-to-reach locations such as rural areas (Sohail 2002b).

The pricing of services in general and the design of tariffs for service provision in particular is a significant issue. In most cases, PPP projects have been accompanied by tariff increases (due to more realistic pricing or greed, depending on one's point of view) that put services beyond the reach of the poor. PPPs may also be accompanied by massive lay-offs, depending on extent of "over-staffing."

Some services are less attractive for private-sector involvement due to their more complex nature; neglect in the area of sanitation is a significant trend that has been noted with PPPs. This could be the case for many reasons: sanitation facilities are often more complex and expensive than water facilities; the demand for the service often does not exist; there is an unwillingness by users to pay; or there may be unnecessary bureaucracy or regulation that constrains service delivery (Sohail 2002c).

PPPs require significant government capacity to be effectively managed, however, such capacity is often lacking. Local government officials need to learn not just how to strategically manage PPPs, but also how to renegotiate and implement them to achieve their objectives.

Successes of PPPs

PPPs haven't always worked, but successes have often received much less publicity than failures. PPPs tend to work best for those who can pay and who live in places where the overall demand makes the provision of services a viable option. If a PPP is to improve access and service delivery for the poor, then this has to be specified in the contract documents that will ultimately be the basis for engaging the private sector. Very few PPP contracts contain explicit pro-poor references. Bidding procedures and contract design should allow sufficient flexibility for innovative solutions to water and sanitation supply, such as lower-cost or alternative technology (for example, pipes at lower depth or condominium sewerage), and flexible billing arrangements as well as payment options, particularly with respect to poor neighborhoods (Hemson and Batidzirai 2002). Multipurpose contacts, such as the combined water and electricity concession in Casablanca, offer opportunities to optimize the demand and sources and should be explored further. In Casablanca the larger electricity side of the services was subsidizing investment in the smaller water division (Hall, Bayliss and Lobina, 2002).

Developing a long-term business model for PPPs to work within a given context is a challenging activity and requires further exploration.

M. SOHAIL and Sue CAVILL
WEDC (Water, Engineering and Development Centre),
Loughborough University

See also in the *Berkshire Encyclopedia of Sustainability* Development, Sustainable; Development, Rural—Developed World; Development, Rural—Developing World; Development, Urban; Health, Public and Environmental; Municipalities; Public Transportation; Water Use and Rights

FURTHER READING

Asian Development Bank (ADB). (2008). Recent experience with infrastructure privatization and PPPs. In *Public–private partnership (PPP) handbook*. Retrieved November 2, 2009, from http://www.adb.org/Documents/Handbooks/Public-Private-Partnership/Chapter2.pdf

Gassner, Katharina; Popov, Alexander; & Pushak, Nataliya. (2009). *Does private sector participation improve performance in electricity and water distribution?* (International Bank for Reconstruction and Development / The World Bank Trends and Policy Options No. 6). Retrieved November 2, 2009, from http://www.ppiaf.org/documents/trends_and_policy/PSP_water_electricity.pdf

Hall, David; Bayliss, Kate; & Lobina, Emanuele. (2002). Water in Middle East and North Africa (MENA)—trends in investments and privatisation. Retrieved November 2, 2009, from http://www.psiru.org/reports/2002-10-W-Mena.doc

Hemson, David, & Batidzirai, Herbert. (2002). *Public private partnerships and the poor. Dolphin Coast water concession: Case study: Dolphin Coast, South Africa*. Retrieved January 11, 2010, from http://www.ucl.ac.uk/dpu-projects/drivers_urb_change/urb_infrastructure/pdf_public_private_services/W_DFID_WEDC_HemsonPPP_and_Poo_Dolphin_Coast.pdf

Marin, Philippe. (2009). *Public–private partnerships for urban water utilities: A review of experiences in developing countries* (International Bank for Reconstruction and Development / The World Bank Trends and Policy Options No. 8). Retrieved January 5, 2010, from http://www.ppiaf.org/documents/trends_and_policy/PPPsforUrbanWaterUtilities-PhMarin.pdf

Nickson, Andrew, & Franceys, Richard. (2001). Tapping the market. Can private enterprise supply water to the poor? Retrieved January 11, 2010, from http://www.eldis.org/id21ext/insights37Editorial.html

Sohail, M. (Ed.). (2002a). *Public private partnerships and the poor. Private sector participation and the poor, part 1: Strategy*. Longborough, UK: WEDC, Loughborough University.

Sohail, M. (Ed.). (2002b). *Public private partnerships and the poor. Private sector participation and the poor, part 2: Implementation*. Loughborough, UK: WEDC, Loughborough University.

Sohail, M. (Ed). (2002c). *Public private partnerships and the poor. Private sector participation and the poor, part 3: Regulation*. Loughborough, UK: WEDC, Loughborough University. .

Sohail, M. (Ed.). (2003). *Public private partnerships and the poor: Pro-poor longer term contracts*. Loughborough, UK: WEDC, Loughborough University.

Sohail, M. (Ed.). (2004). *Tools for pro-poor municipal PPP*. Weikersheim, Germany: UNDP, Margraf Publishers.

Sohail, M. (Ed). (2005). *Public private partnership and the poor. Case study: Revisiting Queenstown, South Africa*. Loughborough, UK: WEDC, Loughborough University.

United Nations Secretary General's Advisory Board on Water and Sanitation (UNSGAB). (2006). Hashimoto action plan: Compendium of action. Retrieved November 2, 2009, from http://www.unsgab.org/docs/HAP_en.pdf

Risk Management

Risk management includes all efforts undertaken by a business to minimize and control hazards that threaten its operations. In the past, uncertainties about quantifying risk led to difficulties in evaluating perceived threats and their possible impact on a company's finances. But new models exist, allowing businesses to more accurately measure risk and even gain a competitive edge in markets once considered too risky.

All companies seeking success in the modern marketplace need to maintain balance between minimizing risk and maximizing opportunities. Risk is any event or action that can impede an organization's ability to implement its strategies and achieve its objectives. While companies continuously face myriad risks, from project failure to industrial accidents, some of the most complex risks relate to social, environmental, and political issues, and managing those risks effectively lies at the heart of successful sustainability strategy.

Social risks are challenges to business practices that emerge from concerns of society. These may include diseases that curtail the workforce, environmental issues that create tension within local communities or trigger financial penalties, human rights violations that damage a company's reputation or lead to litigation, and objections by stakeholders (i.e., an individual or group directly or indirectly affected by a company's polices or actions) due to negative perceptions of business practices.

Environmental risk, often considered a subset of social risk, includes those issues stemming from environmental issues that can impact a company. These include concerns about climate change and potential legislation to minimize corporate impact. It can also include concerns about pollution, both as a result of production and of discarding products like computers and cell phones. Companies can be fined for the pollution generated during manufacturing, and some are held responsible for the proper end-of-life disposal of a product.

Political risk is the exertion of political power in a way that threatens a company's value. This can include the specter of nationalization or forced partnerships facing companies doing business in Venezuela, Bolivia, and other areas of Latin and South America that are drifting farther to the left. It also includes the changed international political landscape heralded by September 11, 2001, and followed by bombings in London, Madrid, and Mumbai, which have impacted the ways in which business is conducted.

The distinction between social and political risk is often blurred. Issues may be experienced differently by different sectors in varied locations—for instance, concerns about climate change may lead to legislation in one geography that can penalize a company but then spur innovation across its manufacturing practices, leading to market success where legislation is not yet in place.

The widely used terms *environmental risk*, *social risk*, and *political risk* are also known as *above-ground risks* (by the mining, oil, and gas industries), *nontechnical risks*, and *noncommercial risks*.

Risk and Sustainability

Issues such as political corruption, child labor, obesity, global terrorism, predatory governments, and environmental pollution pose both challenges and opportunities for business. In fact, setting sustainability objectives is often a result of identifying and seizing opportunities based on the social and political risks facing a company, industry, or region. Corporate sustainability strategy and social and political risk management go hand in hand.

"Leadership" companies view responsiveness to social and environmental issues as assets that produce increased revenues rather than only as liabilities with their associated costs. They recognize that an investment in structures and systems to ensure strong social and environmental performance often pays dividends in terms of improved processes, production quality, efficiency, yields, reputation, and profitability, as well as lower risk. For example, Toyota's leaders tried to envisage what might transform its industry and threaten future market share. They pinpointed climate change and convened a team in 1993 to create the first great car of the twenty-first century, nearly a decade before that century arrived. As a result of a series of technological breakthroughs, manufacturing innovations, and careful marketing, Toyota has sold more than one million Prius gas–electric hybrid cars since introducing them in 1997. That's five times as many hybrid vehicles as its nearest competitor.

Current Practices in Risk Management

Risk management includes all the activities organizations undertake to minimize or control hazards that threaten their objectives. For businesses, access to or analysis of financial information leads to the most rigorous evaluation of options and effective decision making. Companies continue to struggle, however, to integrate social, environmental, and political risks into financial equations in meaningful ways. Failure to consider these risks in investment decisions leaves out critical elements when it comes to allocating resources. According to a 2007 poll by the American Institute of Certified Public Accountants (AICPA), 84 percent of companies don't formally integrate social, environmental, and political risks into financial calculations. Often, therefore, companies make decisions about these risks based on personal biases, or they arbitrarily assign higher risk premiums to projects in unfamiliar locations, failing to focus management's attention on reducing risk. Why? Many analysts mistakenly believe measuring social, environmental, and political risks is not possible. Historically these risks have also been addressed in more descriptive language rather than a format that reflects their financial implications.

Companies have traditionally taken two approaches toward assessing and managing social and political risk—qualitative and quantitative. Neither approach, however, allows companies to use the same formal techniques they employ to evaluate other types of risk, such as business continuity (the risk of disruption to critical functions after a disaster or other unexpected occurrence), information security, or currency fluctuation.

Qualitative Approach

In the 1970s, multinational firms, particularly in the extraction and banking industries, began creating in-house teams to evaluate political and social risks. These teams looked at risk assessment qualitatively, producing detailed briefings that outlined the challenges of conducting business in various parts of the world. Beginning in the 1980s, consultants were often hired to produce similar reports. While providing sound insights about certain risks, such as the likelihood of a coup or a country's use of slave labor, these briefings did not explicitly connect the identified risks to the company's bottom line. Without an understanding of the costs of these risks, executives had no way to integrate the information into business assessments the way they did for other, quantified, data. As a result, important insights contained in those briefs were sometimes relegated to footnotes in the company's business plan.

Quantitative Approach

Realizing the flaws of a purely qualitative approach, some analysts began to quantify political and social risk to make it more relevant to corporate managers. Various methods were developed and put in use.

Scorecards

Indicators of potential political and social risks—such as judiciary independence, corruption, and government turnover—are evaluated and assigned a numerical value. A final "score" is then generated by aggregating and weighting the values of different indicators to calculate a country's overall risk. Such scoring is helpful because it enables a comparison between countries. But it falls short of being directly useful to business decision makers because the risks are not converted into monetary terms.

Statistical Analysis

The emergence of spreadsheet applications, such as Crystal Ball, an analytical tool that automatically generates equations to capture uncertainty, has contributed to quantitative analysis of risk. Results of such software programs show project managers either the most sensitive issues on which to concentrate—sensitivity analysis—or a cumulative probability curve indicating the potential economic performance of a project. The charts, graphs, and dynamic models produced by these calculations, however, cannot be integrated into financial evaluations because they do not generate a return on investment (ROI) number, a political/social risk beta (an indicator used in financial calculations to

compare a company's risk compared to the risk of the overall market), or any monetary results that can be included in financial calculations.

Scenario Analysis

Risk mapping plots the expected degree of exposure to various risks on a graph, with probable frequency on the horizontal axis and expected severity on the vertical axis. Such modeling is beneficial as a communication tool, enabling managers to visualize where to allocate resources, and as a way to measure various types of risk. Mapping as currently practiced does not provide a link to financial statements that are critical for comparisons between competing projects. But, with some modifications, including assignment of monetary values to hypothetical consequences, axis points on such a risk map could correlate to financial data and be integrated into ROI calculations.

Adjusted Discount Rate and Cost of Capital

One method of integrating social and political risks into financial models is to create a discount rate or cost-of-capital calculation that can be used in cash-flow projections. This can be done by creating a social discount rate that employs the weighted average cost of capital (WACC) and the traditional capital asset pricing model (CAPM). (A social discount rate is an important factor in determining the value of contributing funds to a project, such as a school, highway system, or an environmental protection program, that would benefit society in some way.) When dealing with markets that may exhibit hallmarks of social and political risk, this adjusted WACC accounts for social and political factors. Calculations for this risk-adjusted beta, however, have in the past largely relied on the standard country-specific risk-rating methodology generated by political-risk consulting firms, which are too broad to achieve the needed objectives. These ratings are neither industry-, project-, nor company-specific, though social and political risks affect companies and their reputations differently, even those operating in the same country.

Effective Risk Management

Effective risk management involves identifying the sociopolitical and corporate environments that might create risks and then measuring and monitoring them. Reporting these risks in monetary terms is an important step toward integrating them into financial planning and corporate strategies.

One method of monetizing and better managing these nontraditional risks is by including them in slightly modified ROI calculations. Managers commonly calculate ROI, a measure of investment profitability, to make decisions about day-to-day operations and capital investment

planning. ROI is the most popular method for measuring corporate performance because it is the approach CEOs and CFOs are most familiar with. To make such analysis more complete and improve operational and capital investment decisions, political and social risks must be included in the conventional ROI calculation through several phases outlined below, which makes the ROI more explicit and relevant for effective risk management.

Step 1: Generate options. The first step in a modified ROI calculation that incorporates social and political risks is to think about the various options that could potentially minimize risk, such as investing in a range of countries or including a range of suppliers in the supply chain. This thinking is known as "real options." While real options calculations aren't used outside financial settings and stock-option calculations because of their complexity, this type of thinking incorporates financial insights at the strategic stage of project planning rather than as afterthoughts. This helps clarify the risks and their potential repercussions.

Step 2: Calculate benefits and costs. Calculating the savings and costs associated with each issue that could generate social and political risks is the second step. For example, if a corporation considered employing child labor, the savings would be calculated by measuring the wage differential between children and adults. The issue benefit, which is generally assigned a positive value, would be the savings. Next the potential costs associated with the risk of child labor should be calculated, such as lost sales after the public discovers this activity. The reputations of several industries have been seriously damaged by the use of child labor in their supply chains, and some companies have attempted to stop the practice. In 2001, major companies in the chocolate industry like Hershey, Cadbury, and Nestle became aware of kidnappings and forced child labor on cocoa plantations in the Ivory Coast, which tainted their reputations and reduced sales. Had companies in this industry calculated these costs in advance, they may have employed mitigation strategies to avoid sourcing from plantations using these practices. The biggest cost of social and political risk is usually to reputation and lost sales due to consumer boycotts and protests.

Step 3: Estimate probability. After calculating the potential costs of each risk, approximate (in percentages) the likelihood that each risk will occur and hurt the company. This is the *estimated probability*. Assign an estimated probability to each risk identified.

Step 4: Calculate expected value. Calculate the expected value of each risk by multiplying the estimated cost of that risk by the estimated probability it will occur.

Step 5: Calculate net present value (NPV). Calculate the net present value of each risk. Note that each issue has risks that emerge at different times. NPV calculations for social and political risk are determined in the same manner as traditional NPV calculations. Discount back using a set discount rate in the traditional manner used in financial accounting. Carry out these calculations for each social and political risk.

Steps 6: Aggregate NPVs for social and political risks. After calculating all NPVs for social and political risks, add together the social risk NPVs and then the political risk NPVs.

Step 7: Integrate the results into traditional ROI calculations. Insert the social risk NPV and the political risk NPV as line items in the normal ROI calculation. Provide schedules that show the calculations for benefits, costs, probability, and expected value for each social and political risk. This will allow senior managers to see both the results and the processes by which they were obtained.

Defensive and Innovative Risk Management

Identifying and measuring social and political risks, and integrating them into ROI calculations, provides the basis for establishing a comprehensive risk management strategy. While financial risk can be shared or transferred (to joint venture partners, through insurance, or to other entities), this is often impossible with social and political risks. Companies operate in settings where they can be held liable for the misdemeanors of their suppliers or related businesses operating under the same name.

Managing social and political risk includes devising policies and programs to identify, measure, monitor, respond to, and report on issues that generate risk.

There are five methods for managing corporate risk:

- Insuring against risk
- Avoiding risk
- Mitigating risk
- Innovating around risk
- Some combination of the above

Insuring against risk is one of the most conventional methods for managing it. Many insurance policies, however, do not fully cover some of the biggest crises that may arise from political and social issues, such as total expropriation of property, forced joint venture partnerships with the government, or forced renegotiation of contracts. Avoiding certain risks is another option when approaching social and political issues, and it is best achieved by preemptively identifying threats and seeking alternatives. For example, to avoid potential political risks, a company may decide to open operations in a less risky geography. To mitigate a social risk like unpaid overtime, it may implement a working-hours monitoring system in the factories from which it sources its products.

By undertaking the exercise of measuring political and social risk, companies become skilled at recognizing, managing, and even innovating around risk and opening up new business opportunities. In fact, by focusing solely on the downside of risk, companies can overlook opportunities that provide significant possibilities for innovation and creating competitive advantages.

Consider General Electric (GE), which in 2005 launched "ecomagination," its commitment to addressing environmental challenges. The company recognized an opportunity where many others saw only risk. While other companies were litigating and lobbying to avoid liability for their environmental impacts, GE capitalized on growing concerns about the environment by developing products such as energy efficient light bulbs and hybrid locomotives. Ecomagination is a business strategy driving the company's growth—2006 annual revenue from this program exceeded $12 billion—and GE is not alone. Many companies are discovering opportunities to make money from issues traditionally seen as too risky.

McDonald's is another example of a company that transformed risk into opportunity. While the fast-food industry as a whole has been under attack for contributing to increased obesity, McDonald's recognized that its customers' preferences were changing and it responded with healthier foods. McDonald's began offering salads that were more appealing, and it partnered with Newman's Own to provide all-natural gourmet salad dressing and premium coffee. It now also provides sliced apples in Happy Meals. As a result, McDonald's sales and share price have increased in an age when other fast-food chains are scrambling to respond to the threats of obesity litigation and changing customer preferences.

Innovation is central to companies that identify and seize opportunities where others see only risk. Innovation can be a breakthrough idea; it can also be a new model for doing business in a seemingly risky or inaccessible market.

Outlook in the Twenty-First Century

In an increasingly globalized world, companies are becoming aware of the need to better identify and manage social, environmental, and political risks. These risks can emerge along supply chains and from regions in which companies conduct business. Sometimes the risks are related to products or methods of production and their effects on the environment. Corporations are simultaneously beginning to look at these risks, once considered only threats, and creating strategies to capitalize on the sustainability issues inherent in them: employee issues (strategies to address child labor, worker overtime); consumer issues (strategies to address and capitalize on obesity and eating more healthily); environmental issues (strategies to mitigate pollution, global warming, etc. through better methods of production and green products). To realize benefits, risks must be evaluated and handled within a system that adequately identifies, quantifies, and mitigates them. An increasingly robust treatment of risk issues has enabled some companies to identify opportunities to help them gain a competitive edge. As these successes become more widespread, so likely will the practice of monetizing social, environmental, and political issues for inclusion in financial reports and project plans.

Tamara BEKEFI
Daedalus Strategic Advising

Marc J. EPSTEIN
Rice University

See also in the *Berkshire Encyclopedia of Sustainability* Accounting; Climate Change Disclosure; Corporate Citizenship; Fast Food Industry; Financial Services Industry; Human Rights; Investment, CleanTech; Investment, Socially Responsible (SRI); Leadership; Marketing; Performance Metrics; Social Enterprise; Supply Chain Management; Sustainable Value Creation; Transparency

FURTHER READING

Bekefi, Tamara; Epstein, Marc J.; & Yuthus, Kristi. (2007). *Managing opportunities and risks.* New York: American Institute of Certified Public Accountants.

Bekefi, Tamara & Epstein, Marc J. (2006). *Integrating social and political risk into management decision-making.* New York: American Institute of Certified Public Accountants.

Birkbeck, Kimberley. (1999). Forewarned is forearmed: Identification and measurement in integrated risk management. In *The Conference Board of Canada Report 1999* (pp. 249–299). Ottawa, Canada: Conference Board of Canada.

Campbell, Ashley, & Carment, David. (2002). *The private sector and conflict prevention mainstreaming: Risk analysis and conflict impact assessment tools for multinational corporations.* Ottawa, Canada: Carleton University Press.

Day, George S., & Schoemaker, Paul J. H. (2005, November). Scanning the periphery. Retrieved September 7, 2009, from http://custom.hbsp.harvard.edu/custom_pdfs/DSINTR0511H2005103154.pdf

Gale, Bruce. (2009). Identifying, assessing and mitigating political risk. Retrieved September 7, 2009, from http://knowledge.insead.edu/politicalrisk080204.cfm

Kim, W. Chan, & Mauborgne, Renée. (2005). *Blue ocean strategy: How to create uncontested market space and make the competition irrelevant.* Boston: Harvard Business School Press.

McGee, Kenneth. (2004). *Heads up: How to anticipate business surprises and seize opportunities first.* Boston: Harvard Business School Press.

Minor, John. (2003, March). Mapping the new political risk. *Risk Management. 50*(3), 16–21.

PricewaterhouseCoopers. (2005). Predicting the unpredictable: Protecting retail and consumer companies against reputation risk. Retrieved September 7, 2009, from http://www.pwc.com/en_TH/th/publications/assets/risk_whitepaper_v2c01.pdf

Slywotzky, Adrian J., & Weber, Karl. (2007). *The upside: The seven strategies for turning big threats into growth breakthroughs.* New York: Crown Business.

Wood, Duncan. (2009, May 1). Doing business in a volatile world. Retrieved October 5, 2009, from http://www.treasuryandrisk.com/Issues/2009/May%202009/Pages/Doing-Business-in-a-Volatile-World.aspx

Social Enterprise

Social entrepreneurs pursue both social and environmental objectives in addition to economic returns on business investments. The resulting social enterprises are not limited to nonprofit businesses; in fact current emphasis is placed on the involvement of the public and private sectors as well. Underdeveloped countries often are ready markets for these social enterprises.

Tackled in the right way, today's economic, energy, and climate crises will lead to tomorrow's solutions, and the size of the potential market opportunities for solutions is staggering. There are an estimated 4 billion low-income consumers, constituting a majority of the world's population, and they make up what increasingly is called the base of the (economic) pyramid, or BOP. A growing body of research is exploring how to use market-based approaches to "better meet their needs, increase their productivity and incomes, and empower their entry into the formal economy" (Hammond et al. 2007, 3). BOP markets are far from small: it is estimated, for example, that the BOP market in Asia (including the Middle East) is made up of 2.86 billion people with a total income of $3.47 trillion, while in Eastern Europe it is estimated at $458 billion; in Latin America, $509 billion; and in Africa, $429 billion. In total, these markets are thought to be worth some $5 trillion.

But how can mainstream business, financial, and political leaders best come to grips with these emerging BOP trends in value creation? Three answers immediately spring to mind. First, they can experiment with new business models, as much of the BOP literature suggests. Second, as leading business thinkers have long argued, a can-do attitude is much more likely to succeed than don't-do, won't-do, or can't-do mindsets. And, third, it makes sense to find, study, and work alongside can-do and we-can-work-out-how-to-do-it innovators and entrepreneurs

already hard at work developing real-world solutions. In the process, we need to define our terms—particularly the term *social enterprise*. Social enterprises, to quote Social Enterprise London (2009), are "businesses which exist to address social or environmental need. . . . Rather than maximising profit for shareholders or owners, profits are reinvested into the community or back into the business."

When the Seventh Social Enterprise Conference was held at Harvard University in 2006, co-chair Caitrin Moran spotlighted the accelerating convergence between private, public, and nonprofit sectors in this field. "More than ever, social problems are being addressed not just by nonprofits, but by people and organizations in all sectors," she noted. "Involvement in social enterprise is not limited to those who pursue nonprofit careers. It includes those who work in big corporations, in government, and in nonprofits" (Harvard Business School 2006).

Business Models for Social Change

Anything like global sustainability will be impossible without the engagement—and radical restructuring—of business and markets. As the entrepreneur and philanthropist Pierre Omidyar put it, "I have learnt that if you want to have a global impact you can't ignore business. I don't mean corporate responsibility programs, but business models that provoke social change" (Byrne 2006). So where to look for such change and its agents? Time and again in periods of extraordinary volatility, disruption, and change, it turns out that the best place to look for clues to tomorrow's revolutionary business models is at the fringes of the current, increasingly dysfunctional system. In *Out of Control*, a groundbreaking book on twenty-first-century business models, author Kevin Kelly says, "In economic, ecological, evolutionary, and institutional models, a healthy fringe speeds adaptation, increases resilience, and is almost always the source of innovations" (1994, 468).

Although there is new momentum, this is not a new field of inquiry. Among the books already published are excellent works with titles like *How to Change the World, Profits with Principles,* and *Untapped* (which is subtitled *Creating Value in Underserved Markets*). It is clear that there is no standard-issue version of the entrepreneur, but there is a reasonable consensus on what entrepreneurs do. Through the practical exploitation of new ideas, they establish new ventures to deliver goods and services not currently supplied by existing markets. In recent years, however, there has been a growing recognition that there is a spectrum of enterprise, from the purely charitable to the purely commercial. Social and environmental entrepreneurs operate right across that spectrum, though—because of the immaturity of the markets they address—they currently tend to be skewed toward the nonprofit end.

On the purely charitable side, "customers" pay little or nothing, capital comes in the form of donations and grants, the workforce is largely made up of volunteers, and suppliers make in-kind donations. At the purely commercial end of the spectrum, by contrast, most transactions are at market rates. Interestingly however, many of the most noteworthy experiments these days are happening in the middle ground, where hybrid organizations pursue new forms of "blended value"—a combination of social, environmental, and economic value—and where less well-off customers are subsidized by better-off customers.

Against this backdrop, so-called social entrepreneurs develop and operate new ventures (social enterprises) that prioritize social returns on investment. They think in terms of—and aim to measure—social return on investment (SROI). They aspire to improve the quality of life for marginalized populations in terms of poverty, health, or education. One key reason why mainstream business needs to pay attention is that these people try to achieve higher leverage than conventional philanthropy and most nongovernmental organizations (NGOs), often aiming to transform the systems whose dysfunctions help create or aggravate major socioeconomic, environmental, or political problems.

Pursuing the Ideal

While entrepreneurs come from all sorts of geographical, cultural, educational, and religious backgrounds, they share certain characteristics that are immediately apparent the more one gets to know them. These common characteristics color their motivations and influence the kinds of organizations they establish. Social and environmental entrepreneurs share the same characteristics as all entrepreneurs—namely, they are innovative, resourceful, practical, and opportunistic. They delight in coming up with new products or services, or new approaches to delivering them to existing or undiscovered markets. But what motivates the social and environmental entrepreneur is not doing the deal but achieving the ideal. And because the ideal takes a lot longer to realize, these entrepreneurs tend to be in the game for the long haul, not until they can sell their venture to the highest bidder.

One of the burning questions that invariably comes up, particularly when successful business entrepreneurs meet successful social entrepreneurs, is, what motivates you? The implication behind the question is, if you have been so clever in achieving what you have accomplished, why haven't you applied your talents to making money? In response to that question, David Green—one of the world's outstanding examples of entrepreneurial genius involved in creating financial models that deliver quality health technologies to the world's poor—quipped:

> My reasons are purely selfish. I figure I have been put on this earth for a very short period of time. I could apply my talents to making lots of money, but where would I be at the end of my lifetime? I would much rather be remembered for having made a significant contribution to improving the world into which I came than for having made millions. (Elkington and Hartigan 2008, 4)

As interest grows in trying to solve the world's great social, environmental, and governance challenges, definitions—and the boundaries between fields—increasingly blur. In the process, the field of social entrepreneurship has become "a truly immense tent into which all manner of socially beneficial activities may fit," as two board members of the Skoll Foundation (dedicated to supporting social entrepreneurship)—Roger Martin, dean of the University of Toronto's Rotman School of Management, and Sally Osberg, the Foundation's president and CEO—recently put it. Instead, they argue, the real measure of social entrepreneurship is "direct action that generates a paradigm shift in the way a societal need is met" (SustainAbility n.d., 1). What such people do, in effect, is to identify an "unsatisfactory equilibrium" (Martin and Osberg 2007, 32).

Unreasonable People

Any proposed solutions seem improbable given the current consensus that the problems are to all intents and purposes beyond resolution. As a result, many people continue to see the world's leading social entrepreneurs—and, to a degree, those who invest in them—as unreasonable. In fact, a few years ago Muhammad Yunus, the world's leading social entrepreneur, best known as founder of the revolutionary Grameen Bank and winner of the 2006 Nobel Peace Prize, wryly described his breed as "70 percent crazy." (The Grameen Bank, or "village bank," was founded in 1976 and offers small loans to help impoverished people in Bangladesh achieve economic independence through self-employment; in January 2008 the bank opened a branch in the borough of Queens, New York.) It's extraordinary how often these entrepreneurs have been called crazy by the media, by colleagues, by friends, and even by family members. But they are crazy like the proverbial fox. They look for—and often find—solutions to insoluble problems in the most unlikely places.

Many are pioneering and helping map out future markets where most people would see only nightmare problems and risk. Think of it this way: whatever they may intend, these entrepreneurs are doing early market research on some of the biggest opportunities of the century. But they cannot tackle market failures alone. Instead their efforts need to be supported by all levels of government, by business, by the financial markets, and, crucially, by civil society organizations and ordinary citizens—by each and every one of us.

John ELKINGTON
SustainAbility and Volans Ventures

The author wishes to thank Pamela Hartigan, director of the Skoll Centre for Social Entrepreneurship at Oxford University's Said Business School.

See also in the *Berkshire Encyclopedia of Sustainability* Base of the Pyramid; CSR and CSR 2.0; Development, Sustainable; Investment, CleanTech; Investment, Socially Responsible (SRI); Natural Capitalism; Performance Metrics; Poverty; Sustainable Value Creation; Triple Bottom Line; United Nations Global Compact

FURTHER READING

Ashoka. (n.d.) Retrieved June 11, 2009, from http://www.ashoka.org/

Baderman, James, & Law, Justine. (2006). *Everyday legends: The ordinary people changing our world, the stories of 20 great UK social entrepreneurs.* York, UK: WW Publishing.

Bornstein, David. (2004). *How to change the world: Social entrepreneurs and the power of new ideas.* Oxford, UK: Oxford University Press.

Byrne, Fergal. (2006, March 24). Dinner with the FT: Auction man. Retrieved November 10, 2009, from http://www.omidyar.com/about_us/news/2006/03/24/dinner-with-ft-auction-man

Dees, J. Gregory, & Anderson, Beth Battle. (2006). Framing a theory of social entrepreneurship: Building on two schools of practice and thought. In Rachel Moser-Williams (Ed.), *Research on social entrepreneurship: Understanding and contributing to an emerging field* (pp. 39–66). ARNOVA Occasional Paper series, Vol. 1, No. 3. Washington, DC: The Aspen Institute.

Elkington, John, & Hartigan, Pamela. (2008). *The power of unreasonable people: How social entrepreneurs create markets that change the world.* Boston: Harvard Business School Press.

Hammond, Allen L.; Kramer, William J.; Katz, Robert S.; Tran, Julia T.; Walker, Courtland; World Resources Institute; & International Finance Corporation. (2007). *The next 4 billion: Market size and business strategy at the base of the pyramid.* Retrieved November 10, 2009, from http://www.wri.org/publication/the-next-4-billion

Harvard Business School. (2006). 2006 Social Enterprise Conference: Convergence across sectors. Retrieved December 22, 2009, from http://www.hbs.edu/socialenterprise/newsletter_archives/2006spring_5.html

Kelly, Kevin. (1994). *Out of control: The new biology of machines, social systems, and the economic world.* Reading, MA: Perseus Books.

Martin, Roger, & Osberg, Sally. (2007, Spring). Social entrepreneurship: The case for definition. *Stanford Social Innovation Review*, 28–39. Retrieved June 12, 2009, from http://www.skollfoundation.org/media/skoll_docs/2007SP_feature_martinosberg.pdf

Schwab Foundation for Social Entrepreneurship. (n.d.) Retrieved June 11, 2009, from http://www.schwabfound.org/sf/index.htm

Skoll Foundation. (n.d.). Retrieved June 11, 2009, from http://www.skollfoundation.org/

Social Enterprise London. (2009). Social enterprise: Definition. Retrieved December 22, 2009, from http://www.sel.org.uk/definition-of-se.aspx

SustainAbility. (n.d.). The business case for engaging social entrepreneurs. Retrieved January 7, 2010, from http://www.sustainability.com/downloads_public/BusinessCaseforEngagingSocialEntrepreneurs.pdf

Weiser, John; Kahane, Michele; Rochlin, Steve; & Landis, Jessica. (2006). *Untapped: Creating value in underserved markets.* San Francisco: Berrett-Koehler.

Stakeholder Theory

Stakeholder theory addresses the relationships between businesses and those individuals or groups that affect or are affected by the achievement of their objectives. According to this theory, companies that engage in a network of relationships with multiple stakeholders will improve their performance and viability. These stakeholders include environmental organizations that are increasing pressure on companies to improve their sustainability performance.

The term *stakeholder theory* was initially popularized by the professor of business administration R. Edward Freeman in his managerially oriented book *Strategic Management: A Stakeholder Approach* (1984). He adopted and elaborated on the term *stakeholder perspective*, which seems to have originated at the Stanford Research Institute in 1962. Freeman's original book essentially argued, as did his more current iteration with Jeffrey S. Harrison and Andrew C. Wicks, *Managing for Stakeholders: Business in the 21st Century* (2007), that companies would perform better, and hence be more sustainable over the long term, if they paid more attention to their stakeholders (those who affect or are affected by the actions of companies or organizations). Taking stakeholders into consideration was part of what Freeman considered a strategic approach. This approach was inherently managerial—that is, it was intended to help companies improve their performance and viability and be responsive to the interests, demands, and needs of stakeholders who could affect or be affected by that performance. From the perspective of ecological sustainability, environmentalists are among the key stakeholder groups that companies have to consider. Environmentalists place increasing pressure on companies to improve their sustainability performance in light of concerns about climate change, resource overuse, species loss, and other environmental issues.

In *Managing for Stakeholders*, Freeman, Harrison, and Wicks explained that business is about the interaction of stakeholders—employees, investors, customers, suppliers, and others, such as communities, governments, and the media—who both constitute the business itself and interact in ways that implement the business model. Stakeholder theory stands in contrast to theories of the firm, such as neoclassical economics, that place one constituency—shareholders—as the primary stakeholder of concern. Over time, stakeholder conceptualizations have moved from an initial conception of communication from the company to the stakeholder(s), in which the company held much of the power and was frequently pictured in a spoke-and-wheel pattern (with the company at the center of the wheel), to understanding that there is a more interactive or engaged network of relationships that companies must manage if they are to be effective.

This evolution from a decidedly one-way orientation toward a more interactive stance has resulted in new terminology in both theory and practice around issues of stakeholder engagement. Because of this shift, companies are sometimes willing to find ways to both give and get feedback about their activities from different constituencies that are important to them. The newer conception of stakeholder interactions presents a picture of the organization involved in a network of relationships, some of which are critical or primary, and others of which are less direct or secondary. In the realm of ecological sustainability, this shift has meant that companies more frequently engage external stakeholders, such as environmental groups, to hear their concerns and issues, provide feedback, and sometimes shift their business practices. Some companies, such as major chemical companies that have had significant sustainability concerns directed toward them in the past, have begun to seriously incorporate issues of ecological sustainability into their core strategies. They are building sustainability into what many practitioners calls their company DNA.

What Is a Stakeholder?

For most companies and other types of organizations, there are two main types of stakeholders: primary and secondary. Primary stakeholders of corporations are typically considered to be employees, customers, investors, and suppliers. These groups effectively constitute the firm and directly affect or are affected by it (Clarkson 1995). Secondary stakeholders are those groups and individuals that indirectly affect or are affected by a firm's business model, decisions, and actions. Secondary stakeholders are typically considered to be communities, government, and nongovernmental organizations (NGOs), such as external activists and environmental organizations, that are concerned about the company's activities and practices. Some individuals and groups that are less affected by the company's actions or have little interest in the company can legitimately be considered nonstakeholders for that entity. The specific individuals and groups considered to be stakeholders for any given organization differ by organization type and by the specific nature of the organization itself.

Although the environment is not actually a stakeholder, as it is not a person, it is often treated as though it were a stakeholder, because in some way or another all organizations use natural resources to accomplish their objectives. Natural-resource dependent organizations, such as extraction industry companies, would consider the natural environment a primary stakeholder, while more service-oriented companies would think of it more as a secondary stakeholder.

Stakeholders have a "stake" in the organizations of which they are stakeholders. From one perspective, a stake can be viewed as a claim that gives the stakeholder some sort of say over what goes on in the firm or over its impacts, or it can be viewed as a claim that gives the firm some sort of say over its stakeholders. Thus companies can claim that employees owe them certain levels of performance because they are being paid for their intellectual capital, and employees can claim, at least in theory, some sort of loyalty from the company in return for their loyalty to it. Customers can claim certain benefits related to the products and services they are purchasing based on those purchases, and their input can also affect both the nature and quality of those items. Such claims are sometimes based on expectations that are related to ethical principles such as rights (both legal and moral), justice, or fairness; utility (a form of cost-benefit analysis); or principles of care and character. External regulators, such as environmental agencies and NGOs, frequently place demands on companies to improve their environmental performance.

Another perspective on the meaning of *stake* is that stakeholders either have taken some sort of risk or made some sort of investment with respect to the company from which they expect a return. In this sense, stakeholders may have an interest or "stake" in an organization that is somehow at risk, depending on how well the organization performs. Thus investors put financial resources at risk in the firm and can legitimately claim some sort of return for making that investment. Employees can be said to invest human and intellectual capital (physical and/or mental resources) in the firm; customers place their trust in companies' products and services and put that trust at risk if they experience problems. Suppliers and communities can invest in infrastructure that is specific to a company, which is placed at risk if the company chooses to leave or to not use those resources. Depending on the company's business, these groups can either be primary stakeholders, if the company is an intensive user of natural resources, or secondary stakeholders, if the firm's core businesses are not ecologically demanding.

Typically, stakeholders' investments are tangible in that the Earth's resources are used in some way or other, but sometimes they are intangible, as in emotional bonds or ties that can exist between various stakeholders and an organization. Whatever its basis, the reciprocal nature of the relationship between an organization and its stakeholders is increasingly recognized. This recognition has resulted in new activities and terminology around stakeholder engagement, which implies that there is two-way interaction between the company and its stakeholders and, at least to some extent, recognition that there is a degree of influence or power on both sides, not only the company's side of the relationship. In addition, companies frequently view such stakeholder engagement as a means of creating opportunities for learning about the issues they face in society and, sometimes, as a way of providing insights into potential new business opportunities. Sometimes environmental activists will question a company's use of natural resources, creating a sort of "voice" for the natural environment and a platform for engagement on issues of sustainability.

As the notion of primary and secondary stakeholders indicates, different stakeholders have different priorities with respect to any given firm. Ronald Mitchell, Bradley Agle, and Donna Wood (1997) developed a model of stakeholder priorities based on three core variables—power, legitimacy, and urgency—putting primary stakeholders

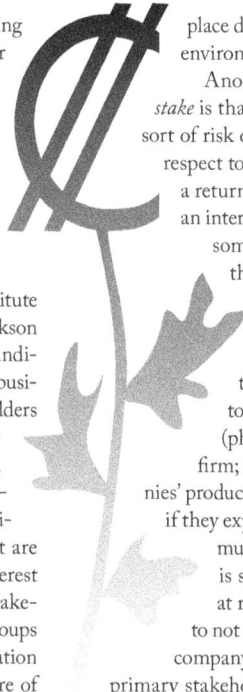

into the category of "definitive" stakeholders because they possess all three attributes. Other stakeholders, who are missing power, legitimacy, or urgency with respect to the company or an issue facing the company, have relatively less compelling means of getting the company's attention. Companies still need to be aware of all relevant stakeholders and their needs, demands, or interests if they hope to be able to deal with them successfully. For example, an environmental regulator has the capacity to become a definitive stakeholder if a company has a serious environmental problem that has come prominently to public attention and drawn regulatory concern. The situation would be urgent because of the public attention and legitimate because of possible regulatory violations, and the regulator would be powerful because of its enforcement capabilities.

This perspective on establishing priorities among stakeholders has the benefit of raising core issues around stakeholder theory. In particular, it raises the issue of power, which is not always equally shared between different constituencies and the company; the company typically has more power, resources, and clout. The other central issue is that of legitimacy, both for the firm and for different stakeholders with an interest in the firm's actions and decisions. In coping with stakeholder claims, risks, and investments, companies have to consider not only the legitimacy of the stakeholder's interest, but also whether its own legitimacy as an actor in society can be questioned on the basis of a decision or action it is considering. For example, although companies typically are larger than most environmental activist entities or NGOs, they increasingly find it necessary to respond when legitimate issues of the sustainability of resource use are raised by stakeholders concerned about the natural environment. At a broader level, the issue of climate change raised by many scientists and governments has created a context in which some large companies have developed comprehensive sustainability programs and are attempting significant internal change to deal with the stakeholder pressures they are experiencing.

Stakeholder Theory and Economic Theory

Stakeholder theory, or what can be called the stakeholder view of the firm, stands in contrast to more traditional economic views of the firm, such as the neoclassical economics view articulated most prominently by the late Milton Friedman. The economics perspective, or what might be called stockholder theory, argues essentially that the sole purpose of the firm is to maximize wealth for one stakeholder group—shareholders. In contrast, the stakeholder perspective argues for a fair return on the investments, claims, risks, and bonds of multiple stakeholders, contending that the company needs to pay attention to these constituencies in order to perform well.

Stakeholder theory can be viewed as an alternative to the stockholder-based theory emphasized in traditional economics. As a theory of the firm, stakeholder theory argues that the fact that firms can function at all is because of their embedment with stakeholders, and that their performance is directly related to the network of relationships that effectively constitute the firm, the values that are brought to those relationships, and how these relationships allow the firm to carry out its business model. In other words, stakeholder theory recognizes the contributions of multiple stakeholders to firm performance, while traditional economic theory essentially limits those contributions to financial ones, "de-peopling" the firm in a sense.

Values, Ethics, and Stakeholder Theory

Stakeholder theory is frequently associated with ethics, although Freeman intended it initially as a managerial approach with an implicit ethic. The link between ethics, values, and stakeholders occurs in the context of the relationships that are developed through a stakeholder lens. Different stakeholders bring different sets of expectations and values to a given company or organization. Companies and organizations respond to their stakeholders in different ways, and their responses reflect their own values and expectations about the appropriate roles that a given stakeholder group might play.

To some extent, managers' decisions and choices always reflect their own and the organization's values. But there is a decided difference between decisions that are made solely with economic or financial considerations in mind, with and for a limited stakeholder set (the shareholders), and decisions that are made with the interests of a wider range of stakeholder considerations. For example, layoffs of employees can seem like the "right thing to do" when only economic considerations are at play, but they may be thought of quite differently when lasting employee relationships, loyalty, and human or ecological costs are part of the equation. Similarly, supply chain relationships may involve arms-length involvement, constant downward price pressures, and resulting sweatshop working conditions, child labor, and serious environmental problems when low cost at any price is the goal. When issues of NGO relationships, supplier relations, and company reputation are taken into account, quite different decisions might be made about what kinds of working conditions are acceptable in suppliers' factories and how the environment is taken into account. The threat of climate change to humanity has made paying attention to sustainability a necessary element of strategy and practice for many companies.

These examples illustrate that stakeholder thinking raises difficult issues about values and objectives that may not always be easily compatible. It is the struggle to find strategies and operating practices that respect fundamental values like human rights and the goal of ecological sustainability that has fundamentally integrated stakeholder theory and the ethics associated with business strategies and practices.

Stakeholder Engagement, Networks, and Social Capital

Companies pursuing stakeholder-engagement strategies develop specific means of interacting with and getting feedback from their stakeholders. Some of these strategies are traditional business practices, such as employee suggestion boxes, employee and customer surveys, and marketing studies. Many companies are involved in collaborative and cooperative endeavors, including multisector alliances, typically aimed at solving social problems, and sometimes called public-private, social, or multistakeholder partnerships or collaborations.

Multistakeholder dialogues are another increasingly popular form of stakeholder engagement. Typically these are forums where stakeholders from different sectors, including government, civil-society organizations, NGOs, educational or academic institutions, and businesses, come together around common problems. One major focus of such dialogues is climate change and the push toward more sustainable enterprise; others can include industry-specific issues, such as how drug companies should engage with the HIV/AIDS crisis in Africa, human and labor rights, and education. Such collaborative engagement with stakeholders is an important way for many companies to build trust with their stakeholders, which helps them establish strong and supportive networks in locales where they operate. This type of collaboration also enhances social capital among all the participants in the engagement or network. Social capital is a sort of social "glue" that connects individuals and groups in a system, providing a degree of coherence (Putnam 2000). Economist Michael Porter (1998) studied the development and success of companies located within networks or "clusters" of related businesses that were supported by other enterprises. He found that companies in clusters tend to do better than others, providing strong support for the importance of social capital in company performance and further supporting the need for companies to build positive stakeholder relationships of all sorts. Similarly, companies in various industries tend to follow the example of leading companies, thus, for example, when a leading chemical company has instituted a comprehensive sustainability program, it can become important for competitors to follow their lead and also implement sustainability initiatives.

Stakeholder Responsibilities

The relationship between stakeholders and companies goes in two directions, with stakeholders influencing companies and companies influencing stakeholders. The management researcher Jeff Frooman (1999) called the tactics that stakeholders use to change companies "stakeholder influence strategies." Some of these influence strategies come from critical outsiders like NGOs that use tactics like boycotts, letter-writing campaigns, and student involvement to call attention to issues that concern them. Other influence strategies might include the tactics of concerned investors who submit shareholder resolutions calling on management to make specified changes.

For both companies and stakeholder groups, the interaction will be unique to the specific situation and nature of the existing or desired relationships. Stakeholders are increasingly demanding that companies pay attention to issues of responsibility, accountability, and transparency, often with respect to the environment as well as employee, customer, and financial performance. Two important reasons that companies need to respond to stakeholders with integrity are reputation and transparency. There is increasing emphasis on corporate reputation because much of a company's value in the twenty-first century resides in intangible assets like goodwill, human or intellectual capital, and innovative capacity. Companies spend millions of dollars to develop both product and corporate brands, and damage to the reputation of those brands can be significant, very costly, and hard to repair. Listening to stakeholders provides an important mechanism to avoid reputational issues proactively, or even interactively if the company is explicitly engaging with stakeholders.

Another major reason for companies' responsiveness to stakeholders is the increased—and sometimes unwitting—transparency provided by electronic communication technologies like the Internet and other media. Stakeholders sometimes demand that companies be transparent about their decisions and actions, as well as the outcomes of those

decisions. Even when companies would prefer that certain things were not publicly known, electronic communication technologies and media make it increasingly difficult to keep things hidden, particularly when critical stakeholders are paying attention to corporate actions. Hence transparency exists whether or not companies themselves deliberately become transparent, simply because it is easier for observers to find out—and communicate widely—what is going on. Today that type of transparency would apply in, for example, the case of a chemical spill or toxic release, or what observers perceive to be excessive or abusive use of natural resources, as happened when an activist publicized Coca Cola's use of India's limited water resources broadly on the Internet; the company was pressured into developing a comprehensive and quite progressive water policy.

Whatever stakeholders do, it is increasingly recognized that they also bear responsibilities for being ethical, proactive, and honest in their engagements with companies. Companies have also come to realize that they are better off understanding what their stakeholders need and want from them, and that sometimes they can forestall problems that otherwise might come as a surprise by directly engaging with stakeholders. With issues of climate change and ecological sustainability now demonstrated to be central to the long-term health and welfare of humanity, many progressive companies are proactively working to build sustainability into their products, services, and operations. These progressive companies are responding to both societal and stakeholder concerns about sustainability and setting an example for companies and other types of enterprise that are slower to respond to these issues.

Sandra WADDOCK

Carroll School of Management, Boston College

See also in the *Berkshire Encyclopedia of Sustainability* Activism—NGOs; Corporate Citizenship; CSR and CSR 2.0; Ecological Economics; Ecosystem Services; Education, Business; Financial Services Industry; Human Rights; Investment, Socially Responsible (SRI); Leadership; Public–Private Partnerships; Performance Metrics; Risk Management; Social Enterprise; Supply Chain Management; Sustainable Value Creation; True Cost Economics

FURTHER READING

Andriof, Jörg, & Waddock, Sandra. (2002). Unfolding stakeholder engagement. In Jörg Andriof, Sandra Waddock, Bryan Husted, & Sandra Rahman (Eds.), *Unfolding stakeholder thinking* (pp. 19–42). Sheffield, UK: Greenleaf.

Andriof, Jörg; Waddock, Sandra; Husted, Bryan; & Rahman, Sandra. (Eds.). (2003). *Unfolding stakeholder thinking 2: Relationships, communication, reporting and performance.* Sheffield, UK: Greenleaf.

Clarkson, Max B. E. (1995). A stakeholder framework for analyzing and evaluating corporate social performance. *Academy of Management Review, 20*(1), 92–117.

Donaldson, Thomas, & Preston, Lee E. (1995). The stakeholder theory of the corporation: Concepts, evidence, and implications. *Academy of Management Review, 20*(1), 65–91.

Epstein, Edwin M. (1987). The corporate social policy process: Beyond business ethics, corporate social responsibility, and corporate social responsiveness. *California Management Review, 29*(3), 99–114.

Epstein, Edwin M. (1998). Business ethics and corporate social policy: Reflections on an intellectual journey, 1964–1996, and beyond. *Business and Society, 37*(1), 7–39.

Freeman, R. Edward. (1984). *Strategic management: A stakeholder approach.* Boston: Pitman/Ballinger.

Freeman, R. Edward. (1999). Divergent stakeholder theory. *Academy of Management Review, 24*(2), 233–236.

Freeman, R. Edward; Harrison, Jeffrey; & Wicks, Andrew. (2007). *Managing for stakeholders: Business in the 21st century.* New Haven, CT: Yale University Press.

Frooman, Jeff. (1999). Stakeholder influence strategies. *Academy of Management Review, 42*(2), 191–205.

Handy, Charles. (2002, December). What's a business for? Retrieved February 1, 2010, from http://www.growthinternational.com/resources/Charles+Handy+HBR+Dec+02.pdf

Jones, Thomas M. (1995). Instrumental stakeholder theory: A synthesis of ethics and economics. *Academy of Management Review, 20*(20), 404–437.

Jones, Thomas M., & Wicks, Andrew C. (1999). Convergent stakeholder theory. *Academy of Management Review, 24*(2), 206–221.

Mitchell, Ronald K.; Agle, Bradley R.; & Wood, Donna J. (1997). Toward a theory of stakeholder identification and salience: Defining the principle of who and what really counts. *Academy of Management Review, 22*(4), 853–886.

Porter, Michael E. (1998). Clusters and the new economics of competition. Retrieved February 1, 2010, from http://www.econ-pol.unisi.it/didattica/ecreti/Porter1998.pdf

Putnam, Robert D. (2000). *Bowling alone: The collapse and revival of American community.* New York: Simon & Schuster.

Supply Chain Management

Virtually all businesses depend on supply chains to move their products from idea to reality and from point A to point B. Globalization, outsourcing, and increased stakeholder expectations all factor into the question of how supply chains may be managed to be more sustainable in the long run. A comprehensive product life cycle management approach can help companies to reduce the environmental footprint of their supply chains while protecting the rights of workers in developing countries.

Increased global competition and international sourcing have magnified the importance of supply chain management (SCM) as a core competency for major manufacturing firms. Supply chains are increasingly seen as strategic assets, and companies are placing greater emphasis on collaboration with suppliers and customers that are part of their "business ecosystem." The scope of SCM is expanding to include all of the business processes involved in fulfilling customer expectations, from product development to end-of-life disposition. As a result, companies are assigning supply chain specialists to the cross-functional teams that manage these business processes. This broader "value chain" perspective of SCM encompasses not only physical assets, such as facilities and vehicles, but also intangible elements such as knowledge and relationships. Accordingly, SCM has been defined as "the integration of key business processes from end user through original suppliers, which provides products, services, and information that add value for customers and other stakeholders" (Lambert 2009, 2).

From this broad perspective, there are a number of global trends that have accentuated the importance of sustainability and corporate responsibility in SCM.

- Globalization has raised concerns about inequities between rich and poor countries, as well as adverse environmental impacts such as energy consumption and greenhouse gas emissions (International Monetary Fund 2002). Tensions between economic opportunities and environmental and social concerns can be obstacles to global expansion, while varying regulatory requirements and cultural barriers tend to complicate the acquisition and integration of international businesses.

- Outsourcing has blurred the boundaries of the enterprise, and companies are challenged to assure that their suppliers and service providers are complying with safety and sustainability expectations. Moreover, outsourcing may simply shift environmental burdens such as carbon emissions to less developed nations. Incidents such as discovery of corrupt labor practices and contamination of product constituents have raised public concerns and given rise to renewed emphasis on supplier auditing and due diligence. Companies are increasingly expected to disclose the origins of products, including raw materials, and the conditions under which they were manufactured.

- Government directives in the European Union (EU) and elsewhere have invoked the doctrine of "extended producer responsibility" in the form of end-of-life product recovery requirements, often called "product take-back." For example, the EU End-of-Life Vehicles directive of 2000 is aimed at reducing the waste generated by scrapped motor vehicles, while the EU Waste Electrical and Electronic Equipment directive of 2003 requires take-back of electronic products such as televisions, computers, and cellular phones. These policies have stimulated adoption of "reverse logistics" (Guide and Van Wassenhove 2002) and have prompted changes in product development practices throughout the affected supply chains, including design for recovery, reuse, or remanufacture of obsolete products, components, materials, and packaging.

- The adoption of "lean" manufacturing approaches, such as "just-in-time" replenishment, has made global supply chains more susceptible to business interruption because their buffers and reserve capacity have been diminished. Supply chains are vulnerable to a variety of disruptions, including deliberate threats, technological failures, and natural disasters. These threats call for heightened awareness and rapid recovery capabilities; they also create opportunities for more agile companies to take advantage of openings for market penetration and growth. Advanced information technology now enables global tracking of assets and shipments, using technologies such as radio frequency identification (RFID) tags. The capacity to monitor market fluctuations, communicate seamlessly with suppliers or customers, and control the flow of products and materials enables real-time, "adaptive" responses to changing supply and demand patterns, thus reducing wasted resources and increasing supply chain resilience (Fiksel 2007).

These trends have magnified the importance of corporate commitments to sustainability, social responsibility, transparency, and responsiveness to stakeholder expectations. Aside from reducing their supply chain environmental footprints, corporations are being held accountable for upholding ethical standards, respecting diversity, and demonstrating concern for employee and community well-being. A company's brand image and reputation can be deeply influenced—either positively or negatively—by the perceptions of customers and other stakeholders.

Linking Sustainability to Business Value

Supply chain business processes such as sourcing, inventory management, warehousing, logistics, and distribution are increasingly viewed as strategic levers in enhancing business competitiveness. Thanks to the Dow Jones Sustainability Indexes and similar rating initiatives, financial analysts have recognized that there is a correlation between shareholder value in capital markets and excellence in sustainability, including both social responsibility and environmental management. Specifically, there are two major categories of business value creation associated with improved sustainability performance.

Avoidance of Costs and Liabilities

The traditional approach to environmental, health, and safety management involves compliance with regulations and standards, minimization of product or process-related risks, and stewardship of natural resources. Sustainable business practices such as pollution prevention, reduction

in hazardous materials use, waste minimization, and improvements in material logistics (e.g., pallet geometry) are important contributors to reducing both operating and capital costs. Paying attention to social responsibility and stakeholder satisfaction also helps to protect a company's reputation and avoid costly business interruptions.

To avoid costs and liabilities, companies have pursued a number of core business practices, as illustrated by the following examples.

- **Assure compliance** of products and business processes with laws, applicable regulations, and industry standards. Texas Instruments anticipated its customers' needs by developing a systematic process for assuring compliance with European Union (EU) requirements regarding banned and restricted substances.
- **Minimize risks** and maintain business continuity by assuring product and process safety throughout the supply chain. Motorola's distribution managers discovered that they could reduce both occupational injuries and solid waste disposal by controlling the quality of incoming wooden pallets from suppliers, yielding estimated savings in lost time and expenses of over $5 million per year (GEMI 2004, 9).
- **Maintain health** and well-being both for employees and local communities through responsible management of operating sites. Abbott Laboratories reduced contractor safety incidents to well below the industry average by integrating safety protocols into its automated contractor performance management system.
- **Protect the environment**, including public health and natural resources, through waste elimination, pollution prevention, and ecological stewardship. FedEx redesigned its overnight letter packaging to utilize 100 percent recycled fiber, strengthening its environmental leadership without compromising product performance or long-term costs.

Economic Value Creation

A more integrated approach to value creation is evident in the increasing level of collaboration between environmental managers and other groups, working in cross-functional teams. The rate of material throughput in industrial supply chains is the single most important driver of (a) operating costs, (b) consumption of energy, water, and other needed resources, and (c) generation of waste and emissions. There are significant business incentives for companies to embrace sustainable SCM practices that reduce the overall flow of materials through the value chain. New technologies such as process intensification and microreactors have demonstrated the potential for order of magnitude increases in process yield and capital productivity.

There are several actions that businesses can undertake to achieve social and environmental benefits:

- **Raise productivity** through material conservation, energy efficiency, and conversion of wastes into byproducts. Intel has saved millions of dollars annually by developing lighter-weight plastic trays used in the fabrication and delivery of its microprocessor units (GEMI 2004, iii). The company is also working with customers to develop closed loop systems for reuse of the trays.
- **Encourage collaboration** among customers, suppliers, and other stakeholders that influence supply chain effectiveness and license to operate. A global coalition, led by HP, Intel, and others, created a uniform Electronic Industry Citizenship Code for suppliers. The code sets forth principles for managing environmental releases, workplace health and safety, labor practices, and business ethics, and includes supplier assessment and auditing procedures.
- **Support innovation** in products, services, and technologies that enhance product differentiation, customer satisfaction, and stakeholder confidence. Eastman Kodak uses "Design for Environment" principles that have helped reduce the weight of its digital cameras while dramatically improving its products' performance.
- **Enable growth** via acquisition, increased market share, or access to new markets by conforming to market expectations such as ecolabeling and ISO 14001 registration. Owens Corning has achieved rapid growth for Atticat fiberglass insulation, which was Cradle to Cradle Certified at the Silver level. (Cradle to Cradle certification is given to companies with production processes and practices that are sustainable and support the recirculation and reuse of materials.) The product utilizes 60 percent recycled material, contains no toxic binder chemicals, and is highly compressible for superior transportation efficiency.

Thus, rather than sustainability issues placing constraints upon the supply chain, environmental and social performance improvements are often consistent with industry efforts to increase supply chain speed, efficiency, effectiveness, and continuity.

Product Life Cycle Management

The vast majority of supply chain environmental impacts, including resource consumption and waste generation, are invisible to product consumers. Life cycle assessment (LCA) methods are frequently used to quantify the "cradle to cradle" environmental burdens of supply chain processes. To incorporate sustainability thinking into SCM, it is essential for companies to consider the *full life cycle* of their products, including all of the supply chain processes involved in sourcing, production, distribution, use, and recovery of the products. The vast majority of supply chain environmental impacts, including resource consumption and waste generation, are invisible to product consumers. In a typical product life cycle, roughly 95 percent of the material throughput is released to the environment in the form of trash, wastewater, and airborne emissions—mainly carbon dioxide. Overall, about 20 billion tons of industrial wastes are generated annually in the United States, and over a third of these are hazardous wastes. This amounts to about 60 tons per capita, by far the highest in the world (Fiksel 2009, 5). Continuation of these patterns threatens to exceed the capacity of ecosystems in terms of resource production and waste absorption, and also poses potential threats to global climate, vegetation, and agriculture.

Increasing awareness of sustainability concerns has led to the development of various methods for estimating the "environmental footprint" associated with supply chain operations. The term "footprint" may connote a single metric, such as a "carbon footprint," or a collection of indicators representing different environmental burdens (such as energy use, solid waste, and air emissions). To estimate a life cycle footprint requires careful definition of scope and boundaries. For example, a material footprint may include only feedstock and supplies used in company operations, may encompass broader supplier and customer activities, or may extend to ecosystem goods and services such as biomass (wood, fish) or fresh water. While efforts to measure total ecosystem service consumption are rare, many companies are beginning to assess their water footprints.

According to the World Business Council for Sustainable Development (WBCSD) publication *The Greenhouse Gas Protocol* (2004), the most common indicator is the carbon footprint, which measures greenhouse gas emissions in terms of carbon dioxide equivalents. The majority of carbon footprint estimates, however, only quantify a company's direct use of energy in the form of fuel or electricity. If a typical company considers all of the energy expended in the supply chain to provide purchased goods and services, its overall carbon footprint can be as much as ten to twenty times larger. A number of organizations, including the World Business Council for Sustainable Development, the World Resources Institute, and the Carbon Trust, have launched initiatives to produce international standards for product life cycle accounting and corporate value chain accounting, expected to be released in 2010.

Having a baseline environmental footprint enables a company to investigate cost-effective opportunities for footprint reduction. Depending on geographic locations and the type of facilities, certain companies in the supply chain may be in a much better position than others to achieve energy and material conservation. The following are examples of such opportunities (Fiksel 2009).

- **Reduce the procurement footprint**—Many companies have begun to examine the environmental practices of their suppliers and encourage greater energy and material efficiency, which also tends to lower procurement costs. The federal government and many state governments have introduced environmentally preferable purchasing guidelines that can be utilized by private-sector decision makers. For example, Walmart has developed sustainability scorecards for packaging and energy use, and has requested environmental performance improvements from all of its suppliers.

- **Reduce the operational resource footprint—** Companies have found a great deal of "low-hanging fruit" (or easily attainable goals) by tightening up energy management practices (heating, cooling, and lighting systems) and materials management practices (maintenance, inventory, and waste management). Newer facilities are being designed with recycled materials and advanced energy-saving features, as interest in "green building" has mushroomed. But the largest gains in resource conservation come from redesigning production processes to reduce throughput requirements and install more efficient equipment. From 2005 to 2007, General Electric conducted a "Lean and Energy" initiative that has yielded over 250,000 metric tons in greenhouse gas reductions and $70 million in energy cost savings.

- **Reduce transportation requirements—**It is common for products or components to go through several shipment stages by various modes before arriving at their ultimate destinations, which adds to supply chain costs as well as packaging and energy consumption. Options for increasing transportation efficiency include shipping outsourced modules directly from the supplier to the final customer; reducing transportation urgency by allowing greater lead times; redesigning the product geometry, packaging volume, or stacking configuration so that less space is wasted; and reducing temperature requirements or other energy-consuming constraints.

- **Reduce consumption of shipping containers—**In many supply chains, disposal of used containers such as shipping pallets is a major source of solid waste. Significant cost savings and material efficiency can be achieved by designing containers that can be recovered and reused for the same application. In some cases, containers can be eliminated. Duke Energy was able to redesign the cable storage and handling systems used for electric power lines so that wooden reels were no longer necessary, saving over $650,000 per year.

- **Reduce waste generation—**Supply chain throughput can be reduced by identifying and minimizing nonproduct output—by recycling pallets, solvents, catalysts, scrap materials, or process water. Lean process design can help to reduce unnecessary inventory, which requires extra resources and can lead to product spoilage and waste.

- **Ensure supply integrity—**The globalization of material procurement has created vulnerabilities in the supply chain for many products, and there have been many examples of product contamination with harmful substances (for example, melamine from China). To avoid such incidents, manufacturers should establish programs to screen and audit their suppliers, and ensure that all product constituents can be obtained from reliable sources.

- **Use refurbished components—**Durable products can be manufactured with refurbished components, resulting in lower costs and reduced material consumption, often with the same level of quality as products manufactured with brand-new components. Ideally companies can develop a reverse logistics system whereby spent materials and used components can be recovered, reprocessed, and recycled back into their supply chain. For instance, Caterpillar has established a profitable Remanufacturing Division that exchanges used engines for new ones.

- **Recover materials at "end of life"—**When products are disassembled, materials and components need to be sorted into different categories for purposes of recovery and recycling; companies can facilitate material identification by means of coding or marking. As recycling technologies and materials science improve, we are reaching the point where recyclable materials can be found for virtually any application. Many industries have formed alliances to support establishment of a recycling infrastructure for obsolete products and packaging.

Generally, there are two different supply chain perspectives that need to be balanced in product life cycle management—upstream and downstream. The upstream view, focusing on suppliers, is mainly concerned with maximizing operating efficiency, anticipating safety and security risks to assure business continuity, and minimizing the environmental footprint in terms of resource utilization. The downstream view, focusing on customers, is mainly concerned with assuring that the product is used safely, delivers value to the customer, and is properly managed at end of life.

Future Opportunities

Perhaps the greatest opportunity for quantum improvements in sustainability is collaboration between customers and suppliers to jointly explore the redesign of supply chain operations. Collaborative innovation can enable solutions that might not have been possible if the parties worked separately. For example, electronic device manufacturers are limited by the performance characteristics of available materials and components, while chipmakers are constrained by the technologies of fabrication equipment. By lifting constraints and pooling their talents, they can develop innovative technologies that benefit the entire value-added chain, such as developing new fabrication processes that eliminate the use of chemical solvents.

One promising approach is based on mimicking nature through the practice of "industrial ecology." Natural systems generate virtually no waste; dead biomass provides nutrients for microorganisms, which in turn enrich the soil. Similarly, industrial systems can convert waste materials from production or consumption activities into "food" for industrial processes. Rather than discarding their wastes, companies can discover alternative uses in their own supply chain or in other industry sectors, and thus convert them into by-products. By substituting local waste streams for virgin material and energy inputs, companies are able not only to achieve cost savings but also to reduce their supply chain footprints. Over the past decade, the US Business Council for Sustainable Development (2009) has stimulated adoption of this approach, called "by-product synergy," to a number of US metropolitan areas and has inspired the development of a national network in the United Kingdom called the National Industrial Symbiosis Program.

Another increasingly common style of collaboration is the formation of joint sustainability initiatives among companies within an industry sector, often including direct competitors. Examples include the Beverage Industry Environmental Roundtable, the Electric Utility Sustainable Supply Chain Alliance, the Pharmaceutical Supply Chain Initiative, and the Electronic Industry Citizenship Coalition, mentioned above. In each case, the parties have decided that it makes more sense to work collectively on managing environmental and social performance in their upstream supply networks. In addition, many companies and industry groups are forming alliances with nongovernmental organizations that have traditionally been critical of industry. These engagements have helped to promote creative dialogue about potential solutions and have enabled companies to leverage the competencies and credibility of external groups with diverse perspectives. Examples include partnerships of the Environmental Defense Fund with SC Johnson Wax, Sierra Club with Clorox, and World Wildlife Fund with Coca-Cola.

A Global Commerce Initiative/Capgemini study suggested that by 2016, supply chains would be characterized by increased collaboration among supply chain participants, including sharing of information, sharing of physical assets such as warehousing and transport channels, and more efficient consolidation of shipments for final delivery. The estimated benefits of such a supply chain redesign, even without energy technology improvements, include a 30 percent reduction in transport costs per pallet, 20 percent reduction in handling costs per pallet, 40 percent reduction in lead time, 25 percent reduction in carbon dioxide emissions per pallet, and improved on-shelf availability (Global Commerce Initiative/Capgemini 2008, 42). While creating a more efficient infrastructure is laudable,

these incremental gains are not sufficient to offset rising demand due to population growth, economic development, and urbanization around the world. Fundamental innovations will be needed to enable sustainable growth, such as "dematerialization" of supply chains by converting physical products into knowledge-based services.

Joseph FIKSEL
The Ohio State University

See also in the *Berkshire Encyclopedia of Sustainability* Chemistry, Green; Cradle to Cradle; Design, Industrial; Energy Efficiency; Facilities Management; Integrated Product Development (IPD); Investment, Socially Responsible (SRI); Life cycle Assessments (LCAs); Manufacturing Practices; Natural Step Framework, The (TNSF); Product-Service Systems (PSSs); Remanufacturing; Risk Management; Stakeholder Theory; Sustainable Value Creation; Transparency

FURTHER READING

Fiksel, Joseph. (2007). Sustainability and resilience: Toward a systems approach. *IEEE Management Review, 35*(3), 5–15.

Fiksel. Joseph. (2009). *Design for environment: A guide to sustainable product development* (2nd ed.). New York: McGraw-Hill.

Fiksel, Joseph; Low, Jonathan; & Thomas, Jim. (2004). Linking sustainability to shareholder value. *Environmental Management, 34*(1), 19–25.

Fiksel, Joseph; Lambert Douglas M.; Artman, Les B.; Harris, John A.; & Share, Hugh M. (2004, July 1). Environmental excellence: The new supply chain edge. *Supply Chain Management Review.* Retrieved September 2, 2009, from http://www.scmr.com/article/CA629971.html

Guide, V. Daniel R., Jr., & Van Wassenhove, Luk N. (2002) The reverse supply chain. *Harvard Business Review, 80*(2), 25–26.

Global Commerce Initiative/Capgemini. (2008). *Future supply chain 2016: Serving consumers in a sustainable way.* Retrieved September 2, 2009, from http://gci-net.org/gci/content/e29/e5015/Documents5017/item_d5641/2016_Future_Supply_Chain_Report-full.pdf

Global Environmental Management Initiative (GEMI). (2004). *Forging new links: Enhancing supply chain value through environmental excellence.* Retrieved September 19, 2009, from http://www.gemi.org/resources/GEMI-ForgingNewLinks-June04.PDF

International Monetary Fund. (2002). Globalization: Threat or opportunity. Retrieved September 2, 2009, from http://www.imf.org/external/np/exr/ib/2000/041200to.htm

Lambert, Douglas M.; Cooper, Martha C.; & Pagh, Janus D. (1998). Supply chain management: Implementation issues and research opportunities. *The International Journal of Logistics Management, 9*(2), 1–20.

Lambert, Douglas M. (2009). *Supply chain management: Processes, partnerships, performance* (2nd ed.). Sarasota, FL: Supply Chain Management Institute.

US Business Council for Sustainable Development. (2009). By-product synergy. Retrieved September 2, 2009, from http://www.usbcsd.org/byproductsynergy.asp

World Business Council for Sustainable Development. (2004). *The greenhouse gas protocol: A corporate accounting and reporting standard* (Rev. ed.). Retrieved September 2, 2009, from http://www.ghgprotocol.org/files/ghg-protocol-revised.pdf

Sustainable Value Creation

In business, the meaning of sustainability has changed since the 1980s. Originally it indicated the ability to remain profitable over time; it now includes social and environmental issues as well as economic ones. The global context has changed, and, with many major corporations leading the way, businesses that promote sustainability must acknowledge their responsibility to both shareholders and stakeholders to succeed.

In the business world, the term *sustainable* has long been associated with economic viability. *Sustain-ability* is usually taken to be the ability to sustain shareholder returns above the cost of capital. A sustainable company is one that is profitable over time.

The terms *society* and *ecology*, when used in the context of business, have long been associated with compliance to government regulations and the moral obligation of companies to be environmentally and socially responsible. They represent the obligatory costs of doing business.

This backdrop of meanings has contributed to confusion and even rejection by business managers of the composite term *environmental and social sustainability*. Executives everywhere are confronted with it, yet they do not understand what it means for their company, and they certainly don't see it as a source of strategic advantage. They don't see how growing societal constraints can be a matter for the CEO agenda.

Yet the global competitive context has changed to make environmental and social sustainability a huge business opportunity—for those executives who have the right knowledge and competencies. *Sustainable value*, a term coined by Chris Laszlo in his 2003 book *The Sustainable Company*, implies that a company can address the "social and environmental dimensions of their business activities" (Laszlo 2008, 119) and create value for both shareholders

and stakeholders. Leading companies are jumping on the sustainability bandwagon: just a few global players who have recently done so include DuPont, General Electric, Walmart, Marks & Spencer, Toyota, Unilever, Danone, Alcoa, Philips, and JPMorgan Chase. They are not only "doing well by doing good," they are doing better as a result (Laszlo 2008).

A New Competitive Context

Since the 1990s, massive changes in the competitive landscape have increased the influence of a broad range of stakeholders, from nongovernmental organizations (NGOs) and activist bloggers to the media and government regulators (Assadourian 2005). Low-cost communications and the sheer availability of information have educated the general public and increased its awareness of environmental and social issues. Corporate disasters from Bhopal to Enron have sown a mistrust of big business, while tougher government regulations and new environmental laws have raised the requirements (and costs) of operations. Companies find it increasingly difficult to hide environmental and social transgressions, even in far-flung markets where the risk of discovery—and subsequent YouTube exposure—is ever present.

As a result of these trends, stakeholders instantly and globally access information about a company, mobilizing against those seen as doing wrong and enhancing the reputation of those seen as leading positive change.

A separate but immensely important development is the rise of intangible value as a component of stock price performance. The economist Baruch Lev (2001) has shown the extent to which accounting value has fallen as a driver of market capitalization—from 70 percent in 1900 to 30 percent in 2000—while intangibles such as goodwill, knowledge, brand value, and strategic relationships have risen accordingly (Low and Kalafut 2002).

A growing number of CEOs understand that their company's environmental, social, and governance performance affect their ability to attract and retain talented employees, drive innovation, and enhance corporate reputation. Such intangibles help in turn to differentiate their company's offering, leading to superior earnings and share price. Today the value created or destroyed for stakeholders carries strategic business risks or opportunities, demanding that business leaders rethink environmental and social sustainability in terms of value creation.

The Sustainable Value Framework

Stakeholder value requires managers to think "outside-in" about how their companies create and sustain competitive advantage. Outside-in thinking, which sees the world from the perspective of stakeholders, is a powerful new lens through which managers can discover new business opportunities and risks. Leaders who engage stakeholders and proactively address stakeholder issues can better anticipate changes in the business environment, reducing the risk of being unpleasantly surprised by emerging societal

expectations. Ultimately, stronger stakeholder engagement allows leading companies to discover new sources of value through innovation.

Figure 1 (below) describes company performance along two axes—shareholder value and stakeholder value. Shareholder value is exemplified by increased dividends and stock prices for company "owners"; stakeholder value emphasizes responsibility to all the stakeholders—employees, customers, community, and shareholders—over profitability and "is created when a business adds to the capital or well-being of its stakeholders" (Laszlo 2008, 120). Managing in two dimensions represents a fundamental shift in how managers think about business performance. In this framework, companies that deliver value to shareholders while destroying value for other stakeholders have a fundamentally flawed business model, while those that create value for stakeholders are cultivating sources of extra value that can fuel competitive advantage for years to come. Sustainable value occurs only when a company creates value that is positive for its shareholders and its stakeholders.

Starting in the upper left of Figure 1 and moving counterclockwise, consider the following four cases of value creation.

Figure 1. The Sustainable Value Framework

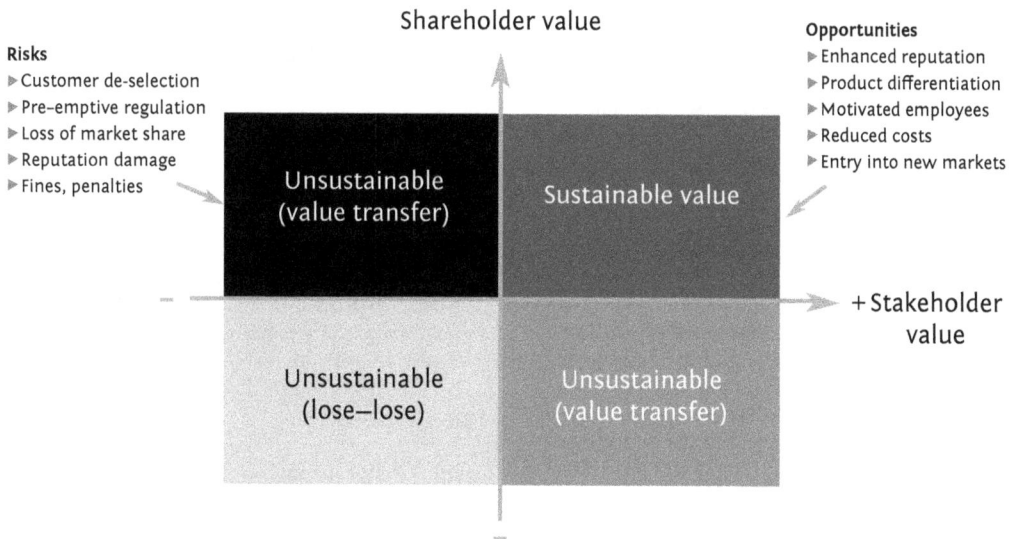

Source: Laszlo 2003, 126.

Sustainable value (top right) is created only when both shareholder and stakeholder values are incorporated by business, resulting in positive opportunities for all interested parties. Unfocused charity and action by well-intentioned environmentalists (for instance, actions that cause a business to go bankrupt) fall into the bottom right sector. A business that pays no heed to societal or environmental concerns and pays the price in lost customers falls into the top left sector. Actions that benefit neither the shareholders nor the stakeholders (the least desirable situation) fall into the bottom left sector.

Upper left quadrant: When value is transferred from stakeholders to shareholders, the stakeholders represent a risk to the future of the business. Leaded paint and asbestos are historical examples; today, carbon dioxide emissions from coal-fired power plants, phthalates in cosmetics, toxic additives in children's toys, volatile organic compounds in carpet adhesives and paints, heavy metals in fabric dyes, and lead solder and brominated flame retardants in consumer electronics are examples of products that create risks to employees, customers, and society even while they create value for shareholders. Companies that avoid environmental regulations in their home markets by exporting production to countries with lower regulatory standards create similar risks. Also in this quadrant are firms that create shareholder value through a low-cost strategy that tolerates management actions to cut expenses by avoiding overtime pay, undertraining on employee safety, or discriminating on the basis of gender and ethnic background. Shareholder value in these cases is created "on the backs" of one or more stakeholder groups, thereby representing a value transfer rather than true value creation.

Bottom left quadrant: When value is destroyed for both shareholders and stakeholders, this represents a lose-lose situation of little interest to either. Monsanto and its European competitor Aventis lost large sums of money by underestimating consumer and farmer resistance to their genetically modified (GMO) crop products. Before Aventis sold its CropSciences division to Bayer in 2001, it is estimated to have lost $1 billion in buyback programs and other costs associated with its genetically modified corn, StarLink, which was approved only for use in animal feed but was found by NGOs to have contaminated a number of human food products.

Bottom right quadrant: When value is transferred from shareholders to stakeholders, the company incurs a fiduciary liability to its shareholders. Actions intended to create stakeholder value that destroy shareholder value put the company's viability into question. Environmentalists often unintentionally pressure companies to take actions in this quadrant without realizing that the pursuit of activities that generate losses is not sustainable either. It is interesting to note that philanthropy, when it is unrelated to business interests and represents pure charity, is also located in this quadrant. Unfocused philanthropy is implicitly a decision to take financial value from the company's shareholders and transfer it to one or more of its stakeholders (Porter and Kramer 2002).

Upper right quadrant: When value is created for stakeholders as well as shareholders, stakeholders can represent a potential source of hidden business value. Sustainable value is created only in this case. When companies design manufacturing facilities that cost less to build and operate than conventional facilities and that use less energy for heating and lighting, they are creating sustainable value. The same

is true when they eliminate packaging waste by rightsizing their products, or when they add environmental intelligence to their products by making them more recyclable, reusable, biodegradable, less toxic, or otherwise healthier. Sustainable value is also created when companies find ways to profitably meet unmet societal needs, for example, by providing nutrition and clean water to the poor. The key is to provide environmental and social benefits to stakeholders without asking customers to accept higher prices or worse quality. Companies that are global industry leaders cannot afford to require their customers to pay the "green premium" that specialty companies have historically charged for their products. Only through process or product redesign and innovation can leading companies create new business and societal benefits without consumer trade-offs.

Managers assessing opportunities to create shareholder and stakeholder value (in other words, opportunities that drive a company further into the upper right-hand quadrant of figure 1) need to make the business case for taking action. Without a clear articulation of business value, managers will be unable to obtain the approval needed to obtain the required resources. The six levels of strategic focus described in the following section is an essential tool used to apply the sustainable value framework.

Six Levels of Strategic Focus

The six levels of strategic focus shown in figure 2 on the following page constitute an important tool for managers seeking to identify how business value is created from sustainability projects. The six levels represent distinct types of sustainability-related business value that can be found in every sector.

Companies have made great strides in compliance-oriented risk mitigation (level 1) and process cost reduction (level 2) through eliminating waste and improving energy efficiencies. Relatively few have focused on top-line (gross revenues) growth based on product or brand differentiation (levels 3 and 5). Even fewer have used stakeholder value creation as a way to drive new markets and business context change (levels 4 and 6). Each of the levels is described in greater detail below.

Level 1: Risk Mitigation

Actions that companies take to comply with government regulations and industry standards (one of the earliest examples being Responsible Care in the chemicals industry, adopted in 1988 by the American Chemistry Council) have historically been seen as a financial burden: they are the necessary cost of doing business and of maintaining license to operate. Yet efficient risk mitigation strategies can create significant value to both shareholders and stakeholders.

Figure 2. The Six Levels of Strategic Focus

Levels of Strategic Focus

Sources of Business Value

Changing the "rules of the game"

Developing a sustainability culture & brand identity. Becoming Employer-of-Choice

Addressing new markets driven by customer and societal needs

Creating product differentiation based on technical and environmental/social features

Reducing energy, waste or other process costs

Compliance-oriented management of risks and protecting license to operate

Source: Laszlo (2003, p. 140).

Implementing the six types of business value, which are applicable to every business sector, is an important tool in creating sustainable value.

They include the avoidance of penalties and fines, reduced legal fees, and reduced site-remediation costs.

Level 2: Process Cost Reductions

Process cost reductions are often one of the first sustainability initiatives a company undertakes. Reducing energy consumption, eliminating waste, and minimizing materials intensity are all initiatives that save the company money while reducing environmental, health, and safety impacts on stakeholders.

Level 3: Product Differentiation

The growing segment of consumers for whom social and environmental attributes are important criteria provides an opportunity for leading companies to differentiate themselves on a dimension other than price or technical performance. Al Gore's film, *An Inconvenient Truth* (David and Guggenheim 2006), along with a changing political

awareness of climate change, is helping to push sustainability issues into the forefront of public consciousness. On the supply side of the equation, mainstream players such as Walmart and General Electric are democratizing green products by bringing unit costs in line with the products' traditional (non-green) counterparts. It is now possible to buy an organic cotton shirt at Walmart for about the same price as one made from conventionally grown cotton.

When consumers are not asked to pay more for environmental and social benefits, and when they are not forced to compromise quality or performance, sustainability attributes become a "plus one." The recent experience of leading companies, including Unilever, Toyota, JPMorgan Chase, and Aviva, shows that consumers prefer green products and services if they do not have to give up anything in return.

Level 4: New Markets

Technological innovation that creates stakeholder value increasingly opens up new markets. Examples include

DuPont's push into soy-based nutritional products and Procter & Gamble's development of water purification products in emerging markets. Aviva, one of the world's largest insurance companies, has begun selling life insurance in rural India for households where the disability or death of the principal wage earner can be devastating. Celanese AG has parlayed its expertise in plastic polymers to develop high-temperature membrane electrode assembly (MEA) for fuel cells suitable for use in cars—itself a new market driven by climate change–related concerns. The French materials giant, Saint-Gobain, is finding new applications for its high-performance materials from particulate filters in diesel cars to solar panel components and windmill tips.

Level 5: Enhancing Corporate Image

DuPont, Walmart, Unilever, General Electric, Alcoa, and many other leading companies are finding that a brand/culture based on creating stakeholder value is rapidly becoming a source of competitive advantage. Among other business benefits, a sustainability image draws in higher-income consumers, attracts and retains talented people, and can ease negotiations with government regulators concerned about industry impacts. It contributes to an image of innovation—in some cases attached to a single product, such as Toyota's Prius—that confers reputation benefits to the entire company.

Level 6: Business Context

At this level, companies attempt to shape the regulations, practices, and rules that govern how business can be conducted in their favor. An example is the US Climate Action Partnership (2007), which began by urging President George W. Bush to support mandatory reductions in greenhouse gas emissions and to propose federal reduction targets. Rather than slowing down climate change legislation, industry leaders are encouraging it. They see their efforts to reduce emissions, reduce energy use, and provide climate change solutions as a source of future comparative advantage in a carbon-constrained world. These companies don't want the price of oil to fall back to twenty dollars a barrel, since they would lose that advantage relative to competitors who are less energy efficient and who have a higher intensity of greenhouse gas emissions. Influencing the business context is not only about lobbying government; increasing

the overall stakeholder value in an industry can create goodwill for the entire industry. Conversely, negative stakeholder value can shrink the potential market size and reduce the ability of players in the industry to make enduring profits.

Companies can use the sustainable value framework to think in strategic terms about their existing portfolio of products and services. With the framework, managers are able to assess the business value and obtain the resources for sustainability-related initiatives. Perhaps the single biggest obstacle to taking action, however, is not making the business case for the initiatives, but establishing the leadership mindset required to even consider sustainability as a business opportunity.

Leadership Challenge

Sustainability-related business opportunities are often poorly managed in companies that are otherwise global industry leaders, even where a great many strategic business opportunities exist. Several factors can contribute to this situation. An incomplete awareness exists about the company's impacts on stakeholders and how these might in turn affect future business value. Responsibility for social and environmental issues are typically fragmented across the organization and often delegated to those outside the core management team. Line managers are naturally focused on short-term drivers of shareholder value and view stakeholder-related issues as a distraction from their business objectives.

These factors are usually symptoms of what is the most critical barrier to effectively managing stakeholder value—our mental models. A new leadership mind-set is needed to capture the systemic interrelationships between a company and its societal context. In this mind-set, the goal is not only competing with industry rivals, but also meeting the changing expectations of an ever-growing and diverse set of stakeholders. Capturing sustainable value requires the CEO and leaders with profit-and-loss (P&L) responsibility to see stakeholder value as essential to the growth of their companies. The primary barrier to adopting a stakeholder perspective stems from the leader's mind-set, not from whether there is business value to be found. Mind-set can be understood

as the hidden set of beliefs about the individual, others, and the world. Much as computer operating systems allow only certain software applications to run, our mind-sets dictate the range of possibilities we draw upon to solve problems (Senge 1994). For instance, if an executive believes that an NGO's primary commitment is to put his or her company out of business, the actions to engage with them will be very different than if the executive believes both are committed to solving a common problem.

Historically, the mind-set required to rise to the top of a large corporation has run counter to adopting a stakeholder perspective in the process of value creation. Executives have tended to focus narrowly on maximizing shareholder value. They have privileged activities that, often unintentionally, externalize negative social and environmental impacts. They have risen to their positions of power precisely because they are able to create shareholder value by maximizing "efficiencies" that legally drive externalities elsewhere.

The idea that maximizing the value of *all* key stakeholders is of interest (much less essential) for business success is quite heretical to what has made leaders successful in the past. Yet stakeholder power is now a reality in the new global business environment. Business leaders who fail to adopt a new mind-set risk putting their companies and careers at risk.

Outlook for the Future

In the past, managers often felt forced to choose between two perspectives: business has a moral responsibility to society, *or* it has a fiduciary responsibility to its shareholders. Those who believe in the profit motive consider moral questions in the workplace to be a distraction. Those who believe in a societal role for business consider the single-minded focus on short-term profits to be irresponsible.

In the new global business environment, companies can pursue both simultaneously. Indeed, they must if they want to succeed. Companies that deliver profits to shareholders while destroying value for society are incurring liabilities; those that offer solutions to environmental and social challenges are discovering huge profit opportunities. The corporate path to doing well by doing good has become the smart way to do business, if you have the knowledge and competencies required for it.

Chris LASZLO
Case Western Reserve University; Sustainable Value Partners

See also in the *Berkshire Encyclopedia of Sustainability* Base of the Pyramid; Corporate Citizenship; CSR and CSR 2.0; Education, Business; Equator Principles; Financial Services Industry; Leadership; Natural Capitalism; Social Enterprise; Stakeholder Theory; Transparency; Triple Bottom Line

FURTHER READING

Assadourian, Erik. (2005). The role of stakeholders. Retrieved September 25, 2009, from http://www.worldwatch.org/node/585

David, Laurie (Producer) & Guggenheim, Davis (Director). (2006). *An Inconvenient Truth* [Motion picture]. United States: Paramount Home Entertainment.

Laszlo, Chris. (2003). *The sustainable company: How to create lasting value through social and environmental performance.* Washington, DC: Island Press.

Laszlo, Chris. (2008). *Sustainable value: How the world's leading companies are doing well by doing good.* Stanford, CA: Stanford University Press.

Lev, Baruch. (2001). *Intangibles: Management, measurement, and reporting.* Washington, DC: The Brookings Institution Press.

Low, Jonathan, & Kalafut, Pam Cohen. (2002). *Invisible Advantage: How intangibles are driving business performance.* Cambridge MA: Perseus Publishing.

Porter, Michael E., & Kramer, Mark R. (2002, December 1). The competitive advantage of corporate philanthropy. Retrieved September 26, 2009, from http://custom.hbsp.harvard.edu/b01/en/implicit/p.j html?login=FSGS030708S&pid=R0212D

Senge, Peter M. (1994). *The fifth discipline: The art and practice of the learning organization* (Rev. ed.). New York: Doubleday Business.

US Climate Action Partnership. (2007). *A call for action.* Retrieved September 25, 2009, from http://www.us-cap.org/USCAPCallForAction.pdf

Transparency

Transparency, as it relates to sustainability, entails the disclosure of information. Transparency increasingly has been seen globally as an essential component in efforts to hold governments and private industry accountable for their actions on environmental issues. But the lack of definitive research about whether or not such disclosures reach their targeted audience raises questions about transparency's effectiveness as a sustainability tool.

In the search for sustainability, the idea of *transparency* has gained increasing favor as a means to achieve desired results. More and more it is being looked upon as an essential component for holding both government and private industry accountable. Transparency means many things to many people—general openness, "opposite of secrecy" (Florini 1998), greater flow of information. Here it means *information disclosure*, a phenomenon increasingly central to a diverse range of sustainability initiatives.

Accompanied by freedom of information legislation, the "right to know" movements spreading across the globe reflect an embrace of transparency (Florini 2007). In the context of industrialized countries, transparency underpins what foreign policy expert Ann Florini (1998) calls "regulation by revelation" to address issues such as air pollution, food safety, and vehicle safety. The most prominent example of regulation by revelation is the Toxic Release Inventory (TRI), a chemical release registry established by the United States Emergency Planning and Community Right to Know Act of 1988. The act mandates that companies disclose information about their toxic emissions, with the goals of informing communities exposed to pollutants, holding the companies accountable, and eventually leading to reduced emissions. The TRI has been hailed as a successful sustainability initiative and served as a model for other countries, resulting in a spread of pollutant emission registries across the globe, not only in Europe but also in Mexico, South Korea, and China (Fung, Graham, and Weil 2007; Graham 2002; Stephan 2002; Weil et al. 2006).

In the context of global sustainability, information disclosure as a means of governance includes both mandatory state-led and voluntary private initiatives (Gupta 2008; Langley 2001). For example, a belief in the power of transparency underpins the June 1998 Convention on Access to Information, Public Participation in Decision-Making and Access to Justice in Environmental Matters (the Aarhus Convention), negotiated under the auspices of the United Nations Economic Commission for Europe (UNECE), which is intended to enhance citizens' right to know about environmental decisions (Mason 2008). Transparency is also central to various multilateral treaties governing trade in pesticides, hazardous waste, and genetically modified organisms, such as the Cartagena Protocol on Biosafety under the Convention on Biological Diversity, and the Basel Convention on Trade in Hazardous Waste. Privately initiated ecolabeling programs in forestry, fisheries, and organic foods, such as the Forest Stewardship Council and the Marine Stewardship Council, also rely upon information disclosure as a way to promote sustainable choices and enhance sustainable resource use. Various efforts to promote corporate sustainability also rely on information disclosure and transparency, for example: the Global Reporting Initiative (calling for sustainability reporting by private corporations); the Carbon Disclosure Initiative (calling for disclosure of carbon emissions); or the Publish What You Pay initiative (calling for disclosure of earnings from extractive—oil, gas, and mining—industries operating in resource-rich developing countries).

As evident from this range of examples, transparency can be invoked to help fulfill a variety of sustainability-related aims. This suggests that there are multiple architects of transparency in a global and national context: those in the private sector, for instance, who voluntarily promote transparency to further corporate sustainability goals, improve their public image, and/or avoid government intervention; and those in the public sector who, while promoting transparency to remedy perceived and real deficiencies in their environmentally related decision making, aim to ensure political accountability and greater citizen participation. The diverse motives underlying transparency can thus range from a desire to extend the regulatory reach of the state to scaling back its reach; and from furthering a moral "right to know" (thereby holding government and private sectors accountable) to promoting individual lifestyle choices and market-based solutions (Mason 2008).

Impact on Sustainability

Given diverse reasons to deploy transparency, how effective is it as a tool of sustainability? Answering that question requires a systematic and comparative analysis of transparency-based sustainability initiatives, and that research remains largely undone (Gupta 2008).

The Global Reporting Initiative (GRI) provides an example of how transparency has been perceived to impact corporate sustainability to greater or lesser degrees. The GRI has been lauded by scholars and corporate sustainability practitioners alike for its comprehensive,

stakeholder-driven process of generating reporting guidelines for use by private companies (Dingwerth 2007; Brown, de Jong, and Levy 2009). But emerging research into its effectiveness suggests that despite time-consuming and resource-intensive efforts to generate large amounts of data and disclose it, certain controversial data (about unintentional releases of genetically modified organisms, for example) is not being disclosed (Clapp 2007) and therefore never reaches its intended beneficiaries. Or alternately, disclosed information is inaccessible and/or irrelevant for those it is intended to benefit, hence

resulting in few users of disclosed information (Brown, de Jong, and Levy 2009).

Such findings can relate to various components of transparency-based reporting, ranging from *design of disclosure*, such as the means by which information is to be disclosed (whether electronic or otherwise), to the *attributes of information* disclosed, such as whether it is standardized, comprehensive, and comprehensible. Those with alternative motives sometimes turn the standard intent of transparency on its head by overwhelming reporting authorities and the public with information, a practice called "drowning in disclosure" (Gupta 2008; Mason 2008; Graham 2002; Fung, Graham, and Weil 2007). Finally, newly emerging *intermediaries of transparency*—auditors, verifiers, and certifiers of disclosed information—are becoming more important, and their degree of involvement can vary depending on the potential ramifications the disclosure. These intermediaries are likely to be increasingly significant in shaping the impact of transparency in sustainability governance (Langley 2001).

Outlook: Struggles over Transparency

Many analysts of transparency begin with an optimistic view of its promise only to subsequently highlight various perils in relying on disclosure in the quest for sustainability (Mol 2008). While most would concur that transparency is no panacea in the search for sustainability, discussions about transparency seem destined to take place in the context of larger societal conflicts, particularly in a global context characterized by North–South disparities in capacities to access and use information.

This is also related to the fact that pressing global sustainability challenges, such as climate change or safe use of biotechnology, are characterized by fundamental conflicts over what is valid knowledge and whose information is credible. In such areas, therefore, agreeing on what constitutes "more and better" information, that is, on the scope and content of transparency, will itself become a site of conflict (Gupta 2008). In short, we can conclude that both the quest for transparency and struggles over it are likely to be defining features of future sustainability politics.

Aarti GUPTA
Environmental Policy Group, Wageningen University

See also in the *Berkshire Encyclopedia of Sustainability*
Accounting; Climate Change Disclosure; Corporate Citizenship; Financial Services Industry; Global Reporting Initiative (GRI); Performance Metrics; True Cost Economics

FURTHER READING

Brown, Halina Szejnwald; de Jong, Martin; & Levy, David L. (2009). Building institutions based on information disclosure: Lessons from GRI's sustainability reporting. *Journal of Cleaner Production, 17*(6), 571–580.

Clapp, Jennifer. (2007). Illegal GMO releases and corporate responsibility: Questioning the effectiveness of voluntary measures. *Ecological Economics, 66*(2–3), 348–358.

Dingwerth, Klaus. (2007). *The new transnationalism: Transnational governance and democratic legitimacy.* Basingstoke, UK: Palgrave MacMillan.

Florini, Ann. (1998, Summer). The end of secrecy. *Foreign Policy, 111,* 50–63.

Florini, Ann. (Ed.). (2007). *The right to know: Transparency for an open world.* New York: Columbia University Press.

Fung, Archon; Graham, Mary; & Weil, David. (2007). *Full disclosure: The perils and promise of transparency.* Cambridge, UK: Cambridge University Press.

Graham, Mary. (2002). *Democracy by disclosure: The rise of technopopulism.* Washington, DC: Brookings Institution Press.

Gupta, Aarti. (2008). Transparency under scrutiny: Information disclosure in global environmental governance. *Global Environmental Politics, 8*(2), 1–7.

Kolk, Ans; Levy, David; & Pinkse, Jonatan. (2008). Corporate responses in an emerging climate regime: The institutionalization and commensuration of carbon disclosure. *European Accounting Review, 17*(4), 719–745.

Langley, Paul. (2001). Transparency in the making of global environmental governance. *Global Society, 15*(1), 73–92.

Mason, Michael. (2008). Transparency for whom? Information disclosure and power in global environmental governance. *Global Environmental Politics, 8*(2), 8–13.

Mol, Arthur. (2008). *Environmental reform in the Information Age: The contours of informational governance.* Cambridge, UK: Cambridge University Press.

Pattberg, Philipp, & Enechi, Okechukwu. (2009). The business of transnational climate governance: Legitimate, accountable, and transparent? *St Anthony's International Review, 5*(1), 76–98

Stephan, Mark. (2002). Environmental information disclosure programs: They work but why? *Social Science Quarterly, 83*(1), 190–205.

Weil, David; Fung, Archon; Graham, Mary; & Fagotto, Elena. (2006). The effectiveness of regulatory disclosure policies. *Journal of Policy Analysis and Management, 25*(1), 155–181.

Triple Bottom Line

Triple bottom line reckoning is a form of business reporting that accounts not only for return on investment (the traditional reporting model) but also for environmental and social values. It has become an important tool for businesses pursuing sustainable growth.

The late 1990s saw the rise of the concept of the triple bottom line (TBL). The TBL underscores the fact that companies and other organizations create value in multiple dimensions. Given the nature and focus of modern accounting, the financial bottom line is generally an inadequate (and often misleading) expression of total value. In addition, the TBL concept aimed to help business people think through the question of how to make corporations more sustainable in the context of major emerging economic, social, and environmental challenges, among them corruption, human rights, and climate change.

TBL and the Three Ps

The term *triple bottom line* was coined in 1994 by John Elkington, countering the narrower focus on the then-fashionable term *eco-efficiency*, which focused on the financial and environmental dimensions of performance. TBL thinking, by contrast, extended to social impacts and to the wider economic impact issues rarely captured in the traditional financial bottom line.

The TBL approach was introduced in detail in *Cannibals with Forks* (Elkington 1997) and has been further elaborated in hundreds of company reports aligned with the Global Reporting Initiative (GRI) and in a growing number of books. A linked phrase, "People, Planet, Profit," or, alternatively, "People, Planet, Prosperity" was also coined by Elkington. This phrase was adopted by Shell in its early public sustainability reporting, following the company's

Brent Spar and Nigerian crises in 1995. Known as the three Ps, it became central to the sustainable development discussion in countries such as the Netherlands. It sparked debate about the double bottom line (combining social and financial performance, as in social enterprise) and, variously, quadruple and quintuple bottom lines, in which issues such as ethics and governance were added.

Corporate Life Cycles

The average life expectancy of a company is relatively short. When the oil crises of the 1970s spotlighted the finite nature of fossil fuels, for example, Shell wondered whether there would be life—or at least industrial life—after oil. It investigated how other long-lived firms had addressed earlier market discontinuities. In most cases companies simply died or disappeared. They merged, were taken over, or went out of business. Of the original thirty constituents of the *Financial Times* Ordinary Share Index, an indicator of stock prices on the London Stock Exchange launched in 1935, just nine had survived more or less intact by the late 1990s. And the US corporate death rates turned out to be even higher. Nearly 40 percent of the 1983 *Fortune* 500 companies had dematerialized, as had 60 percent of those so designated in the 1970s, and of the twelve companies making up the Dow Jones Industrial Index in 1900, General Electric (GE) was the only substantial survivor (Visser et al. 2008).

Although the average corporate life expectancy might be in the region of forty to fifty years, there may be several hundred companies around the world that have been operating between 100 and 150 years. This imbalance among the broad mass of companies and the long-winded few is a reflection of many factors, but perhaps most important is the fact that in a capitalist world, companies that fail to deliver stockholder value are starved of capital and die. To date, sustainability factors have only rarely affected capital availability, but understanding of the relevant linkages is likely to grow rapidly.

Corporate Sustainability Challenges

Corporate sustainability is probably better understood not so much as the discipline by which companies ensure their own long-term survival—though that is clearly part of the equation—but as the field of thinking and practice by which companies and other business organizations work to extend the life expectancy of ecosystems and the natural resources they provide; societies and the cultures and communities that underpin commercial activity; and economies that provide the governance, financial, and other market context for corporate competition and survival. By paying attention to such wider issues, it is often argued, companies are better placed to ensure that their own business models remain valid and adaptable.

As for the corporate sustainability agenda, recent decades have seen sustainability issues gradually forced up through corporate hierarchies. They started on the fringes, handled (if at all) by professionals in such areas as site security, public relations, and legal affairs. Through the 1970s, as new techniques such as environmental impact assessment evolved, new groups of professionals became involved, among them project planners, process engineers, and site managers. Then, during the late 1980s, the spotlight opened out to illuminate new product development, design, marketing, and life cycle management. As the triple bottom line agenda of sustainable development spread through the 1990s, with an inevitable growth in the complexity and political impact of key issues, the agenda was driven up to top management and boards. In the next round, in addition to those already involved, expect to see new ventures people—chief financial officers, investment bankers, and venture capitalists—included.

Over time, the agenda has opened out profoundly, increasingly embracing challenging issues such as transparency, corporate and global governance, human rights, bribery and corruption, and global poverty. The key text in this area has been 1987's Brundtland Commission report, *Our Common Future*. Its definition of sustainable development is now widely accepted. It was brought into greater focus in 1994 with the introduction of the TBL concept, which has subsequently been widely adopted—for example by the GRI. The concept has also been adopted by leading companies, most strikingly perhaps by Denmark's Novo Nordisk (2009).

As the agenda has morphed, several other factors have conspired to increase the challenge for business. First, business has increasingly been expected to do things that governments would once have done, if they were done at all. Second, the processes of globalization have enormously extended the areas and timescales over which companies are held accountable while the processes of outsourcing and "offshoring" mean that corporate value chains have become increasingly extensive, complex, and vulnerable to challenge. (Examples are Nike and Gap.) And third, the spread of the Internet and the introduction of search engines such as Google have subjected business to ever-growing levels of scrutiny.

The Impact of Globalization

The TBL agenda played into a period of intense globalization, with growing concerns about the lack of governance and regulatory systems at the global level. As sustainability and corporate citizenship agendas have evolved, the calls on the time and resources of business have increased almost exponentially. In 1999, for example, former UN secretary-general Kofi Annan called on business leaders "to join the United Nations on a journey." He commented that business was already well down the road with a journey of its own, globalization. At the time, globalization appeared like "a force of nature," seeming to "lead inexorably in one direction: ever-closer integration of markets, ever-larger economies of scale, ever-bigger opportunities for profits and prosperity" (Annan 1999).

Ten months before the Seattle protests against the World Trade Organization (WTO), however, the secretary-general also felt it necessary to warn that globalization would only be as sustainable as its social foundations. "Global unease about poverty, equity and marginalization," he stressed, "is beginning to reach critical mass" (Annan 1999). These issues are no less important today, although some focus has shifted to political and security concerns in the wake of 9/11, the war in Iraq, and the Madrid train bombings of 2004, all of which, some would argue, are intimately connected to unresolved problems of poverty and inequity. In tackling such challenges, business is being told it must pay more attention to the need for new forms of global governance.

"Governance" became a buzzword in the 1990s. "Corporate governance," although not a new concept, began its rise in the public agenda in 1992, for example, with the publication of the Cadbury Report in the United Kingdom. That same year the United Nations held its Earth Summit in Rio de Janeiro, spotlighting the urgent need to shift the global economy toward more sustainable forms of development, and the World Bank released its report *Governance and Development*, making the case that governance failures lie behind the poor progress of development efforts to date. A decade later the spotlight had opened out, with those seeking "responsible globalization" now calling for further meaningful "global governance."

But there is a paradox here, and it has two main dimensions. First, the voluntary corporate responsibility (CR) movement has evolved as a pragmatic response to pressing environmental, community, or human rights issues. Companies are asked to address problems and even deliver public goods because governments have been unable or unwilling to do so. But second, because of the weakness—or absence—of appropriate governance systems, CR initiatives are generally disconnected from wider frameworks. As a result, they are at risk of amounting to little more than drops in the ocean when compared to the scale of the challenges. At worst, they may even undermine long-term solutions.

Progress Report

Nevertheless, huge progress has been made. From the defensive stances adopted in the heyday of government-driven responses, companies have begun to explore ways forward with an expanding range of external stakeholders. There has been acknowledgment of the legitimate—and critical—role of companies. While there are still skeptics, there is also an emerging consensus among civil society, government, and business that, in principle, companies play an important role in developing and implementing solutions to pressing sustainable development problems.

In addition, there has been engagement of a significant number of leading multinationals. For example, some 180 companies are members of the World Business Council for Sustainable Development. Nearly 1,000 companies use part or all of the GRI guidelines to report on their social and environmental performance. Business in The Community, a UK business association focused on CR, reports a membership accounting for one in five private-sector employees in the United Kingdom and a global workforce of more than 15.7 million people. Similarly, membership of Brazil's Ethos Institute accounts for more than a quarter of the country's gross national product (GNP). A key question remains: how can this potential critical mass be used to drive forward sustainable development even more powerfully?

Finally, there has been a clearer understanding of the "business case" (and its limits). The business case clearly has limits in driving CR to scale. But the extent of the business case for CR and the links with investment value drivers such as reputation, risk management, corporate governance, and management quality are increasingly recognized both by business and key stakeholder groups (e.g., government and the investment community).

While these certainly reflect accomplishments and progress, and individual companies can also claim substantial performance improvements, the fundamental question is whether the CR movement as a whole has made a real

difference in addressing longer-term sustainability issues. The conclusion must be that current CR initiatives will increasingly run up against system limits. As former president Bill Clinton argued at a World Economic Forum summit, the scale of the challenges the world faces is such that systematic change will not be enough. Instead, he said, systemic change is needed, changes to the system itself.

But these problems are not new. Professor John Ruggie, responsible for Harvard's Corporate Social Responsibility Initiative and a key architect of the Global Compact, explains: "We in the industrialized world were slow to learn the lesson that markets must be embedded in broader frameworks of social values and shared objectives if they are to survive and thrive. Before we got to that point, we had struggled through the collapse of the Victorian era of globalization, a world war, the rise of the left wing revolutionary forces in Russia, right wing revolutionary forces in Germany and Italy as well as the Great Depression." When the lesson did finally sink in, Ruggie continues, "we called the new understanding by different names: the New Deal, the social market economy and social democracy" (Ruggie 2004, 2). The basis of these social bargains was that all actors agreed to open markets, but they also agreed to "share the social adjustment costs that open markets inevitably produce." And governments played a central role in the process, "moderating the volatility of transaction flows across borders and providing social investments, safety nets and adjustment assistance—but all the while pushing liberalization" (Ruggie 2004, 2).

One of the most striking recent trends has been the formation of new forms of partnerships and alliances, linking business with nongovernmental organizations (NGOs) and other civil society actors. But if future corporate efforts and alliances are to bridge the challenge–response gap, the scaling issue will need to be addressed more seriously and effectively. More thought also needs to be given on how to scale geometrically where the challenges are particularly serious. One answer here is to change market conditions to favor particular outcomes, which is where governments have a key role to play.

That is why two additional challenges evolving in the corporate sustainability space have to do with lobbying and tax policy. On corporate lobbying, there is growing concern that companies that give every surface sign of being committed to sustainability are often—directly or indirectly—lobbying behind the scenes to slow progress. The question here is not only how to make such lobbying more transparent but also how, over time, corporate lobbying can be swung around to support initiatives designed to tackle major problems such as climate change. Second, given the growing importance of government in dealing with so many of the challenges that have landed on the business agenda in the early twenty-first century, there is a real question about how government can be properly funded. As a result, the ability of companies in a globalizing world to manage down their tax burdens is coming under growing scrutiny.

The Four Bs

Work on implementing the TBL agenda has shown that there are many points at which it potentially engages with and influences business thinking, strategy, investment, and operations. TBL-oriented organizations, such as the Global Reporting Initiative (2009) and the Dow Jones Sustainability Indexes (2009), provide insights into current practice. Meanwhile, the corporate work of organizations such as SustainAbility (2009) and Volans (2009) have suggested that a potentially powerful way of approaching TBL-focused corporate change is to think in terms of four Bs.

This often starts with external challenges targeting *brands*, often led by activists, NGOs, and the media. Few things stimulate corporate action faster than threats to brand value, with the result that the TBL agenda cross-cuts the world of brand management. Over time, corporate leaders are then encouraged to adapt their management, accounting, disclosure, communication, and external engagement strategies (*balance sheets*). Some companies can hold the challenge at this level, but, increasingly often, the issues have a sufficiently intense political spin so that they are forced up to *boards*, cross-connecting with the world of corporate governance. If the pressures are sustained, presenting new forms of risk and opportunity, then we may see companies adapting their *business models*, as General Electric (already mentioned as a long-term corporate survivor) has begun to do with its ecomagination strategy. This turn of the wheel brings us back to branding, a point underscored by the success of GE's initiative (2009).

The TBL agenda has spawned a broad range of management tools, ranging from auditing and reporting processes to new thinking about how to blend the different dimensions of value creation. (See, for example, the blended thinking of Jed Emerson—the foundation fund manager famous for popularizing the concept that the value of an organization is based on economic, social, and environmental criteria—and other like-minded analysts, at the Blended Value [2009] website.) In the end, however, there are few drop-in TBL solutions. Indeed, GE founder Thomas Edison's comment about his protracted efforts to find a workable electric lightbulb may be a good way to think of the intense period of experimentation that business is embarking on in pursuit of something like sustainability. Faced with yet one more failure, Edison said something to the effect of, well, now I know 10,000 things that don't work. Given that single-dimensional solutions to complex problems are more likely to fail, the hope is that TBL and blended value mind-sets will shorten the odds of hitting gold with the 10,001st attempt.

John ELKINGTON
SustainAbility; Volans Ventures

See also in the *Berkshire Encyclopedia of Sustainability* Corporate Citizenship; CSR and CSR 2.0; Development, Sustainable; Equator Principles; Global Reporting Initiative (GRI); Human Rights; Investment, Socially Responsible (SRI); Natural Capitalism; Social Enterprise; Stakeholder Theory; True Cost Economics

FURTHER READING

Annan, Kofi. (1999). Press release SG/SM/6881: Secretary-General proposes global compact on human rights, labour, environment, in address to World Economic Forum in Davos. Retrieved November 10, 2009, from http://www.un.org/News/Press/docs/1999/19990201.sgsm6881.html

Blended Value. (2009). Retrieved May 11, 2009, from http://www.blendedvalue.org

Dow Jones Sustainability Indexes. (2009). Retrieved May 11, 2009, from http://www.sustainability-index.com

Elkington, John. (1997). *Cannibals with forks: The triple bottom line of 21st century business.* Oxford, UK: Capstone/John Wiley & Sons.

General Electric. (2009). Retrieved May 11, 2009, from http://www.ecomagination.com

Global Reporting Initiative. (2009). Retrieved May 11, 2009, from http://www.globalreporting.org

Henriques, Adrian, & Richardson, Julie. (Eds.). (2004). *The triple bottom line: Does it all add up?* London: Earthscan.

Novo Nordisk. (2009). Retrieved May 11, 2009, from http://www.novonordisk.com

Ruggie, John. (2004, March 15). *Creating public value: Everybody's business.* Address to Herrhausen Society, Frankfurt, Germany. Retrieved November 10, 2009, from http://www.unglobalcompact.org/docs/news_events/9.6/ruggie_160304.pdf

SustainAbility. (2009). Retrieved May 11, 2009, from http://www.sustainability.com

Visser, Wayne; Matten, Dirk; Pohl, Manfred; & Tolhurst, Nick. (Eds.) (2008). *The A to Z of corporate social responsibility: A complete reference guide to concepts, codes and organizations.* Chichester, UK: John Wiley & Sons.

Volans. (2009). Retrieved May 11, 2009, from http://www.volans.com

True Cost Economics

Traditional economics doesn't account for prevailing business practices' collateral damage to the health and well-being of humankind and ecosystems; critics think the free market / cost-price system is detached from these realities and undermines sustainability. True cost economics attempts to incorporate environmental and health damage into product pricing, which could influence consumption patterns and allow the burden to be borne more equitably.

As prepared by the anti-consumerist, not-for-profit organization AdBusters, the "True Cost Economics Manifesto" begins: "We, the Undersigned, make this accusation: that you, the teachers of neoclassical economics and the students that you graduate, have perpetuated a gigantic fraud upon the world" (Bauwens 2009). The alleged fraud consists of conjuring the illusion of perpetual progress and endless growth from theoretical abstractions that obscure a real world of accelerating ecological decay and widespread human misery. One possible wake-up call is the reality check implicit in true cost economics.

The theoretical debate around true cost economics has been simmering for decades but has now begun to boil over. Its proponents believe that the neoclassical (or neoliberal) economics that has dominated the world for at least the past fifty years is hopelessly flawed. Neoclassical free-market models are detached from physical or social realities. They float disdainfully above the ecological, cultural, and ethical contexts within which the real economy is embedded and thus undermine the quest for sustainability.

Neoclassical economists have traditionally been content to allow the prices of goods and services to be determined solely by the law of supply and demand. However, in unregulated markets, only direct producer costs (for rent, labor, resources, and capital, for example) are reflected in consumer prices. The prevailing cost-price system does not account for the collateral damage to ecosystems, human communities, or population health caused by many production processes. These external (outside the market) costs are born disproportionately by third parties or society at large—and, of course, the ecosphere. Because negative externalities represent real costs, the goods and services inflicting them enter the marketplace at prices below their true cost of production. Such underpricing leads to overconsumption, inefficient resource use, and pollution—all classic symptoms of market failure.

True Cost Pricing

By contrast, in a true cost economic system, consumer prices would incorporate environmental, health, and other welfare damage costs of production. When prices "tell the truth" about costs, consumers adjust their consumption patterns accordingly, purchasing fewer ecologically costly goods. Markets would operate more efficiently, producers would innovate and adopt cleaner production processes, total production/consumption would decline (a good thing in a resource-stressed world), pollution and health costs would be would be reduced to insignificance, and third parties would be relieved of an unfair burden.

With so much going for it, why hasn't true cost economics become standard economics? As we shall see, the answer is complicated but, for starters, consider that the true cost approach would result in steep increases in prices for many goods and services that are today within reach of even lower-income groups. For example, some analysts suggest that true cost economics would raise the price of an average car by many thousands of dollars at current production practices. Who would vote for that? Ours is a global consumer culture accustomed to getting more and more for less and less. Correcting for market failure requires government intervention, and any policy that spawned dramatic price increases would spell electoral disaster for the governing party.

Incentive-Based Instruments

Economists have long argued about how best to internalize wayward external costs. By the 1960s, two main schools of thought had coalesced around the competing theories of Arthur Cecil Pigou and Ronald Harry Coase.

Pigovian Taxes

The English economist Arthur Cecil Pigou (1932) argued in *The Economics of Welfare* (first published in 1920) that the existence of externalities justifies government action. He advocated that pollution charges or taxes be applied to offending activities, to better reflect their true social costs and reduce consumption of the relevant goods. (Pigou also suggested that government subsidize private activities generating positive externalities. This would encourage private engagement in those activities and enhance the gains to society at large.)

The mechanics are simple. Imagine an economy in which a number of polluting industries are imposing unaccounted "pollution avoidance costs" on other industries (such as extra expenses for air and water treatment) as well as various "welfare damage costs" on the public (health costs, aesthetic losses, and forgone recreational opportunities, for example). A reasonable public policy objective would be to "internalize these externalities," keeping in mind that, in a total social-cost framework, any solution that imposes pollution-prevention costs on the polluters greater than the anticipated benefits (avoided costs) to other firms and the public would be inefficient.

Government could, in theory, meet this objective through a flat pollution tax per unit of contaminant emitted. The tax would force each polluting firm to decide between treating its wastes and paying the tax. Acting rationally, firms would opt to treat their emissions to the point where their rising, marginal unit-treatment costs just equal the tax. Beyond that, it would be cheaper to pay the tax.

Since different firms have differing "marginal cost of treatment" curves, each will treat a different proportion of its wastes. However, since the tax is uniform, the marginal cost at which firms switch to paying the tax will be the same for all. This ensures that low-cost polluters do most of the cleanup and minimizes the total costs of treatment (a necessary condition for maximum efficiency).

Note that pollution taxes bring the maximum amount of private information to bear on cleanup strategies.

Government need not know the internal processes or cost structures of affected firms. Taxes also pay for their own administration and enforcement. But there is a major problem: in the absence of perfect knowledge, setting the tax rate is just an educated guess. If set too low, the tax will not induce sufficient waste treatment; if too high, firms will inefficiently overtreat their emissions (that is, marginal treatment costs will exceed welfare gains). Subsequent corrective adjustments to the tax are both materially—and politically—costly.

Coasian Bargaining

Despite such drawbacks, the logic of Pigovian taxes charmed most economists until 1960, when it was seriously challenged by the economist Ronald Coase, who argued that if property rights to resources (including sink capacity, or nature's ability to absorb humanity's output and wastes) were clearly defined, then government intervention to correct for externalities was unnecessary, and society could avoid the administrative and enforcement costs of antipollution taxes.

In the absence of significant transaction costs, both polluters and affected parties have a financial incentive to reach an efficient solution through bargaining, regardless of who owns the contested resource. Suppose you, as a papermaker, hold the right to pollute a stream from which I, as a food processor, draw my water. Then I have an incentive to pay you to treat your waste water as long as the cost to me is less than the cost of treating my intake water. Similarly you have an incentive to accept payment because you can profit from treating your wastes. This is because the marginal cost to you of decontaminating your relatively concentrated wastewater is less than the marginal cost to me of cleaning up my more diluted intake water. Of course with more intensive treatment your marginal costs rise to the point where I would save money by shifting to treating my intake water. We bargain around this point—you to maximize receipts, me to minimize pollution avoidance costs.

Now assume I hold the rights to the stream. You have an incentive to pay me to let you pollute as long as my unit price is less than your marginal wastewater treatment costs; I would profit by selling you pollution rights, but only to the point where your payments just cover the cost of treating my now-contaminated intake water. Again, we negotiate an agreement that internalizes costs with no government involvement.

But what if there are thousands of competing firms and myriad other social entities with interests in the negotiated outcome? In the real world, the initial allocation of property rights does matter, and total transaction costs (for research and information, negotiation, administration, and so on) balloon astronomically. Moreover, it is naïve to think that any collection of narrowly "self-interested utility maximizers" will arrive at a solution that is optimal for nature or society at large. As ecological economist Herman Daly constantly reminds us, the "self" in which we are primarily interested is not an isolated atom, but is defined by its relationships in community and by diverse biophysical connections that are affected, but not acknowledged, in economic transactions. This negates any possibility of achieving an efficient or effective solution through private bargaining alone—community (or government) must be involved.

Cap-and-Trade Systems

Government does have one attractive policy option that capitalizes on financial incentives and the allocative efficiency of competitive markets to take the guesswork out of pollution pricing. So-called cap-and-trade programs also combine fixed emission levels with tradable pollution rights and thus separate the public-policy issue of what constitutes acceptable environmental quality from the legitimate economic question of efficient allocation. The US Clean Air Act was based, in part, on caps and tradable permits, as is the early Obama administration's proposed climate change policy (the Waxman-Markey bill).

In an ideal cap-and-trade scenario, government solicits scientific advice and public opinion to set desirable environmental quality objectives and place a firm limit (cap) on allowable emissions that reflects regional assimilation capacity. The allowable emissions are then divided into a fixed number of shares or permits and distributed by some fair means to existing polluters. After initial distribution, subsequent allocation is determined by trading in an open market. The price per share is thus set by the usual law of supply and demand, except that supply is fixed. If demand increases, prices rise, inducing market participants to invest in more efficient (cheaper) production or waste-treatment processes and reduce their need for pollution rights. New businesses, or firms needing additional shares, purchase them from businesses that no longer require their full quota. Inefficient players are forced out of the market.

In theory then, a tradable permit program could achieve ecological and social objectives with certainty, using multiple sources of public and private information to set limits and prices while internalizing erstwhile externalities with market efficiency. And if government charged for the initial distribution of permits or demanded a royalty on subsequent trades (environmental capacity is, after all, a public good), the system would pay for its own implementation and monitoring.

Invisible and Intangible Costs

We have already shown that, despite their theoretical appeal, standard Pigovian and Coasian approaches have serious practical weaknesses. We now consider a fundamental problem that plagues all formal instruments for true cost economics—identifying and monetizing intangible and invisible costs.

Direct production costs and external property damage costs are readily determined from current market prices. But there are no markets for numerous indirect use, nonuse, option, and existence values associated with ecosystems and communities. The market price for a truckload of logs, for example, is mute about the flood control, water purification, biodiversity, carbon sink, and aesthetic and spiritual values sacrificed in clear-cutting the forest. This is why the consumer purchasing a board foot of lumber—or just about anything else—doesn't come close to paying the full social cost of production.

One problem is that assigning a valid money price to something assumes the ability to compress all the values associated with that thing into a single metric. Arild Vatn and Daniel Bromley (1994) identify three theoretical obstacles to such inclusive pricing of environmental (or social) entities:

- A *cognition problem* always exists in the absence of perfect knowledge, and the simple fact is that many critical functions of species and ecosystems are cognitively invisible. This "functional transparency" means that the cost of losing any important element of an ecosystem may be unknowable until that element has been destroyed. We obviously cannot place any value on that which we cannot know.
- An *incongruity problem* exists when the values associated with an ecologically significant good are incongruous or incommensurable with dollar values. How can we conflate the market price of duck breast with the sheer aesthetic rush experienced from witnessing a wedge of mallards in full flight over the marsh?
- A *composition problem* arises because in ecosystems the whole may be dependent on each of its fundamental parts. This means that value of any single component (for example, a species or nutrient) cannot be interpreted independently of the value of the whole.

These and related barriers mean that mainstream efforts to derive accurate, unambiguous *money* values for complex ecological entities (such as contingent valuation) are doomed to failure—we cannot compute costs. Our assumed ability to commoditize nature and basic life support is an arrogant fiction (and in any event, may not be such a good idea).

Transcending Benefit-Cost Analysis

All important decisions involve weighing the relative gains and losses associated with the various options under consideration. As we have seen, pollution charges, one-on-one bargaining, and cap-and-trade programs all force the affected parties to compute private self-interested benefit-cost ratios as the basis for their internal waste management decisions ("Do we treat our wastes or pay the tax?").

More generally, formal benefit-cost analysis (BCA) purports to provide a comprehensive comparison of the discounted future benefits and costs associated with different development options. The efficiency goal is to maximize any positive difference between gains and losses. Because of its conceptual simplicity and theoretical elegance, many economists regard BCA as the definitive tool for both private and public policy decision making. In an ideal world BCA would therefore be critical to true cost economics.

But this is not an ideal world—there are practical flies in the theoretical ointment. Missing data and irreducible uncertainty combined with limited resources and ideologically tainted analyses explode any claim that BCA produces a socially optimal true cost outcome. The fact is that comprehensive true cost economics is beyond our analytic reach.

This is no minor glitch. Ignorance of critical ecological and social costs has arguably long biased modern society toward endless growth even as the ecosphere slowly implodes. It is entirely possible that if we could subject the global economy to a valid BCA, we would find that the ecological and social costs of growth at the margin now exceed the benefits. We may have entered an era of what Herman Daly calls "uneconomic growth"—growth that makes the world poorer, not richer. True cost economics may well mean no-growth economics. The fact that the world's rich and powerful reap most of the benefits of growth, while the poor and the global commons bear most of the unaccounted costs, undoubtedly contributes to present policy paralysis.

Such conclusions are not cause for despair but rather should liberate society from the dictates of oppressively wrong-headed economic models. Governments, the private sector, and nongovernmental organizations must learn to eschew "crackpot rigor." We all share this single planet and cannot afford to be blinded by faulty theory and vacuous analysis. By all means, use BCA for those tangible things to which we can legitimately ascribe a dollar value. This may bring us closer to the efficient market economy to which we aspire. But both business and ordinary citizens must recognize that the results are not in themselves a sufficient basis for decision making.

In the end, sustainability is mainly a political, not an analytic, goal. Society must recognize that even as we strive for true cost economics, the most critical ecological and social choices must be made "without prices, without apologies" (Vatn and Bromley 1994). Given the scale of the problem, multiple conflicting values, gross distributive inequity, and a deepening well of uncertainty, there is no substitute for informed, cautiously practical political judgment, all for the common good.

William E. REES
University of British Columbia

See also in the *Berkshire Encyclopedia of Sustainability* Accounting; Cap-and-Trade Legislation; Consumer Behavior; Development, Sustainable; Ecolabeling; Ecosystem Services; Energy Efficiency; Green Gross Domestic Product (GDP); Human Rights; Investment, Socially Responsible (SRI); Natural Capitalism; Performance Metrics; Triple Bottom Line

FURTHER READING

Baumol, William J., & Oates, Wallace E. (1988). *The theory of environmental policy* (2nd ed.). New York: Cambridge University Press.

Bauwens, Michel. (2009, August 9). True cost economics manifesto. Retrieved August 26, 2009, from http://blog.p2pfoundation.net/the-true-cost-economics-manifesto/2009/08/09

Coase, Ronald H. (1960). The problem of social cost. *Journal of Law and Economics, 1*(3), 1–44. Retrieved August 31, 2009, from http://www.sfu.ca/~allen/CoaseJLE1960.pdf

Dales, John. (1968). *Pollution, property and prices: An essay in policy-making and economics.* Toronto: University of Toronto Press.

Daly, Herman E. (1981). *Steady-state economics* (2nd ed.). Washington, DC: Island Press.

Daly, Herman E., & Cobb, John B., Jr. (1989). *For the common good: Redirecting the economy toward community, the environment, and a sustainable future.* Boston: Beacon Press.

Daly, Herman E. & Farley, Joshua. (2004). *Ecological economics: Principles and applications.* Washington, DC: Island Press.

Daly, Herman E., & Townsend, Kenneth N. (1993). *Valuing the Earth: Economics, ecology, ethics.* Cambridge, MA: MIT Press

Hahn, Robert W. (1989). *A primer on environmental policy design.* Chur, Switzerland: Harwood Academic Publishers.

Jacobs, Michael. (1991). *The green economy: Environment, sustainable development, and the politics of the future.* London: Pluto Press.

Lave, Lester B., & Gruenspecht, Howard K. (1991). Increasing the efficiency and effectiveness of environmental decisions: Benefit-cost analysis and effluent fees—a critical analysis. *Journal of the Air and Waste Management Association, 41*(5), 680–693.

Manno, Jack P. (2000). *Privileged goods: Commoditization and its impact on environment and society.* Boca Raton, FL: Lewis Publishers.

O'Neill, John. (2006). *Markets, deliberation and environment.* London: Routledge.

O'Neill, John; Holland, Alan; & Light, Andrew. (2008). *Environmental values.* London: Routledge.

Pearce, David W. (1993). *Economic values and the natural world.* Cambridge, MA: MIT Press.

Pigou, Arthur C. (1932). *The economics of welfare* (4th ed.). London: MacMillan,

Prugh, Thomas; Costanza, Robert; Cumberland, J. H.; Daly, Herman E.; Goodland, Robert; & Norgaard, Richard B. (1995). *Natural capital and human economic survival.* Solomons, MD: ISEE Press.

True cost economics. (n.d.). Retrieved November 10, 2009, from http://www.investopedia.com/terms/t/truecosteconomics.asp

Themes, Brendan. (2004, August 26). True cost economics. Retrieved August 26, 2009, from http://www.utne.com/2004-08-01/TrueCostEconomics.aspx

Vatn, Arild, & Bromley, Daniel W. (1994). Choices without prices without apologies. *Journal of Environmental Economics and Management, 26*(2), 129–148.

Victor, Peter A. (2008). *Managing without growth: Slower by design, not disaster.* Cheltenham, UK: Edward Elgar.

United Nations Global Compact

The largest corporate citizenship initiative in the world, the United Nations Global Compact serves as a framework to help companies align strategies and operating practices with a core set of ten principles that address the areas of human rights, labor standards, the environment, and anti-corruption. Formally launched in 2001, it had approximately 6,000 international businesses as signatories by 2009.

In 1999, then United Nations secretary-general Kofi Annan spoke at the World Economic Forum in Davos, Switzerland. In that speech, Annan made the following call for greater corporate citizenship on the part of business:

> I want to challenge you to join me in taking our relationship to a still higher level. I propose that you, the business leaders...and we, the United Nations, initiate a global compact of shared values and principles, which will give a human face to the global market.
>
> Globalization is a fact of life. But I believe we have underestimated its fragility. The problem is this. The spread of markets outpaces the ability of societies and their political systems to adjust to them, let alone to guide the course they take. History teaches us that such an imbalance between the economic, social and political realms can never be sustained for very long....
>
> We have to choose between a global market driven only by calculations of short-term profit, and one which has a human face. Between a world which condemns a quarter of the human race to starvation and squalor, and one which offers everyone at least a chance of prosperity, in a healthy environment. Between a selfish free-for-all in which we ignore the fate of the losers, and a culture in which the strong and successful accept their responsibilities, showing global vision and leadership.

Annan had recognized a changing reality for corporations: corporate citizenship, also called corporate responsibility, was becoming increasingly important both to companies themselves, particularly large companies in the public eye, and to the stakeholders (and, not incidentally, the natural environment) with whom companies interacted as they went about their businesses. In challenging corporations to take action, Annan laid the basis for what has become the largest corporate citizenship initiative in the world, the United Nations Global Compact.

Defining Corporate Citizenship

Corporate citizenship can be defined as a manifestation of a company's vision and values as expressed through the strategies and operating practices by which the company develops relationships with societies, stakeholders, and the natural environment as core elements of its business model. In addition, fundamentals of corporate citizenship are found in the responsibility, accountability, transparency, and sustainability practices (processes, programs, and policies) of the firm. Corporate citizenship includes but goes beyond the company's corporate social responsibilities, which are manifested in their practices that directly benefit society, stakeholders, and the natural environment.

This definition explicitly distinguishes corporate citizenship (or responsibility) from corporate social responsibility by recognizing the inherent and frequently discretionary (Carroll 1979) social-betterment aspects of corporate social responsibility, and the intrinsic relationship of corporate citizenship to the company's business model and practices. It also recognizes that the major impacts of a corporation derive not from its social-betterment activities but from the ways in which it implements its business model, hence its treatment of primary stakeholders (such as investors, employees, customers, and suppliers) as well as secondary stakeholders (including communities, governments, and others affected by the firm's business model).

The Global Compact's Ten Principles

The United Nations Global Compact (UNGC), which was formally launched as an entity under the banner of the UN in 2001—two years after Kofi Annan's speech at the World Economic Forum—is now, by its own estimation, the world's largest corporate citizenship initiative. The UNGC bills itself as a framework that helps companies align their strategies and operating practices with ten principles drawn from globally accepted UN documents.

The Global Compact asks companies to embrace, support, and enact, within their sphere of influence, a set of core values in the areas of human rights, labor standards, the environment, and anti-corruption. The following ten principles appear on the UNGC website (The Ten Principles n.d.).

Human Rights

- **Principle 1**: Businesses should support and respect the protection of internationally proclaimed human rights; and
- **Principle 2**: make sure that they are not complicit in human rights abuses.

Labor Standards

- **Principle 3**: Businesses should uphold the freedom of association and the effective recognition of the right to collective bargaining;
- **Principle 4**: the elimination of all forms of forced and compulsory labor;
- **Principle 5**: the effective abolition of child labor; and
- **Principle 6**: the elimination of discrimination in respect of employment and occupation.

Environment

- **Principle 7**: Businesses should support a precautionary approach to environmental challenges;
- **Principle 8**: undertake initiatives to promote greater environmental responsibility; and
- **Principle 9**: encourage the development and diffusion of environmentally friendly technologies.

Anti-Corruption

- **Principle 10**: Businesses should work against corruption in all its forms, including extortion and bribery.

Developing Corporate Citizenship

The Global Compact is a network organization at its core, consisting of its signatories and supported by the UN Global Compact Office in New York and six UN agencies: The Office of the High Commissioner for Human Rights, the United Nations Environment Program (UNEP), the International Labor Organization (ILO), the United Nations Development Program (UNDP), the United Nations Industrial Development Organization (UNIDO), and the United Nations Office on Drugs and Crime.

By 2009, UNGC had nearly 6,000 corporate signatories, of which about 5,200 were companies, both large and small, from around the planet, each of which had agreed to uphold the UNGC's ten principles and report on an annual basis. The UNGC, which is entirely voluntary, moves the corporate citizenship agenda forward through two main objectives: mainstream the ten principles into business activities globally, and catalyze actions in support of broader UN goals, such as the Millennium Development Goals (which are attempting to vastly reduce the number of people living in extreme poverty by 2015).

The UNGC works to achieve its objectives through a variety of means, including policy dialogues, learning, local networks, and partnership projects. Policy dialogues are multistakeholder meetings around specific issues related to corporate citizenship. Learning involves sharing best practices on the UNGC's website, including in-depth case studies, which are sometimes presented at conferences. More than seventy local networks have been developed globally as a way of supporting signatories as they attempt to live up to the ten principles. The UNGC organizes workshops and training for participants, as well as regular conferences, to share learning and best practices, and it encourages companies to participate in partnership projects with their stakeholders, especially when they are related to other UN objectives, like the Millennium Development Goals, human rights, labor rights, sustainability, or anti-corruption initiatives.

Because the UNGC is a voluntary initiative, it has no authority to sanction signatories that are noncompliant with the principles. In that sense, the ten principles are aspirational in that they set a standard that companies agree voluntarily to meet. To deal with criticisms that it lacked sanctioning capacity, the UNGC has implemented integrity measures, which include limiting the use of the UN and UNGC logo and name only to authorized users and delisting

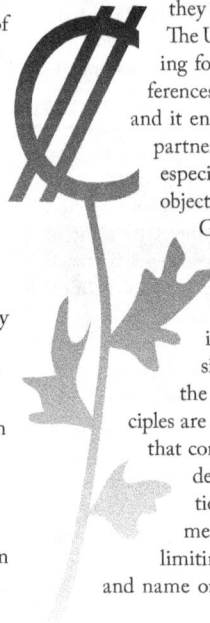

signers who fail to "communicate on progress" on a regular basis, which is a simple requirement for signatories.

The UNGC has identified several benefits for companies that join, including association with the UN with its global reach and convening power. The Global Compact believes that signing on demonstrates leadership and advances responsible corporate citizenship, and that the learning shared among signatories can help develop practical solutions to problems related to globalization, sustainable development, and responsibility, especially when multiple stakeholders are interested in issues. Further, joining the UNGC suggests that the signatory is taking a proactive stance on important issues, thereby managing risks and potentially enhancing reputation, which is a key resource for many companies when they think about corporate citizenship.

The Global Compact has established a foundation to support its work and also has helped to launch other initiatives, including in 2007 Geneva Declaration at the tri-annual International Leaders Summit, held at the UN in Geneva, Switzerland. Endorsed by the one thousand CEOs and executives attending the summit, the Geneva Declaration affirmed the participants' commitment to following a principles-based approach in their business models, including encouraging other business partners (such as suppliers and distributors) to uphold the Global Compact's principles. In line with Kofi Annan's original "call to action" to the business community in 1999 to engage in positive ways with society, the 2007 Geneva Declaration states that "globalization, if rooted in universal principles, has the power to improve our world fundamentally—delivering economic and social benefits to people, communities and markets everywhere."

The Geneva Declaration, which was signed by the largest gathering of business leaders ever brought together by the United Nations, was endorsed in a global context of widening gaps between rich and poor, with more than a billion people living in extreme poverty on less than one dollar per day, and the expectation of a serious lack of jobs for youths. The declaration also noted that "Through a commitment to corporate citizenship and the principles of the UN Global Compact, companies can continue to create and deliver value in the widest possible terms. In this way, globalization can act as an accelerator for the diffusion of universal principles, creating a values-oriented competition for a 'race to the top.'"

Recognizing the important role that management education plays in shaping leaders who can contend with issues of corporate citizenship, the UNGC also launched Principles for Responsible Management Education in 2007. These principles were endorsed by two accrediting agencies—the US-based Association to Advance Collegiate Schools of Business (AACSB) and the European Foundation for Management Development (EFMD)—and numerous management education programs.

Corporate Citizenship and the UNGC

By focusing directly on the business model, good corporate citizenship asks companies, as did Kofi Annan, to take care in implementing their business models and also to participate actively—as individual citizens do—in ensuring that their roles in society are beneficial rather than harmful. Taking this perspective, there are two additional key aspects of corporate citizenship that need attention.

First is the recognition that some level of corporate citizenship or responsibility is present in whatever actions and impacts a company has—from good to poor, whether effectively managed or not. Outside observers looking at the company's impacts can and frequently do make assessments about the level of responsibility inherent to given activities.

Second, there is some concern and criticism about corporate involvement in political activities, a notion that is implicit in the use of the term *citizenship*. Unlike individuals, corporations are not people who can participate in democratic processes. Corporations have been granted the rights of individuals to some extent by various judicial rulings; however, the reality of the size and power, particularly of large multinational corporations, which frequently become involved in the political process through donations to campaigns, lobbying, and other means, has caused critics to question whether this corporate personhood is helpful or harmful to democracy. In addition, some criticize the UN's involvement with corporations at all, claiming that an initiative like the Global Compact provides an opportunity for what critics label "bluewashing," meaning that companies attempt to look good by using the UN's blue-flag logo while continuing business as usual.

Despite these criticisms, the UN's involvement with companies through the Global Compact has provided opportunity for many companies to learn how to better implement their own corporate citizenship practices. To enhance these efforts, the UNGC provides numerous opportunities for engagement among and between companies and

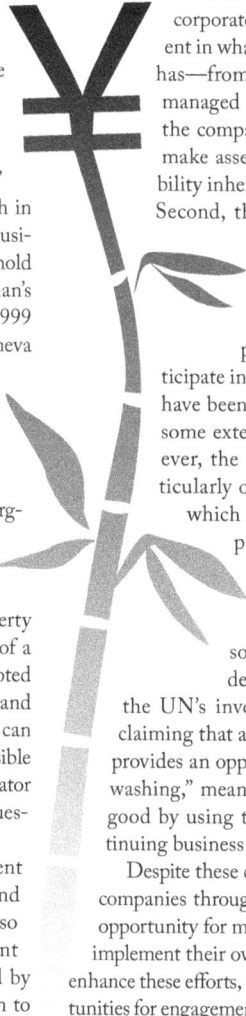

with other stakeholders, for dealing with issues that companies are facing for which relatively little has been known in the past (for example, how to cope in situations of conflict), and for moving forward a broad agenda of corporate responsibilities that encompass the most universal and aspirational qualities embedded in globally accepted UN documents, which are the basis of UNGC's ten principles.

Sandra WADDOCK

Carroll School of Management, Boston College

See also in the *Berkshire Encyclopedia of Sustainability* Corporate Citizenship; CSR and CSR 2.0; Development, Sustainable; Equator Principles; Fair Trade; Human Rights; Stakeholder Theory; Social Enterprise; Transparency

FURTHER READING

Annan, Kofi. (1999). Press Release SG/SM/6881: Secretary-General proposes global compact on human rights, labour, environment, in address to World Economic Forum in Davos. Retrieved November 10, 2009, from the United Nations Web site: http://www.un.org/News/Press/docs/1999/19990201.sgsm6881.html

Carroll, Archie B. (1979). A three-dimensional conceptual model of corporate social performance. *Academy of Management Review, 4*(4), 497–505.

Geneva Declaration. (2007). Retrieved March 25, 2008, from http://www.unglobalcompact.org/docs/summit2007/GENEVA_DECLARATION.pdf

Principles for Responsible Investment. (2009). Retrieved July 2, 2009, from http://www.unpri.org

Principles for Responsible Management Education. (2009). Retrieved July 2, 2009, from http://www.unprme.org

Scherer, Andreas Georg, & Palazzo, Guido. (Eds.). (2008). *Handbook of research on global corporate citizenship.* Cheltenham, UK: Edward Elgar.

The Ten Principles. (n.d.). Retrieved July 2, 2009, from http://www.unglobalcompact.org/AboutTheGC/TheTenPrinciples/index.html

United Nations Global Compact. (2009). Retrieved March 25, 2008, from http://www.unglobalcompact.org

Waddock, Sandra. (2009). *Leading corporate citizens: Vision, values, value added* (3rd ed.). New York: McGraw-Hill.

Index

A

accountability, 86, 105, 129
accounting, 66
Anderson, Ray, 57
Annan, Kofi, 77, 129
antiwar activism, 49
Australia, 82

B

Base of the Pyramid, 1–2, 51, 99. *See also* **Investment, Socially Responsible (SRI)**
    layers/levels of, 1–2
benefit-cost analysis (BCA), 127–128
biological nutrients, 14
Biomimicry, 67, 79. *See also* **Life Cycle Assessments (LCAs); Natural Capitalism**
Bourdieu, Pierre, 3
Bowen, Howard Rothmann, 17
Braungart, Michael, 14, 15, 62, 78. *See also* **Cradle to Cradle**
Brower, David, 77
Building Research Establishment Environmental Assessment Method (BREEAM), 34. *See also* buildings, design and operational sustainability
    aims, 34

buildings, design and operational sustainability, 33
    Building Research Establishment Environmental Assessment Method (BREEAM), 34
    capital *vs.* running costs, 36–37
    carbon *vs.* costs, 35–36
    Energy Performance Directive for Buildings (EPDB), 33–34
    energy use, 34
    Leadership in Energy and Environmental Design (LEED), 34–35
Burns, James MacGregor, 56
business value creation, 108. *See also* **Sustainable Value Creation**

C

C2C. see **Cradle to Cradle**
cap-and-trade carbon trading system, 127
carbon footprint, 70
China, 83
civic intelligence, 7
Community Capital, 3–4
    alternative currency movement, 4
    and civic intelligence, 7
    and ecological capital, 6
    community culture, 4–5
    cooperative movement, 3–4

Bold entries and page numbers denote article titles in this book.

Image Credits

The illustrations used in this book come from many sources. There are photographs provided by Berkshire Publishing's staff and friends, by authors, and from archival sources. All known sources and copyright holders have been credited.

Bottom front cover photo is of fireflies (*Pyractomena borealis*) on an Iowa prairie, by Carl Kurtz.

Photo used with the Introduction and Index is of daffodil shoots growing outside of Berkshire Publishing's offices.

Money-plant illustrations by Anna Myers.

Front cover images, left-to-right:

1. *Work horses near Junction City, Kansas.* Photo by John Vachon: Library of Congress.
2. *Praekestolen, Geiranger Fjord, Norway.* Photo courtesy of the Library of Congress.
3. *General view of the city and the Atchison, Topeka, and Santa Fe Railroad, Amarillo, Texas; Santa Fe R.R. trip.* Photo by Jack Delano, Library of Congress.

Back cover images, left-to-right:

1. *Buddhist cairns alongside Qinghai Lake, China.* Photo by Thomas Christensen.
2. *Tassel on a stalk of corn, Minnesota, USA.* Photo by Flip Schulke (1930–2008). National Archives.
3. *Wind turbines in Somerset, Pennsylvania, USA.* Photo by Eric Vance, Chief Photographer, USEPA, National Archives.

Page 1, *Landscape, northeast Utah.* Photo by John Vachon: Library of Congress.

Pages 3, 8, 14, and 17, *Pink sedum.* Photo by Anna Myers.

Pages 22, 25, and 27, *Azaleas in the fall.* Photo by Anna Myers.

Page 32, *Kongen og Dronningen, Bispen, Norway.* Photo courtesy of the Library of Congress.

Pages 39, 43, and 46, *Windmills (going home).* Photo by Jusben: Morguefile.com.

Page 49, *Bamboo.* Photo by Anna Myers.

Pages 53 and 59, *Bands of sheep on the Gravelly Range at the foot of Black Butte, Madison County, Montana.* Photo by Russell Lee: Library of Congress.

Pages 65 and 71, *Grasses.* Photo by Anna Myers.

Page 77, *Work horses near Junction City, Kansas.* Photo by John Vachon: Library of Congress.

Pages 82, 86, and 90, *Basilicata, Italy.* Photo by Gianfranco Franci: Morguefile.com.

Page 94, *Ailsa Craig, Scotland.* Photo by Library of Congress.

Pages 99, 102, 107, and 112, *Longqing Gorge, China.* Photo by Thomas Christensen.

Pages 118, 121, and 125, *General view of the city and the Atchison, Topeka, and Santa Fe Railroad, Amarillo, Texas; Santa Fe R.R. trip.* Photo by Jack Delano, Library of Congress.

Page 129, *Open mine.* Photo courtesy of the Library of Congress.

Author Credits

Base of the Pyramid
by **Mark B. Milstein, Erik Simanis, Duncan Duke, and Stuart Hart**
Johnson Graduate School of Management, Cornell University

Community Capital
by **Liam Leonard**
Institute of Technology, Sligo

Consumer Behavior
by **Tim Jackson**
University of Surrey

Cradle to Cradle
by **Hsin-Neng Hsieh**
New Jersey Institute of Technology

CSR and CSR 2.0
by **Wayne Visser**
CSR International

Ecolabeling
by **Maria Proto**
University of Salerno

Ecological Economics
by **Robert Costanza**
University of Vermont

Education, Business
by **Nicola J. Acutt**
Presidio Graduate School

Facilities Management
by **Gillian F. Menzies**
Heriot Watt University

Global Reporting Initiative (GRI)
by **Elizabeth F. R. Gingerich**
Valparaiso University College of Business Administration

Greenwashing
by **Norm Borin**
Orfalea College of Business, California Polytechnic State University

Green GDP
by **Jianguo Wu**
Arizona State University
Tong WU
Northern Arizona University

Investment, Socially Responsible (SRI)
by **Jacob Park**
Green Mountain College

Leadership
by **Benjamin W. Redekop**
Christopher Newport University

Life Cycle Assessments (LCAs)
by **Henrikke Baumann**
Chalmers University of Technology

Manufacturing Practices
by **Robert B. Pojasek**
Harvard University

Marketing
by **Norm Borin**
Orfalea College of Business, California Polytechnic State
    University

Natural Capitalism
by **L. Hunter Lovins**
Natural Capital Solutions

Packaging
by **Anne Chick**
Kingston University

Performance Metrics
by **Marc J. Epstein**
Rice University
and **Priscilla S. WISNER**
Montana State University

Public—Private Partnerships
by **M. Sohail** and **Sue Cavill**
WEDC (Water, Engineering and Development Centre),
    Loughborough University

Risk Management
by **Tamara Bekefi**
Daedalus Strategic Advising
and **Marc J. EPSTEIN**
Rice University

Social Enterprise
by **John Elkington**
SustainAbility and Volans Ventures

Stakeholder Theory
by **Sandra Waddock**
Carroll School of Management, Boston College

Supply Chain Management
by **Joseph Fiksel**
The Ohio State University

Sustainable Value Creation
by **Chris Laszlo**
Case Western Reserve University; Sustainable Value
    Partners

Transparency
by **Aarti Gupta**
Environmental Policy Group, Wageningen University

Triple Bottom Line
by **John Elkington**
SustainAbility; Volans Ventures

True Cost Economics
by **William E. Rees**
University of British Columbia

United Nations Global Compact
by **Sandra Waddock**
Carroll School of Management, Boston College

This **BERKSHIRE** *Essentials* book was distilled from the

Berkshire Encyclopedia of Sustainability VOLUMES 1–10

Knowledge to Transform Our Common Future

In the 10-volume *Berkshire Encyclopedia of Sustainability*, experts around the world provide authoritative coverage of the growing body of knowledge about ways to restore the planet. Focused on solutions, this interdisciplinary print and online publication draws from the natural, physical, and social sciences—geophysics, engineering, and resource management, to name a few—and from philosophy and religion. The result is a unified, organized, and peer-reviewed resource on sustainability that connects academic research to real world challenges and provides a balanced, trustworthy perspective on global environmental challenges in the 21st century.

Ray C. Anderson

General Editor

Sara G. Beavis, Klaus Bosselmann, Robin Kundis Craig, Michael L. Dougherty, Daniel S. Fogel, Sarah E. Fredericks, Tirso Gonzales, Willis Jenkins, Louis Kotzé, Chris Laszlo, Jingjing Liu, Stephen Morse, John Copeland Nagle, Bruce Pardy, Sony Pellissery, J.B. Ruhl, Oswald J. Schmitz, Lei Shen, William K. Smith, Ian Spellerberg, Shirley Thompson, Daniel E. Vasey, Gernot Wagner, Peter J. Whitehouse

Editors

10 VOLUMES • 978-1-933782-01-0
Price: US$1500 • 6,084 pages • 8½ × 11"

"The call we made in *Our Common Future*, back in 1987, is even more relevant today. Having a coherent resource like the *Encyclopedia of Sustainability*, written by experts yet addressed to students and general readers, is a vital step, because it will support education, enable productive debate, and encourage informed public participation as we join, again and again, in the effort to transform our common future."

—Gro Harlem Brundtland, chair of the World Commission on Environment and Development and three-time prime minister of Norway

"This is undoubtedly the most important and readable reference on sustainability of our time"

—Jim MacNeill, Secretary-General of the Brundtland Commission and chief architect and lead author of *Our Common Future* (1984–1987)

www.ingramcontent.com/pod-product-compliance
Lightning Source LLC
Chambersburg PA
CBHW080557220326
41599CB00032B/6509